DATE DUE

APR 17 1998	

HIV-NEGATIVE

How the Uninfected Are Affected by AIDS

HIV-NEGATIVE
How the Uninfected
Are Affected by AIDS

WILLIAM I. JOHNSTON

Foreword by
Eric E. Rofes
Board Member, National Gay and Lesbian Task Force
San Francisco, California

✦ INSIGHT BOOKS

Plenum Press • New York and London

Library of Congress Cataloging-in-Publication Data

Johnston, William I.
    HIV-negative : how the uninfected are affected by AIDS / William
  I. Johnston ; foreword by Eric Rofes.
        p.   cm.
    Includes bibliographical references and index.
    ISBN 0-306-44947-1 (hardbound). -- ISBN 0-306-44951-X (pbk.)
    1. AIDS (Disease)--Psychological aspects. 2. Gay men. 3. AIDS
  phobia.   I. Title.
  RC607.A26J654   1995
  155.9'16--dc20   95-6962
                                                                   CIP

The excerpt from the *Decameron* by Giovanni Boccaccio, translated by Frances Winwar, is reprinted by permission of The Limited Editions Club, New York.

"Fog" appears in *My Alexandria*. Copyright © 1993 by Mark Doty. Used with permission of the University of Illinois Press.

"Faith" and "Atlantis" are copyright © 1994 by Mark Doty. Used by permission.

ISBN 0-306-44947-1 (Hardbound)
ISBN 0-306-44951-X (Paperback)

© 1995 William I. Johnston
Insight Books is a Division of Plenum Publishing Corporation
233 Spring Street, New York, N.Y. 10013-1578

An Insight Book

10 9 8 7 6 5 4 3 2 1

Printed in the United States of America

Witnessing the Epidemic

TESTIMONY IS CRUCIAL for survivors of any disaster. Amid the earthquake detritus and hollowed-out shells of buildings at the battlefront, men and women emerge compelled to bear witness to horror and atrocity. The recounting of these stories is part of an age-old cycle which eases contemporary tragedy into the realm of history and integrates what once appeared unimaginable into the individual and collective psyche.

The narrators of *HIV-Negative* have much to teach about surviving and witnessing the current mass disaster we call AIDS. As the epidemic widens and deepens, those who remain standing at Ground Zero face daunting challenges. Why are we still living when so many of our peers have died? Are we survivors or merely the last among our crowd to become infected? When our daily lives teem with infirmity, mutilation, and gruesome deaths, what kind of "mental health" is possible?

Gay men, in particular, face disturbing and painful questions. Those of us who inhabited the nation's urban centers during the "golden years" of gay liberation in the 1970s are among the increasingly few members of a lost generation caught between memory and regret. Our sexual congresses—once sites of safety, affirmation, and joy—have become twisted by fear, sadness, and intrusive thoughts of death. The social fabric of our community has been torn asunder. On a daily basis we discover frightening new aspects of ourselves and our world which we cannot understand and do not want to face.

Yet few people want to hear the pain faced by uninfected individuals. A simple assertion of issues influencing the HIV-negative is met with a barrage of rage. When we have attempted to bring these issues into a public forum we are accused of robbing resources from the "truly needy"—those who are HIV-positive or who have AIDS. We are mocked as having "antibody envy" or derided as self-centered survivor queens yearning for victim status. The severity of the impact of the epidemic in our lives has been denied, minimized, and discounted every step of the way. So we, a population of supposed survivors, are left to walk the earth like robots or zombies, telling ourselves and others that everything's fine while we are actually numb, cut off from our emotions, entrenched in a state of denial.

I lived in this village of denial for years. As I watched friends, lovers, and colleagues sicken and die, my psyche shifted from a state of simple grief to multiple loss to complex repeated trauma, without awareness or self-knowledge. The circuits of emotion within me became bizarrely redirected and sometimes fully disconnected; a close friend would die and I would feel nothing. Funerals ceased to serve a restorative function. I knew I wasn't alone in what seemed to be a warping of internal response, because at AIDS memorial marches and displays of the NAMES Project quilt, I watched others engaging in social banter, gossiping, or joking, doing anything except confronting the direct experience of grief.

No one tells survivors of an earthquake that they are wrong for being profoundly shaken by the experience. Midwest farmers who lost homes, livelihoods, and entire communities were not expected to be "doing fine" in the aftermath of the floods of 1993. The destruction of the human psyche visited on survivors of Hiroshima or Nazi death camps was viewed as an understandable fallout of these unique historical catastrophes. Yet survivors of a dozen years of the AIDS epidemic are expected to be well-adjusted, grateful people; specific psychological, spiritual, or existential needs should remain unspoken. There's more important business at hand.

AIDS is a disaster, different from though parallel to earthquakes and fires, plane crashes and shipwrecks, the bombing of Hiroshima and the Vietnam War. Like a long, slow train collision occurring over years rather than seconds, the AIDS epidemic presents us with survivors who have suffered enormously, witnessed extraordinary human mutilation, and are left wondering why they survived while others perished. Is it any wonder that individual survivors of the AIDS epidemic are experiencing a broad range of clinical symptoms usually seen in the wake of mass disaster? Yet, as often occurs amid certain kinds of trauma, a mass architecture of denial has been constructed which insists that the uninfected are "doing fine."

Not only are HIV-negative individuals crashing under the weight of so much sickness and death, but we judge the manifestations of this trauma within us as indications of our own personal weaknesses. When we experience depression, anxiety, panic attacks, or listlessness, we attribute it to failings in our character rather than to a natural response to decimation. And we are aided in our self-blame by psychotherapists, journalists, and community activists who occupy this same contradictory terrain of decimation and denial.

We can afford to ignore the impact of the epidemic on the uninfected no longer. Over half the gay men in San Francisco are estimated to be infected with HIV; another 14,000 have died in the past dozen years. The majority of my peers who were here in 1980 are either dead or infected. The handful of us who are as yet uninfected struggle to avoid succumbing to self-destructive behavior indicative of the demons inside us. Therapists I've spoken with estimate that almost half of us are on antidepressants and antianxiety medication. Anecdotal evidence of drug and alcohol relapse and suicide activity is mounting; the statistics on the prevalence of unprotected anal intercourse and subsequent seroconversion are again on the rise. Something is happening to us which no one wants to face.

HIV-Negative is the first book published which begins to describe the emotional and psychological landscape of the uninfected after a dozen years of plague. In account after account, the real-life conflicts we face spill out and the struggles to escape or hide, resist or adjust, loom large. HIV hasn't gotten into our bloodstream; nevertheless it has twisted and distorted our identities, self-esteem, and relationships. We read of the difficult social and sexual dilemmas posed by antibody status and the many ways our lives have been interrupted and redirected without our knowledge or consent. The lives we live now are not the lives we expected to be living; we are not now—nor will we ever again be—who we once were. This cataclysm has changed us in deep and permanent ways.

The testimony in these pages is shattering, destroying silences in the community, in the media, and within the souls of HIV-negative people. The tenuous grasp we have held on our fragmented selves becomes difficult to maintain. As the HIV-negative narrators in this book strip away the cloak of secrecy and reveal the complex ways in which living in the center of a cyclone transforms the human spirit, we find pieces of our own lives spinning madly through the air. Through bearing witness to this epidemic, we are able to transmit our testimony to others and begin to integrate the horror into the story of our lives.

Such activity must take place before individual and social restoration can begin. This book encourages all of us to speak the truths of our lives, however ugly, painful, or bizarre. The disaster of AIDS demands much of us; our testimony is the key to our continuing survival.

Eric Rofes
San Francisco

CONTENTS

ix

PROLOGUE

Boccaccio's Lesson

In the year of Our Lord 1348 the deadly plague broke out in the great city of Florence, most beautiful of Italian cities. Whether through the operation of the heavenly bodies or because of our own iniquities which the just wrath of God sought to correct, the plague had arisen. . . . It spread without stop from one place to another. . . . Neither knowledge nor human foresight availed against it, though . . . advice was broadcast for the preservation of health. . . .

. . . Various fears and superstitions arose among the survivors, almost all of which tended toward one end—to flee from the sick and whatever had belonged to them. In this way each man thought to be safeguarding his own health. Some among them were of the opinion that by living temperately and guarding against excess of all kinds, they could do much toward avoiding the danger; and forming a band they lived away from the rest of the world. Gathering in those houses where no one had been ill and living was more comfortable, they shut themselves in. They ate moderately of the best that could be had and drank excellent wines, avoiding all luxuriousness. With music and whatever other delights they could have, they lived together in this fashion, allowing no one to speak to them and avoiding news either of death or sickness from the outer world.

Others, arriving at a contrary conclusion, held that plenty of drinking and enjoyment, singing and free living and the gratification of the appetite in every possible way, letting the devil take the hindmost, was the best preventative of such a malady; and as far as they could, they suited the action to the word. Day and night they went from one tavern to another drinking and carousing unrestrainedly. At the least inkling of something that suited them, they ran wild in other people's houses, and there was no one to prevent them, for everyone had abandoned all responsibility for his belongings as well as for himself, considering his days numbered. . . .

Many others followed a middle course, neither restricting themselves in their diet like the first, nor giving themselves free rein in lewdness and debauchery like the second, but using everything to sufficience, according to their appetites. They did not shut themselves in, but went about, some carrying flowers in their hands, some fragrant herbs, and others divers kinds of spices which they frequently smelled, thinking it good to comfort the brain with such odors, especially since the air was oppressive and full of the stench of corruption, sickness and medicines. . . .

Although the members of these different factions did not all perish, neither did they all escape. . . .

. . . So great was the multitude of those who died in the city night and day, what with lack of proper care and the virulence of the plague, that it was terrible to hear of, and worse still to see. Out of sheer necessity, therefore, quite different customs arose among the survivors from the original laws of the townspeople.[1]

Giovanni Boccaccio
From *The Decameron* (1353)

Climbing to Angels Landing

HALFWAY ALONG THE TRAIL from Scout Lookout to Angels Landing in Zion National Park, Utah, the path narrows along an exposed sandstone rib so that hikers must walk single file. On the right side, the rock underfoot tumbles hundreds of feet into Refrigerator Canyon. On the left, it drops a thousand feet to another canyon floor, where the North Fork of the Virgin River meanders.

I hiked this trail with my younger brother a few years ago, and when we came to this place he went first. He moved effortlessly across, using a step carved into the rock like the stairs of a Roman amphitheater. As I followed him, I found myself crouching and moving slower and slower, until my knee joints began to creak. A single misstep, I realized, could send me plummeting to my death. I froze.

"Just don't look down," my brother called out as he turned and saw me immobilized with one foot on the stone step.

Poised at this juncture on the trail to Angels Landing, I saw the ground hundreds of feet below me on both sides. It barely seemed to move as I walked, much as the moon hardly appears to move as you cross a field at night. Heeding my brother's advice, I glanced up toward him. Even so, my peripheral vision continued to register the canyon floor far below.

Along the trail to Angels Landing, chains are embedded in the stone as handrails to assist hikers. My brother, nimble and sure-footed, hardly touched the chains. I clasped the chains and pulled myself along one step at a time. I envied my brother's poise.

"Don't worry so much," he said to me. "Just stand up and you'll balance fine."

"I'm not afraid of heights," I yelled back as the wind whipped across the space between us. "I'm afraid of falling."

THE GRAVITY OF HIV INFECTION

Gay men who test HIV-negative often find themselves fearful and immobilized much as I was on the trail to Angels Landing. When we learn of our HIV-negative status, we feel relieved, redeemed, saved. And yet often this relief is short-lived. The possibility of becoming HIV-positive lingers in the periphery of our minds just as the canyon floor lingered in the periphery of my vision as I walked along the trail in Zion National Park.

Some gay men have little difficulty adjusting to the knowledge of their HIV-negative status. Like my brother, they walk nimbly along the trail with assurance. Others of us, however, are not so fortunate. Our position seems precarious. One misstep, one moment of carelessness during our lovemaking, we fear, might send us hurtling to an unwelcome fate. Some of us are convinced that we cannot escape becoming HIV-infected, just as we cannot escape the inexorable force of gravity. Often these feelings lead to a kind of sexual and emotional immobility akin to the immobility I experienced on the trail to Angels Landing.

I suggest the metaphor of falling because it expresses the one-way nature of HIV infection. According to our current under-standing of HIV,[1] the uninfected can become infected but the infected cannot become uninfected. Being HIV-negative—unlike being HIV-positive—is not necessarily a permanent position. It is unstable, and this instability makes it difficult for many HIV-negative gay men to feel secure.

I sympathize with my HIV-positive friends who object to equating HIV infection with falling. The metaphor of a fall is sometimes used to imply that those who have fallen are inferior to those who have not fallen. Good is equated with up, and bad with down, much as heaven and hell have been visualized in spatial terms. Most of my HIV-infected friends do not view their HIV infection as evidence of a moral lapse or a fall from grace. In many cases, their HIV infection occurred before the mechanism of HIV transmission was understood. And even if their infection occurred later, many people find it unhelpful to dwell on the question of whether they could have prevented it had they been more cautious.

Even if we avoid adopting a moralistic hierarchy, those of us who learn we are HIV-negative often find ourselves freighted with a moral charge: if we become infected in the future, we will have to face those who reprove us because "we should have known better." The responsibility to remain uninfected is a burden whose psychological costs are not fully understood.

THE POSITION OF THE HIV-NEGATIVE

Before I got tested for HIV, I did not imagine that HIV-negative gay men faced unique psychological and social issues. I had been a volunteer for an AIDS hot line run by the AIDS Action Committee of Massachusetts since 1987, so I knew that many gay men felt anxiety about HIV and wondered whether they should be tested. But I had not given much thought to the ways in which HIV testing[2] might raise different issues for the HIV-positive and the HIV-negative.

Like most people who consider HIV testing, I supposed that testing negative would eliminate my anxiety about HIV and AIDS. I was surprised, therefore, to discover when I tested negative in 1989 that my concerns about HIV were not resolved by testing. On the contrary, testing HIV-negative brought forth new concerns I had not predicted.

Finding out I was HIV-negative put me in a new position—psychologically, socially, ethically, and philosophically—a position very different from not knowing my HIV status. Suddenly I began asking myself all kinds of new questions: Do I believe my test results? Why don't I feel like telling other people my "good" news? Will knowing I am HIV-negative influence my sexual behavior? How should I act with HIV-positive friends? Should I ask sexual partners about their HIV status? How will I feel about myself if I become HIV-positive?

I did not know if other men who tested HIV-negative were also asking themselves these questions. Then in February 1991, a meeting was held in Boston for HIV-negative gay and bisexual men to talk about their concerns. The meeting drew almost 90 men, clearly revealing that an unmet community need was being addressed. I attended that meeting and later became a facilitator of the group when it continued to meet monthly at the Fenway Community Health Center in Boston.

I participated in the Boston HIV-Negative Support Group because I wanted to hear what other HIV-negative gay men were thinking. I was relieved to learn that I was not alone in my concerns. Other men too were experiencing anxiety, grief, and hopelessness in the face of the epidemic. Other men too were tired of pretending they were coping well in the midst of an epidemic. Other men too were experiencing numbness as a result of repeated loss, and worrying that they might not be able to remain uninfected for the rest of their lives.

The support group revealed to me that many issues remain unresolved—or are brought forth—by a negative HIV test. Although most gay men report relief at learning they are HIV-negative, there are many other responses, including surprise, disbelief, hope, doubt, guilt, and grief. The variety of those responses is the subject of this book.

NEGLECTING THE HIV-NEGATIVE

Why did it take nearly ten years for the issues facing the HIV-negative to become apparent? One practical reason stands out. During the first decade of our response to the AIDS epidemic, we focused energy and resources on supporting HIV-positive people and researching ways to combat HIV and its associated infections. This focus was—and continues to be—understandable and appropriate. One unforeseen consequence of this focus, however, is that the effect of the epidemic on HIV-negative people remains poorly understood.

There are also historical reasons why the position of being HIV-negative has remained unexamined until recently. HIV testing did not become widely available until 1985, and when it did, many gay men avoided testing because they feared discrimination and there were no treatments for asymptomatic HIV infection. One consequence of this early reluctance to be tested was that both infected and uninfected gay men inhabited the same position. In the absence of information about HIV status, we all had to assume that we might be infected and behave accordingly. Safer sex guidelines were developed that treated all individuals the same. The psychological result was that both infected and uninfected gay men were "living with AIDS" in much the same way. There did not appear to be a need to discuss the position of the HIV-negative individual.

When therapeutic advances in the late 1980s made early knowledge of one's HIV-positive status more useful, more gay men got tested. As more people learned they were HIV-negative, the position of the HIV-negative individual became clearer, and social and sexual divisions based on HIV status were brought into stark relief.

Even so, there remained powerful reasons why the issues facing the uninfected were not addressed. Sometimes HIV-positive people disparaged support networks for the uninfected: "What could HIV-negative people possibly talk about? That sounds like a group of rich folks sitting in a circle deciding how to spend their money." Far more influential than such comments, I believe, was the survivor's guilt commonly found among the HIV-negative. Many of us felt we must not dwell on our own problems when those of the HIV-positive were so much greater. After all, shouldn't testing HIV-negative be a cause for celebration? What did we have to complain about, when we were not facing the challenges that the HIV-positive must face? Such feelings for a long time kept HIV-negative gay men from recognizing that they have unique mental-health concerns that need to be addressed.

ADDRESSING THE HIV-NEGATIVE

I believe gay men will pay dearly if we do not begin addressing HIV-negative issues directly. Not only will we see increased rates of new infection among HIV-negative gay men, but what psychotherapist Walt Odets has called "the silent epidemic"—widespread community depression among the HIV-negative—will continue to damage our physical, emotional, and spiritual health. I am dismayed by the thought that gay men might self-destruct because we cannot figure out how to live well.

By the end of 1991, I realized that the Boston HIV-Negative Support Group had been profoundly helpful to me. It had provided me a window into the lives of other HIV-negative gay men, helped me feel less isolated, and allowed me to explore and accept my complicated feelings about being HIV-negative.

Because the group had been so useful to me, I imagined that a book in which gay men offered their views about being HIV-negative could be useful to others who did not have a similar forum to discuss these issues. Such a book might begin a much-needed discussion about how HIV-negative gay men can sustain themselves during the continued onslaught of the AIDS epidemic.

SCOPE OF THE INTERVIEWS

In 1992 and 1993 I interviewed more than 45 HIV-negative gay men from the metropolitan Boston area. My intention was to gather information about the psychological and social issues facing gay men who have learned they are HIV-negative.

During my two-hour interviews, I used a sequence of questions that followed a roughly chronological order, exploring the past, present, and future. In the first part of each interview, I asked people questions about their past experiences of the AIDS epidemic and HIV testing:

- What was it like not to know your HIV status?
- What led you to get HIV testing?
- What were your experiences getting tested?
- What were your reactions to testing HIV-negative?

In the second part of each interview, I asked people to discuss how learning they were HIV-negative influenced their present social and sexual relationships:

- In what ways are there divisions between the HIV-positive and the HIV-negative?
- Does your sexual behavior depend upon the HIV status of your partner?
- Why do you think some uninfected men have unsafe sex?
- When do you have difficulty practicing safer sex?

In the third part of each interview, I asked people to discuss their concerns about the future, including retesting, seroconversion (becoming HIV-positive), and survivorship:

- Have you been retested? Why?
- How would you feel if you seroconverted?
- What does it mean to be a survivor of the AIDS epidemic?
- What is in our future?

I structured this book by alternating interview-based chapters and thematic chapters. The even-numbered chapters are based on individual interviews selected for their interest and insight, and the odd-numbered chapters (aside from the first and last) are based on general themes I uncovered during my interviewing. The thematic chapters follow roughly the same sequence as my interview questions. I have tried when possible to place the interview-based chapters so they comment upon the surrounding thematic chapters.

INTERVIEW SOURCES

The people I interviewed, unless otherwise indicated, were HIV-negative gay men from metropolitan Boston. Many of them have participated in the Boston HIV-Negative Support Group. As participants in a support group, they may exhibit greater anxiety or more caution about HIV than others. Ages ranged from 23 to 52. Other people I interviewed were professionals in the field of AIDS, including HIV-test counselors and public-health educators.

To supplement my research, I posted a list of interview questions on the Internet. I got over 50 replies, mostly from men but a few from women. Responses came from California, Colorado, Delaware, the District of Columbia, Illinois, Indiana, Iowa, Kentucky, Massachusetts, Michigan, New York, Ohio, Oregon, Pennsylvania, Rhode Island, Texas, Virginia, and Washington. Other responses came from Australia, Canada, Denmark, and the United Kingdom. Ages ranged from 19 to 48. These replies reiterated many of the things I had learned in my interviews.

Because the people I interviewed and the replies I received via the Internet were not a random sample, it would be unscientific to conclude that they are representative. I believe, however, that they voice concerns shared by many. To protect privacy, I have in most cases changed the names of my sources.

AUDIENCE

The principal audience for this book is HIV-negative gay men. In addition, I trust this book will appeal to many of the following:

- People considering HIV testing for the first time
- HIV-positive gay men, especially those in positive-negative couples
- Family, friends, and coworkers of HIV-negative gay men
- HIV-test counselors
- AIDS educators working in primary prevention
- Mental-health workers, counselors, clinicians, and therapists working with HIV-negative clients

Readers who are not gay themselves but whose lives are affected by HIV may gain something by considering what gay men have learned about being HIV-negative. To survive this epidemic, we must learn from each other. This book raises issues that resonate with us all. It is about how we live now: how we experience and define the meanings of sexuality, vulnerability, mortality, and responsibility.

I hope the variety of voices in this book allows readers to recognize the wide range of attitudes and responses to the HIV epidemic. Readers may find some of their own thoughts reflected in these voices. I hope they also find new food for thought in other people's experiences. One theme that surfaced as I interviewed people is that when we see how other people have struggled with and resolved difficult issues we are better able to confront these issues ourselves.

RETURNING FROM ANGELS LANDING

As I climbed to Angels Landing with my brother, I was encouraged by the hikers returning from the summit. Their broad smiles and murmurs of sympathy as they saw me clinging desperately to the rock encouraged me in a way that my brother's poise had not.

Listening to someone telling me not to worry because I test negative for HIV is like listening to my brother telling me not to worry about falling off the trail to Angels Landing in Zion National Park. Although well intentioned, it doesn't really help. Fears and anxieties cannot always be rationally controlled. But listening to others who have experienced fears and found ways to manage them may help.

I did, after all, make it to Angels Landing. On my way back, I had more confidence as I negotiated the trail. I remembered my initial fears and was not entirely free of them, but I was better equipped to manage them. I passed again the step carved into the rock. From this direction, the step looked like a seat. I paused to sit there for a moment, secure in the niche, and was able to look to my left and right without fearing I would fall.

This book is like the niche carved into the rock at the narrowest part of the trail to Angels Landing: it can serve either as a step or as a resting place. It is designed to act as a step to support people who have recently tested HIV-negative and as a resting place for those who have made that journey and want to sit for a moment, reflect on their experience, and regain strength.

I hope this book helps people who learn they are HIV-negative negotiate their trails without the fear of falling. Or if with the fear, then without the fall. We need ways to find our balance before we can move on. The HIV test provides for some of us a chain to cling to, helping us move slowly along our path. But an excessive reliance on it may inhibit our progress. We cannot learn to trust our inner sense of balance if we never stand up.

1

A Stranger Comes to Town

Anthony Tommasini

I'M OF AN AGE where I really went through the whole thing. I remember very clearly the articles about the gay cancer and the gay plague and people having no idea what the hell was going on. It all seemed very distant from me, but I was scared. My first friend to get sick was somebody I had known at Yale. He died quickly and it seemed mysterious to me at the time. It was frightening. We just didn't understand what was going on.

My first very good friend who died, Bob Walden, also got sick very early. I remember when I got a letter from him saying he had HTLV-something. I didn't know what he was telling me. I literally didn't know what it meant. I asked him, "Do you have AIDS? Is that what you're saying?" And he said yes. I remember going to see him and helping him and dressing him—he had a Hickman catheter—being terrified of getting blood on my fingers, and not wanting to let him know that I was terrified.

One of the most moving things about the movie *Longtime Companion* is that it really did capture the confusion of those early years. In the hospital one character is sick and his lover is standing there in a surgical gown, sobbing. He wants to go hug his lover and he doesn't know what to do. I sat there in the audience wanting to shout, "Hug him! Hug him! It's okay. It's okay." But we just didn't know. We were paralyzed.

❧

When the test came along, it seemed like a big breakthrough to me. I remember there being uncertainty about the test, but it seemed basically like a breakthrough. All the issues about testing didn't occur to me. I remember thinking, "Ah, finally, we've got a test. Well, that's great." It was only later that I really started thinking about the implications.

I didn't get tested right away. I was involved with a guy who had never been tested. He was younger than I. He was terribly worried, terribly afraid of it. I couldn't figure out what his worst scenario would be: that he would be positive, that I would be positive, that both of us would be positive? It was all just white fear to him, just big, irrational, consuming fear. I wound up getting tested partly for him. I thought I could hold his hand and take him through it.

Now that I think about it, I probably deflected some of my own anxiety into a sort of paternal role. Maybe I used his fear, and my realization that I had less fear, to get myself through it. People in my age bracket had a decade of sex before this even started. It was easy to assume that we were going to be positive.

I went to the Fenway Community Health Center in Boston. I remember when the counselor came to bring us into the room to tell us what the results were, she said, "Oh, that's a nice backpack." I thought, "Uh oh." I thought the chatty remark was proof that she was setting me up for bad news.

We got our results together and were both negative. My friend was elated. I was relieved and happy. But that was also when it really first hit me that I had made it through.

It must have been 1987 when I took that test, because Bob was still alive. I remember visiting him. His mind was slipping. You could talk to him but he would forget things. He was lying in bed, and I was stroking his head, just being there. He started getting a little weepy. He said, "So you, you're not HIV-positive, are you?" And I said, "No. No, I'm negative." He knew that, but he had forgotten. Then he said, "Well, that's good, Tony." Then he said,

"Somebody has got to stay around to tell the story." And that struck me.

This will show you how AIDS affected me: In my class at Yale, there were four of us who were so close. One is my friend Tom, who is a doctor. He's straight, he has three kids, lives in Seattle, and he's fine. Then there's me: I'm HIV-negative. One's my friend Bob, who died in 1988. And then my friend Al, who is in San Francisco and getting closer to death. So 50 percent of us, half of this bright-college-years group.

My friend in San Francisco who is dying, this beautiful black man, this amazing man, is such a life force. He walks into a room and just takes it over. He can't understand why anybody wouldn't think he is completely attractive. And that actually works.

I find it hard to know what to say to Al, to know how to deal with this guy who is dying who should not die. I find it so much harder than if I were the person who was dying and he was the life force helping me through whatever years I had. That's part of HIV-negative survivor's guilt. Why did I survive? I mean, Al of all people! It's incredible to me.

When Bob died, I went to his memorial and something occurred to me to write about him. The *New York Times* ran it as an op-ed piece. I've written a lot since then about AIDS. It was Bob's injunction to me: Somebody has got to tell the story. Maybe that's why I have survived. I have more to say. I'm sure I do. More stories to tell. This is not going away. And even if it does, the stories are still going to be there to be told. Maybe that's my role: to be one of the people that tells the story.

Shortly after Bob died, I felt I could not sit around and just watch my friends die and not do something besides helping them. That's when I went to the AIDS Action Committee of Massachusetts to start working on the hot line.

As part of the training, we were told to write out four items on index cards in four categories: four activities, four roles, four possessions, and four people. Important things. Activities for me: swimming, playing the piano. Roles: I'm an uncle, I'm a friend, I'm a son. Possessions: my condo, my piano. And then four people. It wasn't like you had to pick the four closest people, but just four people you were thinking about. I picked Jon, my best friend in Boston, and my friend Tom in Seattle, and the two other Yale people: Bob, who had just died, and Al, who was HIV-positive, I knew, but not sick at the time.

When I laid out those cards, I remember looking at the floor and thinking, "Wow! There's my life. Look at that." I sort of felt pleased. "Gee. Those are pretty good things. Sort of a nice life."

And then the specter of AIDS, in the form of one of the trainer's helpers, swept through the room, picking up cards. The specter would go through everybody's cards and take a few of them. Not everything, just a few. He'd *select* a few things.

It was very powerful—the idea that this specter could just come through and take things from you. That all of a sudden, AIDS could mean that you don't have your condo, or you can't swim anymore, or you've lost people, or you're no longer one of your roles.

And I remember he was coming toward me and all I could think of was, "Don't take Al. Please don't take Al." He, of the four people, was the one who was HIV-positive. Bob was already gone. I was thinking, "Take Bob. That would sort of be appropriate." I put him on my list because I was thinking about him all that weekend. In a sense Bob was the reason I was there.

Every time people compliment me about my condo and how lucky I am, I think of this exercise. I remember thinking, "Take the condo. Take the condo, please. But don't take Al." So the specter comes and—you won't believe this—he picks up a few cards, and the only person he picks up is Al. And he's done.

❧

They say there are only two stories in all of fiction. One is boy meets girl, boy loses girl, boy gets girl, or some variation of that story. The other is a stranger comes to town. Everything changes because of the stranger. AIDS is the story of the stranger who comes to town. Here we all are, bopping along, trying to be gay and happy, and this stranger comes to town and everything is different. That's what it was like.

2

Like Ripping a Bandage Off

Sandro Costa

To be honest with you, if I thought about AIDS, it was like for five minutes. I went to all the fund-raisers—the dance-athons, the walk-athons—because it was fun to go with your friends and have a good time. We knew it was for AIDS, but we never thought about that. In the club scene in L.A., we'd go to a club on a certain night and AIDS Project Los Angeles would be passing out buttons, safe sex stuff, and condoms. We'd take them, but never really thought about it.

I think a majority of my friends were like that. We never really talked about AIDS, we never really knew anybody that had it. AIDS was something that happened to guys that had group sex, things like that. It wasn't part of our clique. It was something we wanted to forget about. We were just out, meeting guys, and having a good time. It was a rebellious thing to go to gay clubs. Most of the kids at the clubs were underage anyway, and shouldn't have even been there. It was a big deal to get in, to be doing things your parents don't want you to do.

When I think of the way I used to act, I think of myself as a slut. It wasn't like a different guy every night, but there are still days when I remember guys I had forgotten I was with. Sometimes I would practice safer sex, if they wanted it. Other times I wouldn't. There would be nights that I didn't feel like having anal sex, but I would go along with it because—I don't know—I was afraid to say no, he was bigger than I was, he was going to do it anyway. With guys that I really liked a lot, I would do it because they wanted to and I wanted them to like me.

It wasn't until Christmas of 1992 that I heard a couple of stories about people I knew who had AIDS. My friend Walter and I would talk about it, try to separate them from us: "Remember that person we haven't seen for six months? He has AIDS." "Yeah, but didn't he sleep with a lot of people? And didn't he used to have group sex?"

Josh, my ex-boyfriend, was not like that, at least from what he said. He was very monogamous. I was with him for almost a year before we broke up. He had only had a couple of relationships. As far as I know, he didn't have a lot of one-night stands. But then he also didn't tell me that he had AIDS.

In retrospect, Josh had symptoms when we were together. He was always sick, always coughing. He lost his voice numerous times. He had lesions. He never told any of us what was going on. I don't think he even knew. I know for a fact that he didn't get tested. At one point I told him, "Why don't you go see a doctor?" He told me, "No. I hate doctors."

A big part of the reason I never suspected Josh had AIDS was that he did a lot to hide how sick he was. He was suffering more than any of us knew. It never really crossed my mind that he had AIDS, and if it did, it was for a split second before dismissing it. I thought it was a cold that wouldn't go away. We were young and in love. Something like AIDS was inconceivable.

We broke up, and although I thought about Josh a lot after we split, I never thought of his illnesses. A few months later, without a word to any of us, he moved back home. He called me a couple of times from Texas, but that was it. Then one day before Christmas this past year, I called. His brother answered the phone and told me Josh had passed away. He had been put into the hospital a week before he died. His brother told me Josh had been out of work ill for a couple of months, didn't want to go to the hospital, didn't want to know what he had.

Of course, after he was admitted they found out it was AIDS. The doctor told him, "If you had come to me a few months ago, I would be able to help you. I really don't think you're going to last long." And he died a week later, right before Thanksgiving. He died of pneumonia, which is what he had all along. He was 21.

His brother had no idea that Josh was gay. His parents to this day don't know. His brother had taken him to the hospital. When I called that day, his brother said, "I'm happy you called, but don't call here again, because I don't want my parents to find out." I guess he lied to his parents about what Josh had. It seems sad that I spent a year with Josh and I don't know where he is buried. I can't send a card. I can't do anything.

You know what's funny? The day before I called, I was watching an episode of *Designing Women* where one of their friends asks them to design his funeral because he is dying of AIDS. The whole show is about death, AIDS, and safe sex. That night I couldn't stop thinking about it. Then the next day I called and found out Josh had passed away.

I think he suspected all along he had it. I mean, how can you not know? I spoke with his best friend afterwards. I had never really spoken to her before. She had a lot of friends who had died of AIDS. She said, "Yeah, he had all the symptoms that my other friends had. I urged him to get tested and to get help but he wouldn't."

He told me he loved me, for a year almost. I'm surprised that he dropped out of my life. It leaves me upset because he didn't admit, "Hey, Sandro, I may have this. Why don't you go get tested?" He didn't consider me. He didn't consider all the people I could be passing it on to. He had numerous opportunities to call me and tell me. In that sense, I'm bitter. I can't help thinking there must have been a day before he died when he thought to himself, "Look, I have AIDS. I'm dying. I should probably call Sandro and tell him, because we had unprotected sex." Sometimes I think of him with great feeling, but then at other times with great resentment. He had no regard for his life or anybody else's, as far as I am concerned.

&

My first reactions when I heard the news were despair over his death and "I have AIDS." The next day I had the most terrible fever. I was chilly. I remember having no food in the house. I had to take myself to the store. I was dizzy. I thought, "How coincidental! I find out that he had it, and now I'm getting sick." The next day I felt fine. I had no trace of the fever, no trace of a cold. But I had this pain, a burning sensation, in my chest. I had it for weeks. I woke up with sore throats. Because Josh had lost his voice, I naturally thought I had AIDS. I don't know if it was all psychological or what. I thought, "Is this something I am just imagining or is this real?" But I really felt something. I felt sick for weeks.

I made an appointment to get tested through a Latino AIDS group. I don't know why I picked that organization; I just had the number. I called and they scheduled me for an appointment a month later, the day before New Year's Eve.

For that month I was a mess. I was a shut-in. I didn't want to get up and get dressed. I couldn't picture myself trying to get through a whole day at work. I had three weeks' vacation time saved up where I did clerical work at a department store. I told them a very close friend had passed away—which wasn't a lie—and took my vacation time. But even after three weeks, I couldn't go back.

I didn't go out, didn't take calls, didn't do anything. I stayed in my apartment. Friends would come to my door and I would turn off the light and pretend I wasn't there. I slept the entire time. I have no recollection of that whole month. I just slept.

When I was awake, my mind was going a mile a minute. I thought about everything I had done with everybody, especially with Josh. I had been with him for a year and we had totally unprotected sex, more times than I can count. We did everything. I could not conceive of any way that I could not have AIDS.

I was the last person that Josh had sex with, as far as I know. I don't know of anybody he was with in Los Angeles before he left to go home. He was really sick; I doubt he was with anybody. So I know it was not something that he could have gotten later, after our relationship had ended.

I made maybe three phone calls the entire month. I called my best friend Walter and told him, "I called Josh the other day and his brother told me something really shocking." My friend Walter said, "Oh, no. What happened? Did he die?" And I said, "Yeah." He said, "Well, he was sick, Sandro, for a long time." I asked, "So you knew it was AIDS?" And he replied, "Well, no, but I figured it was. I just didn't say anything to you because I figured that you knew." That was interesting.

And then another friend of mine, Oliver, called me and the conversation just naturally got around to it, because I brought it there. He had just had one of his friends find out that her boyfriend had died of AIDS. She had tested negative a few months before, then went to get tested again and tested positive. So he was telling me about that. He told me he was tested every three months. It was a surprise to see that he had been thinking for a long time about things that I was just beginning to think about. We had been friends for a long time, but he had never mentioned it. I felt out of the loop.

Then there was my friend Marco, who was trying to get in contact with me for a long time that month. Since I had broken up with Josh a year before, we had been messing around. Every once in a while he'd call and we'd get together. I wasn't careful when I had sex with him. But he told me that he got tested every six months, and the last time he tested negative. He thinks as long as he's negative, then it's okay. He's always a top. He would never have been a bottom. Maybe that's why he feels he's not as much at risk. I guess he felt that because he tested negative, he was fine, and he wasn't going to worry about it.

So he was calling around that time, and I avoided him like the plague, because sex was just something I could never do again. When I talked to Marco, he could tell over the phone that there was a definite change in my character. He said, "God, you're really worried about this. Well, you have the appointment, you're going to get tested, don't worry about it. You're not going to die tomorrow. You're going to waste this whole month worried about testing positive, and you may not even *be* positive." It's easy to tell somebody that. It's another thing when you're actually waiting to get tested. He had been tested many times; it was my first test. He didn't really know anybody who had passed away; my lover had just died. So it was different.

By Christmas, I was feeling better. I convinced myself that maybe I was lucky and I didn't have AIDS. The day before the test, one of my friends called and asked if I wanted to go to Disneyland the next day. I said, "Sure." So I went to Disneyland instead, and totally blew off the test. In retrospect, that was probably a bad thing to do. There were other people waiting; somebody else could have been tested.

I made another appointment, with AIDS Project Los Angeles. They set me up with an agency at a health center that could do it the next week.

When I got tested, the counselor was very nice. I told her my primary concern was about Josh. She told me something very definitive: "If you're worried about this person you slept with over a year ago, this test will definitely tell you. It will not tell you within the last three months." She used three months as the time that the antibody would take to appear. She was very definitive about it, which surprised me, because all the books I had read—I had read Magic Johnson's book when I was browsing in a bookstore—said it could be anywhere from three months to a year or more before the antibody shows up. It made me feel good to hear a health-care professional telling me this. I imagined she really should know what she was talking about.

I cried when they took the blood. Not because it hurt, but because I couldn't believe I was sitting in a room getting tested for AIDS. The thought struck me: "How many more needles am I going to have to face in the future? This may be the first in a long series."

I was okay waiting for the results. I went to work. It was good for me to go back to work that week, because I socialized. I got my mind off it. I was supposed to get my results back a week later, on Inauguration Day of 1993. I asked for a day off.

I remember waking up that day and there was a talk show on TV about AIDS. There was this little girl with AIDS and they didn't know how she had gotten it. She never had a blood transfusion. Her parents were negative. There was all this controversy about having to change the perspectives about how AIDS could be caught. There was also a woman who had been trying to get pregnant for a long time, and she had artificial insemination and got AIDS.

I was expecting to go in there and hear the counselor tell me that I had it. I looked myself in the mirror and talked to myself for a good half hour before I went. I told myself, "Look, you have it. Don't be surprised when she tells you." I didn't know what I was going to do when she told me, whether I was going to cry. I know that when I get nervous I shake a lot. I took the bus there that day, because I didn't know if I was going to be able to drive home.

I went by myself, went in there, sat down. When the counselor came in the waiting room and got me, the expression I read on her face was, "How am I going to tell this person he has AIDS?" When she sat down, she told me right away, like ripping a bandage off, "You don't have it. You're negative." I couldn't believe it. I was shocked.

She asked some follow-up questions: "How has this changed you? How has your attitude toward safe sex changed?" I said,

"Well, I'm never going to have sex again, basically. Can't get much safer than that." She said, "I suggest you get tested in another six months, just to make sure."

It had been 17 months since I had had sex with Josh. I knew that I didn't get it from Josh. That narrowed the field down a lot. In the year and a half since I had broken up with him, there were numerous instances where—only because the other person wanted to—we did use condoms. And it was anal sex only with Marco, who had told me he was negative. With other people, it was oral sex, which was not that much of a risk. So I thought pretty much that the test was accurate.

I felt I had been lucky, really lucky. I must have been, considering all the times that me and Josh had sex and the things that we did! I mean, you hear about people having sex with one person one time and they get it. I just don't see how I could not have gotten it.

There were a few days when I didn't believe it. I thought about the day I went to get the results. When you're tested, they give you a number that you have to check against the result sheet. But when I went for the results, the counselor just knew me by face. I don't remember if she asked me for my little card. I don't remember her checking the number against the number on the test results. She may have, but I was in a daze at the time. I wanted to get out of there so fast I did not even look at the paper.

So I called and talked to one of the administrators. I said, "I want to come back and take a look at the results, because I don't remember her asking me for my number." And he said, "We really don't do that under normal circumstances. I can just assure you that everybody who tested positive that day we are doing follow-up with. So if you are positive, you would be working with us. You would know."

But I insisted. And I left work early to go back the next day. He was really nice about it when I got there. He dug in and got the test results out. I actually compared the numbers.

❦

I made the decision to come back home to Boston whether I was negative or positive. I had been thinking a long time about coming home. It seemed like a good time to make a transition. I couldn't stay in L.A. and go to clubs for the rest of my life. I left school the year before and was in L.A. only because I had a lot of friends there. I was thinking, "I have family in Boston. How long can I stay in Los Angeles and be doing nothing with my life? I need to go home, be a good boy, and stay away from 'bad' L.A." But Boston can be pretty bad too, I've found out, if you go to the right places.

My parents knew that I was gay, but I didn't tell them a word about what was happening until right before I came back. I told my mom what was going on, but I didn't tell her until I found out for sure I was negative. Even though she knew I was gay, I don't think she ever really pictured me having sex with people. I surprised myself in the amount that I told her. I thought this was something she was not going to be able to handle, but actually she handled it really well.

I said, "I just want you to know I'm going through this, because when I come home, I may be introverted for a while. I don't want you to think I'm unhappy to be home. I don't want you to think I'm unhappy not to be in Los Angeles anymore. I just want you to know this is why."

She said, "This is not the only reason you're coming home, is it?" And I said, "No." She said, "Well, good, because eventually you're going to work through it, and I don't want you to find yourself in Boston really wanting to be in Los Angeles. I hope you're not just running back home because you're running away from it. Because it will take you just as long to get over it in Boston as it will in Los Angeles." For her to say that really surprised me. She has been begging me for years to come back to Boston. She never wanted me to be in Los Angeles. She's Italian, she's Catholic, she's very protective. I think she has accepted the fact that I am 23 years old and am not a kid anymore.

ł

Testing negative I really saw as another chance, the start of another life. I saw it as an opportunity to look for something more meaningful. In Los Angeles, I was going out every night. I thought it was cool to go out and be wild, have fun, party, and have sex. But I really wasn't happy. Everybody needs a loving relationship. That's what you really want.

After I found out Josh died, there was no more sex. I built up a new morality for myself: I was not going to have sex unless it was somebody that I was serious about, in love with, had been going out with for a long time, had just been tested, and I knew was negative. And even so, we would always use a condom. I had all these new rules for myself.

Marco called and wanted to come over a couple of times before I returned to Boston. He did, but we didn't do anything. I explained to him why. He thought I was being stupid, being crazy. He said, "Well, you're negative. I'm negative. We're not going to give it to each other. We'll use a condom if you want." But I just didn't want it. To have sex with him, who I cared about but not enough, would be going against that new morality I had for myself. So we didn't. He was disappointed. I didn't feel too guilty about it.

I've been to the clubs here in Boston. It's the same as in L.A. The people dress the same, they act the same, they are just as wild. I thought it would be different. My friends out there make fun of Boston. They think the clubs are subdued. Eventually somebody asked me to dance. His name was Jerry. We've gotten to know each other over the past couple of months. It was a week before we had sex. I waited a week, which was good, because that's usually something I don't do.

The first time I had sex with Jerry, we were totally safe. There was no exchange of bodily fluids except for kissing. There was no oral sex, no anal sex. Just basically masturbation, and that's it. But I was very guilty after I did it. I kept thinking about what we had done, over and over in my mind, to make sure that there wasn't any possible way I could have gotten AIDS from him. That lasted for about a week.

Because it didn't meet the standards I had set for myself, I wondered, "If this time I give in, then what's going to happen next time? And the time after that?" It was just going to get worse and worse. I'd find myself doing stuff I had done before. That's totally irrational. It really is. Maybe it's part of the morality that sex should be reserved for somebody more intimate.

There's part of me that wants to do all the stuff I used to do before, and there's part of me that wants to be the good little boy and not do anything. The last time I was with Jerry, we sat in the car for the longest time. He wanted me to go upstairs. I was nervous, thinking, "Here we go again, the whole ritual of making sure that we don't do anything that's going to put me at risk." My mind is working more during sex; I'm conscious of everything I'm doing.

Jerry had told me that he was negative and that he got tested regularly. He gave me the name of the place he went to: "I can have them make copies of my results." I was surprised that he was very giving of the information when I asked him what his HIV status was. I figured asking somebody that question would get a negative reaction, as if I had said, "You're a slut, obviously, so what's your status?"

A couple of weeks ago, he started to do oral sex on me and I pushed him away. Luckily he's about my size. We didn't talk about it until after. He said, "Why did you do that? I'm not putting you at risk by doing that. It's inconceivable that you would catch it from me." I really don't know why I pushed him away. I guess it would be bringing the thing to a new level. And that eventually it was going to keep sliding down to stuff that I didn't want to do.

We've had sex three times and that's the only time it came up. He didn't try to force me to have unprotected sex. However, in the future, if there's ever an instance that I'm with somebody I really like a lot who wants to do something I don't want to do, I don't know how I'll react.

If I found somebody I felt strong feelings for, and had gotten to know, and of course knew was negative, I would consider having oral sex without a condom and anal sex with a condom always. But it would really have to be somebody that I felt strongly for. It would be a really gradual thing. At first, it would be protected sex, and I would have to feel comfortable with the person, and know that they're not the type to go out and cheat. That's a big step that I haven't made yet: to have oral sex or anal sex with somebody, even with a condom.

Public service announcements say, "Have protected sex under all circumstances, every time you have sex." You have Liza Minnelli telling you that on TV. My mom and dad don't have protected sex. Why should two gay guys who are in love and are negative have protected sex? I get opposing views.

ta.

How much am I willing to trust a person? That's I guess what it all boils down to. Even though we're in love, did he go out the night before and sleep with somebody? It's not just the question, Did this person go out and cheat on me? It's the question, Did this person go out and risk my life last night? It has life-long consequences. You have to trust somebody not only to not betray your relationship but to not go out and risk your life. This is trust in its deepest form.

That's the only reason why me and Jerry are just doing what we're doing and not anything else, just masturbation. Because I haven't seen the test results. I haven't gone with him to be tested. He could be lying. We don't have a committed relationship.

There are a lot of decisions to make with any relationship about monogamy, about trust. AIDS is just an added factor, something to add into the mix that makes everything more difficult, more complex, and more vague.

ta.

At a meeting of the HIV-Negative Support Group in Boston, we were talking about the effectiveness of condoms at one point.

There was a bearded guy across the circle who said, "If you knew somebody was HIV-positive, would you have sex with him even using a condom?" He expected the overwhelming answer to be, "No way." But a lot of people said, "Yeah, of course. Sure." I was shocked to hear people saying they would have sex with HIV-positive people as long as it was safe sex with a condom. I guess I was naive, or uninformed, or ignorant. I thought it was a given that if somebody is HIV-positive and you're negative, you're not going to have sex with him.

I don't know what I would do if I met somebody, we went out for a month, I fell in love with him, this was the person I had been looking for, and then he told me he was positive, or got tested and found out he was positive. It's asking a lot to be in a relationship with somebody positive, because you know what the end result is going to be. You are basically asking, "Could you fall in love with me, and then perhaps take care of me, and suffer my loss?"

I guess it's an individual choice. You're with who you want to be with, for whatever reasons you want to be with him. Maybe it's selfish to say, "No, I wouldn't want to be with a positive person, because of the risk." You would be excluding a whole group of people. I realize there are a lot of HIV-positive people who are virile and healthy and just as alive as everybody else, and they should not be discriminated against. You don't want to just leave them by themselves, saying, "Well, you're positive. Sorry."

In fact, probably the person I'm looking for is HIV-positive. Who knows? One of those people might be the person I would get along with the best. I can conceive of being with somebody who is positive, but I think every time we had sex, as safe as we might be, I would be worried. Maybe that will change. Maybe I'll become more rational as time progresses and I move away from what happened this past year with Josh. I can't imagine going through the rest of my life with such a big hang-up as far as sex is concerned.

3

Before the Test

GOT AIDS YET?

"I didn't know what caused it. There was a time when I thought just being gay would be enough," said Tucker, a 31-year-old receptionist, when I asked him about the early years of the AIDS epidemic. "I knew it was happening in gay men. Could it have been excessive masturbation? There goes my hobby."

Tucker told me that his early religious upbringing had been Catholic. "Then my parents became Fundamentalist," he said. "They went through everything they could find, from Bible-thumping Baptist to Tammy Faye and Christian Cosmetics. So I had all sorts of imaginable guilt. The mentality of the southern ministers on television—that AIDS is some sort of retribution for being gay—is prevalent throughout a good deal of the country. When I first started hearing about AIDS, something in the back of my mind said, 'Jesus Christ. What if they're right?' I was 21. I have never really known sexual life without the grim reaper standing next to the bed."

It was not only religious Fundamentalists who equated being gay with getting AIDS in the early years of the epidemic. Tucker recalled the reaction of a former sweetheart when he told her he was gay: "She cried and said she had always loved me and had always wanted me to be the one to share her life. She was a nurse. She said, 'I will love you anyway, even if I can only touch you with rubber gloves.'"

Tucker's recollections reminded me of an episode from my college years. Sitting on the dock of the crew boathouse at school in 1983, I overheard one rower ask another, "Do you know what G-A-Y stands for?" The answer was, "Got AIDS Yet?" I sat silently on the dock with heat rising in my face, ashamed that I was not out of the closet enough to confront them. I was hurt and confused. Did people really think that being gay meant you were destined to get AIDS? Did I think that too?

I knew homosexuality had been associated with illness, contagion, contamination, and death for centuries. Gay men, for example, were believed to "recruit" or "corrupt" others by having sex with them, as if homosexuality itself were a kind of sexually transmitted disease. The fact that gay male relationships were not biologically procreative linked them metaphorically with death, and religious scriptures were interpreted as invoking death penalties against gay men. The arrival of a plague that appeared to selectively strike gay men reinforced these old models of viewing homosexuality. Despite my growing awareness of the prejudices implicit in these models, I found it hard to banish them from my thinking, and they poisoned my estimation of myself as a young gay man.

It's not surprising that the equation of being gay with getting AIDS was made. In 1981 the available evidence revealed only that many gay men in New York and San Francisco were dying of opportunistic infections because of severely compromised immune systems. We did not know what was causing the epidemic, which for a time was referred to as GRID, an acronym for gay-related immunodeficiency. Later, when similar illnesses were recognized among intravenous drug users and blood transfusion recipients, the name was changed to AIDS—acquired immunodeficiency syndrome—to reflect that the immune deficiency was an acquired trait, not a characteristic of some people.

What *is* surprising is that gay men sometimes continue to equate being gay with getting AIDS. Gay men who test HIV-negative often wonder why they are not infected. For some men this is an expression of simple disbelief that they have escaped infection. But for others it reveals a more complex identification with AIDS, often tied to a lingering dread of being infected or an expectation that becoming infected is inevitable. This is an unfortunate example of how early reactions to an epidemic can persist for years.

It is worth reflecting on gay men's experiences before HIV testing was available, because our responses to the epidemic were shaped in that time when no one knew who might be infected. This chapter explores some of our early experiences with the epidemic and points out how they continue to influence our thinking today. We cannot understand how profoundly HIV testing has affected gay men unless we first recall the position we were in before testing.

SEARCHING FOR SYMPTOMS

Scientists studying the epidemic, which was first reported in the United States in 1981, suspected a transmissible agent might be responsible. It wasn't until 1984 that Robert Gallo and Luc Montagnier identified the agent believed to be responsible for AIDS—then named HTLV-III or LAV, now referred to as HIV, for human immunodeficiency virus. HIV testing was developed in 1984, but it became widely available only when it was licensed by the United States Food and Drug Administration in 1985. Before then, the only way to learn you were infected was to become sick. All you could do was wait.

In the absence of a test for HIV infection, many gay men began searching for early symptoms of illness. People were being disfigured by Kaposi's sarcoma, a rare form of skin cancer, so we began inspecting our bodies for the slightest sign of lesions, the visible stigmata of AIDS. People were dying from *Pneumocystis carinii* pneumonia, so we began watching for signs of shortness of breath. Chronic lymphadenopathy was a common early sign of infection, so we began palpating the glands under our jaws. Of course, we found the symptoms we were looking for. The fact that so many of the symptoms were nonspecific did not deter us from diagnosing ourselves and inundating our doctors with our concerns. It was easy to imagine being infected.

Many of the people I interviewed recalled finding what they feared might be HIV-related symptoms in the years before they took an HIV test. When I asked what it was like not to know their HIV status, the men I interviewed commonly responded by submitting a list of symptoms that made life miserable.

"I could not have a cold, only an experience with death," said David, a 35-year-old software writer from San Francisco. "Every infection was another notch on some viral gunslinger's belt, every cough another sign of immunity breaking down. I knew the cold feeling in my spirit every time I bruised or tired, the slightly faster heartbeat when I thought of it, like my body was preparing to fight or flee. Of course, there was nothing wrong with me that I knew of, but that's the key: 'that I knew of.'"

Scott, a 24-year-old graduate student from Newark, Delaware, recalled constantly monitoring his health. "The slightest hint of a cold or flu sent all kinds of fears into me," he said. At the age of 16, he said, "I was always looking in my mouth in a mirror to see if I had thrush, or at my legs to see if I had Kaposi's sarcoma. I once had a small boil on my leg and immediately rushed to the doctor. Then there was the time a pen in my jeans pocket broke, and when I saw the black stain on my skin I was sure I was a goner."

The dread of being the next one to succumb loomed large in the early years of the epidemic, and fear about one's own health was sometimes accompanied by another more excruciating fear: the fear of having infected a lover unknowingly. Lewis, a 44-year-old travel agent, remembered watching a television program in which people with AIDS talked about symptoms. "All of a sudden I realized I had this little spot right here," said Lewis, pointing to his ankle. "It was similar to what they had talked about. I had an absolute freak-out. I was convinced that I had AIDS, because I saw this spot. And not only did I have AIDS but I had infected my lover of seven years. It was devastating."

Lewis immediately got up, turned off the television, and walked out of his house wearing no coat. "It was only five degrees above zero. I was in such a state of shock I did not feel the weather. In a daze, I walked to a park. I just sat under a tree and broke down crying. I was horrified. All of a sudden the AIDS epidemic lived in my home. I was dying and my lover was dying too."

When Lewis went to a doctor a few days later, he learned that the spot on his ankle was a harmless blemish. "I see nothing wrong with you anywhere," his doctor told him. "There is nothing to worry about." Was his doctor right? I think not. Lewis's anxiety about the spot on his ankle revealed not only concern about his own health but a sense of responsibility for the health of his lover as well.

Men who were partners of people with AIDS sometimes developed symptoms, just as the sympathetic strings in an old violin vibrate with the strings the bow touches, even though they remain untouched themselves. Sandro, 23, whose narrative appears in chapter 2, remembered that his lover with AIDS was always itchy, sometimes scratching his skin until it was raw. "On his hands he had little welts," Sandro said, "and he would scratch them so much that they would get bloody. You know what's funny? At the time I was with him, I would scratch myself, too. There was really nothing there, but I would itch. When we broke up, I didn't itch at all anymore. It was only when we were together." This kind of imaginative link to an ill partner is found among spouses of cancer patients who believe they too have cancer, and among husbands who gain weight during wives' pregnancies.

Searching for symptoms was not confined to the years before HIV testing was available. It continues today among people who experience AIDS anxiety. When I worked on an AIDS hot line in Massachusetts between 1987 and 1993, nearly every week I heard callers convinced that they were experiencing symptoms of HIV infection. Even when the possibility of HIV infection was remote, AIDS was so frightening to these callers that they did not discuss their concerns with their health-care providers. Fearful of having acquired HIV and fearful of learning this truth through HIV testing, they preferred to agonize over the telephone with an AIDS hot-line worker.

Hypochondria is nothing new, of course, and HIV provides a useful hook for the hypochondriac. The earliest symptoms of HIV infection are so nonspecific that it is easy for hypochondriacs to invoke them by autosuggestion. Alice, a 40-year-old HIV-test coordinator for the Red Cross in Massachusetts, discussed how anxiety about HIV was related to the symptoms people present when they come in for HIV testing. "Many people seem to have waited several years before making the decision to get tested," she said. "Their anxiety in many cases goes to the point where the stress manifests itself in physical problems, like diarrhea, loss of appetite, chest pains, and rashes. A little digging finds out that these are things people were prone to before. Now the stress is just causing symptoms to come back."

"One problem," Alice added, "is that people look at the list of symptoms, tell themselves they have a symptom—such as swollen lymph glands—then palpate their glands so much that they bruise and say, 'Well, now I do have them.' People who are really far gone just make things up."

INVENTING SAFER SEX

Even before we learned that AIDS was caused by a virus, gay men invented the practice of "safe sex"—later renamed "safer sex"—to deter the epidemic. At first, safer sex was defined as limiting the number of partners you had, and avoiding ejaculation in the body. In Boston, AIDS educators passed out buttons with the slogan "On me, not in me," a message that was interpreted to mean that withdrawal before ejaculation was a safer practice. Later, when epidemiologists found that insertive as well as receptive partners could be susceptible to infection, the use of latex condoms was recommended to protect both partners during intercourse. When HIV was identified in 1984, many gay men had already begun to adopt safer sexual behaviors.

Before HIV testing existed, no one knew who was infected and who was not. In the absence of information about HIV status, it was useful to believe either that you were infected and your sexual partner was not, or that you were not infected but your partner was. If you believed you were infected, safer sex was an ethical responsibility to avoid infecting others. If you believed you were not infected, safer sex was a pragmatic method of avoiding infection. You could justify safer sex either as an altruistic gesture to protect others or as a self-serving device to protect yourself.

Curiously, some people justified safer sex both ways at once. Some men I interviewed mentioned that they simultaneously held beliefs of being both infected and not infected, of being both infectious and capable of becoming infected. "There was a way in which I assumed I was positive and a way in which I assumed I was negative," said Alan, a 31-year-old editor at a university publishing house. "I tried to look at each day as if I were positive and it was my last healthy day, and to look at the future as if I were negative and I was going to be there forever. I was trying to get the best of both worlds: Live today like it's the last good day, but there's going to be a million tomorrows anyway."

Early efforts at preventive AIDS education encouraged people to practice safer sex "with every partner, every time," stressing that it was impossible to know just by looking whether someone was infected. These guidelines were analogous to the universal precautions adopted in health-care settings, which required health workers to assume that every incoming patient might be infectious, and to take precautions accordingly. Conveniently, the behavior to adopt whether you believed you were infected or not was the same: using a condom during intercourse protected an uninfected partner, whether insertive or receptive.

Rudy, a 47-year-old teacher, described this universal approach to sexual encounters. "Everybody that you have sex with, you have to have in mind that they are infected and treat it that way," Rudy said. "When you don't know for sure, you treat everybody as if they have it. And you do what you would do with somebody if they were infected."

The "universal precautions" approach to safer sex helps

explain why many gay men found it ethically acceptable to avoid HIV testing when it first became available: you did not have to get tested if you practiced safer sex. It was ethical not to learn your status as long as you behaved as if you or your sexual partner were infected.

FEARING BEING INFECTIOUS

Given the stigma attached to AIDS, the assumption of being infected led to unwelcome feelings about being "tainted" by HIV. When it became evident that HIV was infectious, many gay men created new attitudes toward their own bodies and the fluids coursing through them, because of the risk they might pose to others.

The mystery surrounding the infectiousness of HIV led some men I spoke with to worry about whether they might be putting loved ones at risk. "I remember having irrational worries about being around my very young nieces and nephews," said Edward, a 39-year-old faculty development specialist at a music college. "I knew my worries were irrational, because I knew it was difficult to catch AIDS. Now they seem silly, but that was an issue for me. Not that I would breathe anything, or that I would cut myself. I don't know what. I feared that somehow or other these children—who I had very strong feelings for—would become ill as the result of their gay uncle spending time with them. I felt a little dangerous around them, and I was careful around them."

Although saliva is not generally considered an infectious fluid with respect to HIV, uncertainty about its infectiousness in the early years of the epidemic led some men to worry about whether kissing might transmit HIV. Sam, 30, whose narrative appears in chapter 10, told me that his worries intensified when someone he had sex with in 1983 was diagnosed with AIDS in 1984. "When my friend became sick, I didn't want to kiss anyone, family members or partners. I didn't kiss anybody because I was convinced that I was infected and I was going to pass it on to someone and that I shouldn't do that. When I would visit home, I would kiss people on the forehead."

BAD BLOOD

Quite early in the epidemic, scientists hypothesized that HIV was transmitted by blood, because the pattern of infection was similar to that of hepatitis, and because cases were found among intravenous drug users. That HIV can be present in and transmitted through blood evokes an enormous number of cultural resonances. Blood has been revered as a life-giving force and yet feared as a taboo substance. The idea that their blood might be "bad" because of the possible presence of HIV had a powerful psychological influence on gay men. Many people already viewed homosexuality as evidence of sickness; now there was a physical correlate to this view.

One of the few helpful things that gay men could do to limit the epidemic before HIV testing was available was to refrain from donating blood. Preserving the safety of the national blood supply was an important priority. Even before HIV testing, members of what were called "risk groups"—gay men, hemophiliacs, Haitians, intravenous drug users, and blood transfusion recipients—were asked to voluntarily remove themselves from the donor pool. Membership in one of these stigmatized groups was seen as evidence that you were more likely to be infected.

I remember the impact that the new regulations about donating blood had on me. Donating blood was something I had viewed as an act of generous altruism. Suddenly altruism was defined in opposite terms, in terms of withholding rather than giving. As a gay man, I was being asked to help others by *not* donating my blood. Guidelines about blood collection do not permit any man who has "had sex with" another man since 1977 to donate blood, regardless of the kind of sexual behavior and regardless of his HIV test results. I obliged, and I continue to refrain from donating blood, even though I have tested HIV-negative. By following the recommendation not to donate, have I in some ways acquiesced in a definition of myself as "tainted"?

Through the regulations surrounding blood donation, the concept of "risk groups" became officially institutionalized. Later campaigns that emphasized that "it's not who you are, it's what you do" that puts you at risk for HIV infection have done something to discredit the reactionary concept of "risk groups." And yet blood-collection regulations continue to encourage the uninfected to imagine they are infected, equating gay sex of any kind with the risk of HIV infection. Even if this is done with the goal of keeping the blood supply as free of HIV as possible, it reinforces the equation of being gay with getting AIDS.

What is it like to imagine that your blood is HIV-infected? It is to wonder every time you floss your teeth if kissing a loved one could lead to his death, or your own. It is to wonder every time you nick yourself shaving if HIV is there on your chin. It is to wonder when you have hemorrhoids if you should let someone come near your ass. Even if you assume you are not HIV-infected, the sting of bleeding is made sharper by ruminations about HIV, because bleeding makes you more vulnerable to infection. Blood is supposed to sustain life, not be the initiator of death.

PRECIOUS BODILY FLUIDS

Semen also has life-affirming connotations that are at odds with the presence of HIV. When I was a teenager, I looked at my own semen through a toy microscope and was amazed to actually see spermatozoa swimming around, the seeds of life. Now when I look at a pool of semen in my hand, I sometimes wonder, "Does it contain HIV?" If I repeated my childhood experiment, I would not be able to tell. HIV is too small.

For many gay men, semen is important. Ejaculating semen into a partner's body and taking a partner's semen into one's own body are an important part of sex. In heterosexual couples, semen represents the possibility of generating a new life. In gay male couples, even though conception is not an issue, semen has important life-affirming characteristics. That semen has become entwined with death is deeply troublesome for gay men. Psychologically, the affiliation of HIV with semen is even more problematic than its affiliation with blood, because whereas the appearance of blood is associated with injury and pain, the appearance of semen is associated with ecstasy and pleasure.

"I am pissed I have to do it," said Blake, a 33-year-old library clerk from Portland, Oregon, referring to safer sex. "Sex is a pretty intimate thing to me. I feel that it is a sharing, and I feel that body fluids are part of that sharing. Physically a person does become part of you; you become 'one.'" Jeremy, a 27-year-old graduate student from Lexington, Kentucky, said, "When I've been in a long-term relationship, I begin to care for a person and in some way want to exchange fluids as an almost spiritual need to share part of that person. Sounds sort of weird, but I know of two other men who have said the same thing."

It saddens me that Jeremy describes his desire to exchange fluids as "weird." Because our culture does not approve of homosexuality, the celebration of semen exchange is not something widely supported. And now that HIV is with us, that celebration is muted even among gay men. Jeremy's language reveals that what gay men used to consider "ordinary sex" is now problematic as a result of having to consider semen dangerous.

We have yet to fully appreciate the complex psychological damage that occurs in people who believe they are HIV-infected, who imagine that their body fluids are dangerous when they may not be. Even though such beliefs may have helped encourage the development and practice of safer sex in the early years of the epidemic, it has been at great cost to gay men's attitudes toward their bodies and their sexual behavior in general.

Unfortunately, beliefs about being infectious continue to influence our attitudes toward sexual behaviors and our definitions of safer sex even after we find out we are not infectious. These attitudes, which developed very early in the epidemic, restrict us from adapting our early definitions of safer sex to take into account knowledge of HIV status.

INVENTING UNSAFE SEX

The invention of safer sex before HIV testing involved a simultaneous invention of unsafe sex, the categorization of certain behaviors as being "high risk." The earliest risk-reduction campaigns used our limited early knowledge about the mechanisms of HIV transmission, largely based on case histories, to place sexual behaviors along a rough spectrum of "riskiness," labeling anal sex "high risk," oral sex "possibly risky," and masturbation "low risk" based on the unspoken assumption that the two people involved in sex were of different HIV status.

The drawback of this kind of risk analysis was that gay men began to identify their body fluids as dangerous, and to define certain sexual behaviors, such as anal sex or oral sex, as *unsafe in and of themselves*, without regard to whether one of the people involved had HIV and the other did not. In the early years of the epidemic, before HIV testing was available, this kind of risk analysis was unavoidable and prudent, since it was impossible to know if someone was infected with HIV. Now that HIV testing is available, however, such risk analysis is somewhat outmoded. Gay men nowadays do take their own and their partner's HIV status into consideration—even though it is difficult to know whether someone is truly uninfected—when deciding what kinds of sex to engage in.

But the categorization of certain sexual behaviors as "risky" persists even after people have begun to learn about HIV status. Gay men in the United States persist in calling anal sex without a condom "unsafe" without regard to whether one of the people involved has HIV and the other does not. It is common for gay men now to say that anal sex is "unsafe" even when practiced by two HIV-negative people. Does this merely reiterate our mainstream culture's proscription of same-sex behavior, under the guise of public health? Or is it perhaps evidence of the durability of our early definition of safer sex, developed before HIV testing, which was predicated on a belief that every sexual encounter was potentially between two people of different HIV status and therefore a site of possible new infection?

STANDING BEFORE THE TEST

Although it is tempting to think of the time "before the test" as something that ended when HIV testing became available in 1985, the truth is that those who have never been tested are in a sense standing "before the test" even now. And those of us who have tested HIV-negative sometimes find ourselves standing "before the test" as well. We may find ourselves uncertain about our HIV status, wondering if we can be confident about it, especially if we have had sex that puts that status into question. This is not the case for those who learn they are HIV-positive.

Wondering about HIV status, then, can be a recurring concern for those of us who test HIV-negative. Because becoming infected with HIV remains a possibility, it is easy to find ourselves returning to a position we thought we had left behind, vulnerable once again to the search for symptoms, the simultaneous belief that we are infected and uninfected, and a reconsideration of how to define safer and unsafe sex. HIV testing has not entirely done away with the psychological and social issues we experienced before its existence.

4

Something Tremendously Valuable

Robert Newman

MY MOTHER WAS ILL with cancer for a few years and I was her primary caretaker. I didn't want to deal with the knowledge of being HIV-positive while she was sick, nor would I have wanted her to know about it, because of the worry it would have caused her. I might not have been able to keep it a secret, so I waited until after she died before I got tested for HIV.

I wasn't sure if I'd be negative or positive. I was always alert to what might be AIDS symptoms: excessive fatigue, weight loss. I'd look at my skin and examine it more than I ever had. I found things that had always been there and are harmless. I felt a swelling under my arm and was afraid it was a swollen gland. My doctor said it didn't seem out of the ordinary. I was not ready to deal with a positive test result, so I decided not to get tested.

I worked up to it. It took me a lot of thinking over two or three years before I finally decided to do it. For a while, I believed the anxiety of knowing I was positive would exacerbate my condition, increase the likelihood that I'd get sick. I thought I'd stay well longer if I didn't know. One of the things that pushed me to get tested was encouragement in some gay publications that it was better to know than not know, because you could do things to improve your likelihood of staying healthy: prophylactic drug treatments, AZT, and other things. I had to work up to it over months. I kept telling myself, "I'm almost ready."

Another factor that led me to get tested was that I was anticipating quitting work and going to graduate school full time. A friend of mine in San Francisco had made a major financial commitment only after getting tested. That stuck with me. Before he made the commitment, he wanted to know his status, and it encouraged him to know he was negative. Before I quit my job to go to graduate school full time, I wanted to know I was healthy and that I would be able to carry out my plans.

I had a dramatic meeting with this person later. I was visiting him in California, having dinner with him, and I said, "I have something important to tell you, some good news, and it has to do with you. I recently got tested and I was negative. I remembered that you got tested before making a big commitment of money and energy, and that's why I did it." Then, sadly, he told me that he had recently tested positive. That threw me for a loop. My story evaporated and I listened to his story: he had tested negative several times; it surprised him when he found out he was positive; his lover of several years also was positive. I don't know if they're sure how it all happened. I gave him a long hug. The hug expressed more than words could have.

ف

I don't know how I'm so lucky. I had unprotected anal sex in the early eighties. I got fucked numerous times by strangers. I tried once to count how many times and by whom. I came up with maybe 20 people from 1980 through 1985, before people used condoms. With that activity, I could easily have become infected. I'm glad it was in Boston. I lived in San Francisco until 1979. Had I done that in San Francisco, think of the risk. I'm here by great luck. It could be me in the hospice and not the people I see there when I volunteer.

I feel I've been delivered, given a second chance that other people weren't given, people who had exactly the same behavior as I did and who got sick. I've got a chance to be safe and not get AIDS, just through choosing my behavior. For other people there is no second chance.

I'm not a rabid religionist, but I have a feeling for what God means to me and I feel deeply grateful that I am HIV-negative, deserving or not. I feel grateful to God. I don't feel grateful to myself. I don't particularly deserve to not have AIDS.

So I feel a moral obligation—almost truly religious—to stay HIV-negative. If you have a relationship with God and feel God is instrumental in your health, and you know what sexual practices are safe and unsafe, there is a moral obligation to yourself and your values and your God to treat yourself lovingly. To respect the gifts you are given. When I don't take care of myself, I feel I've wronged myself and done something immoral in a way, by not protecting my health. I feel guilty about it.

෴

Last summer my friend from San Francisco came to visit me. I knew he was HIV-positive. When I was visiting him in San Francisco, we slept together regardless of his status and had safe sex. I don't recall exactly what we did, but I felt comfortable with it, knowing he was HIV-positive. He's in the health-care field; I felt he'd be scrupulous and careful.

In August 1991, he came for a week in Boston and spent it with me. We went down to Provincetown and stayed in a fancy guest house. During that time, we had what I consider an unsafe sexual episode. We were having sex: mutual masturbation and some kissing. When he came, he was positioned over me. I didn't realize it right away—being involved in my own self-amusement—but he came in my crotch and the semen ran down near my anus. After I realized I was wet down there, I was upset that his HIV-positive semen was touching my anus. I thought, "Jesus Christ, of all the stupid things, the things you want to be careful about!" I didn't get angry with him; I didn't want to hurt his feelings. But I did let him know I was concerned about it.

I realized after he went home that I was angry and worried. I wrote him a strong letter, saying, "How could you possibly not have been more careful? I trusted in you as a health-care professional, as a friend who would look out for me." My feelings toward him won't ever be the same. I'll always wonder if he was knowingly careless, knowing that he was positive and I was negative. I don't think he aimed at my anus; he came on top of me. The way he expressed it to me in a letter and phone call later was that he didn't think it was particularly dangerous.

The problem was that I assumed a person who is my friend, who is intelligent, who is a health-care professional, and who is HIV-positive will come in the right way when he comes—on unbroken skin, or not on me at all—just out of caution. The reason I didn't discuss this with him beforehand was I didn't want to insult his intelligence. I thought it would be insulting to even suggest that he wouldn't be careful. Afterwards I regretted it deeply.

So now, I would certainly ask somebody if they're infected. I'd say, "Do you know your status?" That's a little more euphemistic. I treat everybody's ejaculate the same way, really. It's just that what happened with him was much more anxiety-producing and traumatic. Since that time, I haven't knowingly had sex with anybody positive.

If I ever had sex with somebody I knew was HIV-positive, I would say, "If and when you come, we have to do it this way: on my stomach, or my chest, or my leg. Preferably you just come on yourself." I feel like saying, "Be careful with your cum if you're positive, especially if I'm negative." I'm not afraid of saliva, some moist kissing if I don't have any cuts in my mouth. I would kiss somebody who is HIV-positive. I'm willing to take that risk. I *am* concerned about semen. Certainly somebody who is HIV-positive isn't going to fuck me, with or without a rubber.

❧

I called the AIDS Action Committee hot line two times after that episode in Provincetown. Both counselors felt there was little likelihood of transmission. That reassured me to a degree, but not entirely. I told my doctor eventually. He didn't think it sounded too dangerous. I waited six months and got tested. Although I had tested two times before that, routinely, this was the first time it was worth having a test.

After that scary sexual experience, I was much more anxious when I went to get my results. It wasn't difficult to keep the appointment, but I was scared. I went to the same place I had gotten tested the other times and had the same counselor. I felt so relieved when I learned I was negative, I can't tell you. When I left, I resolved to volunteer, either as an AIDS buddy or at the hospice.

Although I've tested negative, I've never felt secure that I'm negative, never absolutely. I'm still nervous about false negatives, just thinking about it. Something like 96 percent of positives will show up after six months. I'm still scared I could be in the other 4 percent, so I'll be nervous the next time I get tested.

If I continue to be active sexually, I'll probably get tested every year, because I don't feel what I'm doing is 100 percent safe. And suppose I didn't have any more sex: I guess there's still a little anxiety about the past.

&

I feel a tremendous pressure—an obligation—to keep myself negative. I'm responsible from now on for not becoming infected. I can't take credit for being HIV-negative. But I *can* take credit for staying HIV-negative.

Suppose I lose willpower, engage in unsafe sex, and get the virus. I'll probably go through a period of terrible emotions, including guilt. I'd feel stupid, really dumb. I like to think I'd be easier on myself. I hope I would forgive myself and other people, make peace with it, and not condemn myself. I've seen people with that serenity at the hospice where I volunteer.

I think I'm more motivated to stay negative, having found out the lucky result. I feel I got something tremendously valuable by getting a negative test result. I want to protect that wonderful gift. I worry about career, money, having a lover, and other things, but I can't think of anything more precious than having an HIV-negative test result. Maybe somebody who is positive would feel offended by that. I feel a little troubled saying it.

&

49

There are some cruisy areas in the Blue Hills, south of Boston. There are miles of marked hiking trails. Both on the marked trails and off, beaten paths have been created in certain areas by horny gay men. People cruise each other, talk, meet, take walks, play there. Sometimes they go other places to have privacy. Sometimes you see condom packages and condoms, a pair of underwear, or a porn magazine. Condoms indicate that maybe people are fucking in the woods. I've seen plenty of blow jobs. That's common. It's not unlike any outdoor cruising area anywhere.

Bars used to be my prime place to meet new sexual partners. An ear condition I have makes it uncomfortable for me to go to loud bars, so my carousing has decreased. I'm not entirely displeased with not going out to bars as much. When I have a couple of drinks and it's late and I'm tired, my judgment is lessened, my willpower is lessened. Instead, I meet people in the Blue Hills. I like hiking, getting exercise, not just visiting the cruising areas. I might meet somebody and go home with him, if I want to. Safe sex is a big issue, still, but at least I'm not having any drinks there, so my judgment is strong.

I might jerk off with somebody in the Blue Hills. I don't feel it matters what their status is if I jerk off with them. I met one guy there who didn't look terribly well and I wondered if he had AIDS. And yet we played around. He went down on me.

It's easy to be safe if you're just masturbating. But some people want to suck dick. Suddenly they drop to their knees and they're sucking your dick. They've chosen to not care about the risk they might get from me. I assume I'm negative because I've tested negative. But what am I exposing myself to in the other direction? I believe there's no proven transmission of HIV that way, but certainly there's opportunity for other sexually transmitted diseases. I feel a little uncomfortable. Suppose somebody is carrying the virus. Can he transmit it from his mouth to my penis? I think probably not. But it goes through my mind.

Once in a while I'll take a guy's penis into my mouth. I don't do that very much, but once in a while I do. There's risk in that. I don't know how much. Very small, I think. I'd prefer to avoid having cum or precum in my mouth. I've lost much desire to go down on strangers. I used to like that years ago. That was a hot thing. With somebody I was getting closer to, dating, I'd probably want to do that among other things.

Occasionally I'll engage in aggressive kissing with somebody, with a lot of saliva. I don't know if I have any microscopic cuts from eating pizza with a sharp crust earlier in the day. I get canker sores every now and then. Who knows? Maybe in their saliva there is a little HIV "virus-ette" and it lands right on a canker sore. I know it's really a minuscule chance, but still it feels very good to get tested and find out you're negative.

Some people have come home with me from the Blue Hills. I like it when people mention safety, or if they agree when I mention it. I don't go over the menu or the specifics, necessarily. When you're going to have sex with somebody—this may be more true with a trick, where you hardly know each other—you don't want to destroy the mood. If we refer to safe sex when we've met, that means that when we get in bed, it's going to be easy to bring it up, because we've already said it and we both know we agreed to it, at least nominally. I feel comfortable saying, "I don't feel safe about this." I do not mind being specific about what I consider safe. I can easily have that conversation with people, and I have.

৯৯

I've discovered the phone-sex lines in the past six months. I've had phone sex a number of times. There's a routine way people exchange information: What town are you from, what's your name, what are you into? People sometimes say, "Anything safe," or a few specific things they like to do. It's interesting that people mention safety even if you're not getting together. They're expressing themselves and their personality, even though there is no risk in having sex over a telephone.

The recording on the line says you should not give out your home phone number or address. But the computer cuts conversations at certain points; you're only allowed to be on half an hour.

You can lose track of time and be in the last moments when you're cut off. So people give each other their real numbers. I have met three or four people that way.

People have a variety of attitudes towards safety, especially people in their early twenties. They seem to be more cautious. They grew up in the age of AIDS. Some of them have never entertained the thought of fucking. When I was in my early twenties in San Francisco, you either had tried it or were going to try it. Nobody didn't do it because of safety reasons; you only didn't do it because you didn't like it.

§

My first reaction when I heard about the HIV-Negative Support Group in Boston was that it was a silly, superficial thing. Maybe a snotty thing for HIV-negative men so they could meet each other and shed tears for people who are HIV-positive. It sounded a little elitist: "Hey, we're all negative. We're all clean. We're all pure." Most of it is not that. I realized, "My God, I found out I'm HIV-negative and yet I'm still anxious about it. The group must be for me." There are no other groups specifically having to do with being HIV-negative and where you go from there.

I wanted to go to the HIV-Negative Support Group before my HIV-positive friend arrived last summer. For some reason it didn't work out; I can't recall why. The first time I went to the group was after the traumatic incident where my friend came on me and for me it represented unsafe sex. I regretted that I had not been to the group earlier, because I might have asked for some ideas from the group. Somebody might have said to lay out the ground rules before we had sex. I might have done that. It might have been very useful for me. But the timing was wrong.

I told you how much I value being HIV-negative and how grateful I am and how I'd like to protect that. Just hearing somebody else say that would reinforce it in me and make me feel that other people feel that way. I want to hear negative men stating what they do to stay negative, their fears, and their desires—gut-level stuff.

&.

What it all boils down to is this: What does sex mean to people? What does not having sex mean when you have to give it up? Why are we driven to have sex? Is it purely hormonal sexual drive? Or in gay men does it meet multiple needs? In some respects, sex is an answer to loneliness. It fulfills a need for intimacy, closeness, and love. Promiscuous sex can be a temporary filling of an emotional need.

What do I get out of sex? Is there love missing from my life? Companionship? Is there an aching loneliness that sex in the woods seeks to fulfill just for a short while? Does it meet deep emotional needs, even if it's through ultimately unsatisfying transitory encounters?

Sometimes I get into a pattern of seeking sex and stop thinking about why I'm doing it. It's hard to figure out what sex is answering in my life, but if I gain some insight into that, I might be able to say, "Maybe I don't have to have sex in that way. Maybe I can get my needs met in some other ways." It's an idea I'm curious about exploring.

5

Considering Testing

I was 22 when HIV testing became available in 1985, and I remember that I did not want to learn if I was infected. I did not want to know I had a potentially life-threatening illness. In the summer of that year, I spent a weekend with my parents on Cape Cod, Massachusetts. I had been working long hours at a summer job, so when I arrived in Dennisport, I was rundown. I felt achy, I had a burning sore throat, and the glands at the sides of my neck were swollen.

I knew that swollen glands were one of the common early signs of HIV infection, but I knew too that they could be a sign of many other illnesses. I prayed it was not HIV infection causing my symptoms, but I secretly feared it might be. Although it was unlikely that my past sexual behavior had put me at risk for AIDS, I was not sure. There has always been a degree of uncertainty about the transmission of HIV, so I was uneasy.

My parents were uneasy too. I had come out to them as a gay man a year earlier, and when I did, they told me they were concerned about my health and hoped I was "being safe." That was all they said out loud. They didn't talk about AIDS and neither did I. So when I was with my parents on the Cape that weekend, a silence overwhelmed us. I sat on the beach with my parents, but instead of speaking to them, I gazed out over the water of Nantucket Sound and remained silent.

A seagull hovered over the water, riding a draft of wind that kept him suspended in midair. Several times the gull rose high above the stone jetty that protects the beach, each time carrying a clam in his beak. When he was high enough, the gull would drop the shell onto the rocks below, hoping to break it open and reveal its contents. Sometimes the shell would break; sometimes it would remain fixed shut.

The subject of AIDS hovered over my parents and me that weekend, like the clam carried aloft in the seagull's beak. Even if we had wanted to open that clam and see what was inside, we could not. Nothing would break open against our stony New England reserve. I didn't want to entertain the thought that I might have HIV.

When I went to my childhood pediatrician after returning from the Cape, I did not raise the question of whether my symptoms might be AIDS-related. I didn't tell him I was gay or that I was fearful about AIDS. I didn't discuss with him the possibility of taking an HIV test. He gave me a probable diagnosis of mononucleosis. When I returned home from the doctor's office, my father obliquely referred to AIDS. "I hope you asked all the questions you needed to ask," he said. But of course, I hadn't. The prospect was too frightening.

TWO SIDES OF THE PAPER

In 1985, four years after AIDS was first reported, the technology of HIV testing became widely available in the United States, and gay men were unprepared for the profound effects it might have on their lives. When the test arrived, gay men were faced with an ethical and emotional dilemma: To test or not to test?

Opinion was divided. Gloria, a 55-year-old HIV-test counselor, told me that this division was eloquently expressed by an informational flyer printed when HIV testing first became available in Boston. "I still have the broadside," she said. "One side says, 'Take the test' and the other side says, 'Don't take the test.' I think those issues are just as relevant now as they were in 1985." As an experienced HIV-test counselor, Gloria knew that the decision to get tested is a complex one, with many aspects to be carefully weighed.

In chapter 7 I explore the reasons why the gay men I interviewed decided to get tested. In this chapter, conversely, I explore the decision by gay men *not* to get tested in the early years of the epidemic. Studying the reluctance of gay men to get tested when the test first became available not only offers insight into why some gay men today choose not to get tested but also helps us understand the ways in which remaining *untested* was valuable for gay men in the early years of the epidemic.

THE EARLY PURPOSE OF TESTING

When HIV testing first became available, many gay men were opposed to it. One man I interviewed remembered going for an HIV test during the first week it was publicly available in San Francisco: there were protesters outside the testing site, and he had to struggle to get past them.

A large part of the protest was that there were no medical treatments available if you found you were infected. There were a few therapies for the opportunistic infections that struck people with AIDS, but nothing proven effective for retarding HIV in asymptomatic HIV-positive people. Learning you were infected seemed equivalent to a death sentence, because people with AIDS did not live as long as they do now, and there were few long-term survivors to look to as examples.

To many community activists, it seemed that HIV testing was not intended to help people who were infected but rather was a vehicle for surveillance, discrimination, and possibly even quarantine. Alan, 31, who has performed a show about HIV testing, recalled early attitudes against HIV testing:

> Early on, it was a political decision. It sure seemed to me—and to almost everyone else I knew—that the agenda of testing was not treatment, because there weren't treatments. The end products being talked about were things like quarantine and isolation, and those hardly seemed

57

something I wanted to be part of. Given the history of the way our government and the medical establishment have treated queers—or minorities of any kind—there seemed very little reason to trust that there was anything good about the idea. For a long time, there was no reason to get tested and lots of reasons not to.

Was Alan's distrust of the purpose of HIV testing justified? Recall that in 1985, there were no protections against discrimination for people who were HIV-positive or diagnosed with AIDS. People understandably feared they might lose their jobs, their insurance, or their housing if it became known that they were HIV-positive, because such losses routinely happened to people after HIV-positive test results were disclosed. For these reasons, many community activists and physicians recommended caution about testing.

In addition, there were—and still are—no federal protections against discrimination based on sexual orientation, and in the early years of the epidemic, being HIV-positive was viewed as an almost surefire indicator of homosexuality. Gay men already had decades of experience with witch-hunts based on sexual orientation, so the prospect of witch-hunts based on HIV status—as a surrogate for sexual orientation—was not welcome.

Fear of discrimination from outside the gay community was mirrored also by a personal fear of discrimination from within the gay community. If you found out you were HIV-positive, you might feel obliged to tell sexual partners, which could result in rejection. After all, the reasoning went, who would want an HIV-positive partner?

FEARING A POSITIVE RESULT

Behind the reasons publicly put forth by community activists when testing was discouraged early on—lack of medical treatments and fear of discrimination—lay other more personal fears: the fears of illness, of stigma, and of death, and the fear of learning you might have infected others or were capable of infecting others.

These fears kept me from getting tested when testing first became available. I did not want to learn I was ill, I did not want others to shun me because of my HIV status, I did not want to die, and I did not want to accept the emotional burden of finding out that I had infected someone else or was capable of doing so. Such fears are human responses to the awareness of mortality and are part of the character of life in times of sexually transmitted plague.

Austin, a 36-year-old medical professional, captured some of my own feelings when he described why he did not get tested. "Not getting tested was the most comfortable place for me to be, because I didn't know what I was going to do with the information once I found out," Austin said. "I thought, 'God, if it comes back positive, am I going to be like a time bomb waiting to go off?'"

Austin was not alone. Surveys in the 1990s asking why gay men had not gotten tested revealed that the lack of medical treatments and fear of discrimination were less often reported than more psychological reasons, such as "I don't think I'm at risk," "I'm afraid of the results," and "I'm not sure I could handle a positive test result."[1] If similar surveys had been done when testing first became available, I suspect these psychological reasons would have appeared as well.

In the face of the bleak prospects for the infected early in the epidemic, some gay men voiced the intention to kill themselves if they found out they were HIV-positive. Those in drug treatment expected their sobriety would be threatened by learning they were HIV-positive: they would have little reason to pursue treatment for addictions if they believed they were already "doomed" to die. A positive test result could thus lead to anxiety, despair, self-destructive substance use, or even attempted suicide.

All of the above concerns make it easy to understand why gay men who suspected they were HIV-positive might not have wanted to take a test to find out. But what about gay men who suspected they were HIV-negative? Surely they would want to know they weren't infected, wouldn't they?

FEARING A NEGATIVE RESULT

It may sound strange that gay men who believed they were uninfected would not immediately want to learn they were HIV-negative, but this was so in the early years of the epidemic. Although fear of a positive result probably accounts for most of the reluctance among gay men to get tested, fear of a negative result cannot be entirely discounted.

I believe several factors fueled gay men's reluctance to learn they were HIV-negative. These factors have not often been acknowledged, and I mention them because they help us understand why some gay men chose—and still choose—not to get tested, and why others have reacted—and still sometimes react— with disappointment, confusion, or despair when they learn they are HIV-negative, reactions which I explore further in chapter 9.

One reason some gay men did not want to learn they were HIV-negative was they feared this knowledge might lead them to feel immune to HIV and therefore to take greater risks. HIV-test counselors were aware early that some people misinterpreted the HIV test as indicating susceptibility to infection rather than infection itself. Test counselors therefore frequently cautioned people not to assume that a negative result meant they were invulnerable to HIV infection. Nowadays, ignorance about the scope of the test is less common, but there is another way in which this idea persists. Some HIV-negative gay men use HIV testing as a way of justifying continued unsafe sexual behavior, with the reasoning that if they repeatedly test HIV-negative, then whatever risks they are taking must not be truly dangerous.

Another way in which finding out they were HIV-negative was undesirable for many gay men was that it took away one of the important motivations to practice safer sex: the fear that they might infect a sexual partner with HIV. For some gay men, uncertainty about their own HIV status helped them to maintain safer sex consistently. As long as they did not know they were uninfected, it was easy to imagine being infected, and this strengthened the ethical resolve to practice safer sex. If protecting other people from infection is a moral imperative more compelling even than protecting oneself from infection, then remaining ignorant of one's lack of infectiousness might be desirable.

In practice, it is not clear whether these two beliefs—that one is uninfectable, and that one is uninfectious—actually result in unsafe behavior. Studies exploring the link between learning one's HIV status and subsequent sexual behavior have been inconclusive. Some have suggested that there is no correlation between learning one's HIV status and subsequent risk reduction. Other studies have suggested there may actually be a *negative* correlation between learning one is HIV-negative and subsequent risk reduction.[2] Therefore, the fear that learning you are uninfected might lead you to unsafe sex may indeed have operated to make some gay men reluctant to test.

Finally, learning you were uninfected meant that you might become infected in the future and therefore would bear a responsibility to stay uninfected. Seroconversion—the event of moving from being HIV-negative to being HIV-positive—is a possibility much feared by HIV-negative men because of the blame that it entails. Not getting tested in the first place allowed men a unique comfort: if they did not know for sure that they were uninfected, then they did not have to feel responsible for staying that way. If they later found out they were infected, they could not be blamed or blame themselves for "knowing better." Staying untested thus allowed some men to escape the burden of feeling they had to remain uninfected.

FEAR OF DIVISION AMONG GAY MEN

Another reason gay men were reluctant to learn they were HIV-negative was the fear that it might establish a distance between them and their HIV-positive peers. Some men didn't want to learn they were HIV-negative because of its impact on current or prospective relationships.

Kevin, a 46-year-old child-development specialist, told me that he decided not to get tested as long as his lover with AIDS was still alive. "I was very sure I did not want to know before he died," Kevin said, "because if I found out I was negative, that would have created a barrier between us. It was clear there was a difference between us: he was getting sicker and sicker; I wasn't. I did not want something more that might separate us. It would be like saying, 'You are really sick, and I am not.' I didn't feel comfortable holding that up to him."

Some men looking for relationships found that learning they were HIV-negative made them feel as if they were in a different social category, an issue I explore in chapter 11. "There are some incredibly hot men in Rochester who are HIV-positive. Two of them work out at my gym," said Cal, a 42-year-old software training specialist from Rochester, New York. "I'd like to roll in the sack with them, but they are difficult to get close to. It's not that I'm unattractive or anything, but they seem to prefer being around other HIV-positive men or guys who have lost lovers to AIDS. It's like a private club. I resent their attitude at times."

The idea that HIV-negative gay men might feel resentful at not being part of the "HIV-positive club" strikes some HIV-positive gay men as odd. "I'd be glad to trade places with you any day" is a common response. It is hard for HIV-positive gay men who are blinded by their own feelings of being excluded to see that HIV-negative gay men can also feel excluded. Yet being HIV-negative in the 1980s was in some ways a kind of disenfranchisement from the gay community, because so much of the community's identity at that time was wrapped up in AIDS.

Staying untested allowed gay men to maintain a solidarity with HIV-positive friends and peers in the community. Just as people who believed they were positive anticipated rejection, people who believed they were negative feared that verifying this might place them beyond the borders of the gay community, which was rapidly becoming redefined in the popular imagination as an AIDS community. Not getting tested, then, was for some a deliberate strategy to not distance themselves from the HIV-positive.

In a related way, I remember not wanting to test because I was afraid it might influence my commitment to doing volunteer work in AIDS education. I feared that if I learned I was uninfected, I might not feel that the issue was important. By staying untested, I was able to identify with the HIV-infected community. It was easier for me to imagine that I too might be HIV-infected, that I too might suffer discrimination, that I too might need HIV-related services. Part of my motivation in working at the AIDS hot line in Massachusetts was to be part of the services for people with HIV, so that one day if I needed such services, they would be in place. Staying untested felt for me like a way of linking myself to a besieged community. As long as I did not know that I was HIV-negative, then there was a way in which I was "like" people with HIV or AIDS.

THE VALUE OF AN UNDIFFERENTIATED COMMUNITY

Before HIV testing, the absence of differentiation by HIV status created a kind of unity in the gay community: we were all threatened by HIV equally. The "universal precautions" approach to safer sex developed at this time supported this unity. The same rules applied to everyone. There were no differences in the actions that the uninfected and the infected should take. This unity was threatened when HIV testing became available.

HIV testing appeared to have the power to divide gay men into two camps: the HIV-positive and the HIV-negative. That there might be adverse social or sexual consequences to learning about HIV status raised the ugly issue of whether a kind of "AIDS apartheid" might develop in the gay community.

By not getting tested, gay men were able to maintain the fiction that there were essentially no differences between HIV-positive and HIV-negative gay men that needed to be addressed. If no one knew his HIV status, then everyone would have to behave in the same way, and no apartheid could be established. It was a way of securing cohesion in a community threatened by division.

This reluctance to acknowledge division or difference within the gay community was politically motivated in part. Community cohesion has often been important to gay men because of our socialization as members of an oppressed minority. Already under attack by the mainstream culture for being different because of our sexual orientation, we did not want to splinter ourselves further into factions based on differences in HIV status. For if we did, we reasoned, what could we accomplish? How could we develop and maintain a cohesive community identity?

The need for community cohesion was especially apparent to gay men in the face of the epidemic, because we recognized that governmental indifference and neglect were forcing us to create and sustain most of the AIDS care and prevention efforts in our communities. Gay men were caring for each other, whether we were infected or uninfected. We were all in it together. In addition, as a community, we wanted to remind people that all of us were at risk, and that cordoning off some people because of HIV status was wrong. If HIV status became a source of division within our own community, we would be enacting precisely what we feared from outside our community: the shunning of some people by others based solely on HIV status.

It is precisely the desire for unity within the gay community, the desire to maintain an undifferentiated community, that early in the epidemic inhibited gay men from getting tested. Later, this same desire for unity made it difficult for gay men who were HIV-negative to admit that they had unique mental-health needs that needed to be addressed if they were to survive the epidemic. We still do not always want to admit difference.

6

Hope Is Victory

Paul Fielding

IN THE EARLY EIGHTIES, when there wasn't a test, you didn't know whether you had done something that could have infected you or not. There were horror stories of people waking up, having some bizarre symptom, and within 90 hours they were dead. For me, it created a sense of urgency. I felt I had to try to achieve as many of my long-term life goals as quickly as I possibly could.

It influenced my decisions about what to do career-wise. I had always had a pipe dream of owning my own business. So just two years out of college, I decided, "I'd better do this, because I may not have the opportunity to. I don't know what is going on in my body." I opened a little store, but it was grossly undercapitalized. I was very young and there was no money to back it, but I did have my new VISA and MasterCard. So I kept a full-time job and at the same time put this business together. My hope was that it would snowball, which it did during points in its history, but it eventually folded.

In my junior year of college, I had met somebody and had had a monogamous relationship with him for about four years. That relationship ended about that time. I felt angry and somewhat deprived: I felt as though I couldn't explore my sexuality the way I should have been able to, because of the epidemic.

In the late seventies, the ideal was to be as promiscuous as you could. That was a sign of masculinity, virility, and gay identity.

You were comfortable with your sexuality and you were genuinely a gay man if you fucked your brains out 24 hours a day, anywhere, anytime.

I was angry because I couldn't experience a lot of these different things. I felt that if I could be a real slut and do all kinds of incredibly nasty things, it would somehow be freeing for me. I'm older now. I understand that no sexual escapade is going to give you that kind of freedom. Sex is not going to do it. But I used to think that way.

I wanted to kick up my heels and have a good time, but I really couldn't do that without fear. In retrospect, I see that a lot of my sexual appetite and behaviors were repressed. I had inhibitions as far as anal interaction was concerned. I was more of a top. Being a bottom was something that I considered too painful and didn't pursue. I was always relaxed as far as oral sex was concerned, thinking that's less of a risk. If my desires had been different, I think I would have been much more at risk. Looking back on it in a parochial way, I think that was my safeguard, a little bit of a guardian angel.

§

In 1985 I began a relationship, the most powerful, committed relationship I've ever been in. The love of my life. We put together as close to what would be considered a traditional marriage as you could. We exchanged rings and vows and tried as best we could to honor our commitment. We were wrapped up in being in a relationship. There was a feeling like, "Oh, boy, we've found each other. And because we've found each other we won't have to worry about AIDS anymore. We've probably escaped." That was in 1985 and 1986.

My partner, Brad, was about seven years older than I was and had lived through the heyday of the seventies in New Orleans and Provincetown. He had had multiple partners. He had gone through his thing with being anal-receptive. From what I understand, if you were right in the thick of it, you had to adapt to being anal-receptive or you weren't really gay. You weren't really part of the whole thing unless you could do that as well. In San Francisco there was a course on getting fucked that men would take. There was that much of a value placed on it.

Brad was really caught up in living the eighties kind of life, having to do it all, and do it all quick. He was a psychotherapist, which provided a healthy income, but in addition he liked to dabble around with real estate. That was the peak of the real estate boom. He would leverage one thing against another and have all sorts of credit available. He bought himself—and me—wonderful toys and gifts. It was a lavish period. He felt justified indulging himself, because of the AIDS thing. But also, that was what was going on in our society.

Testing was an issue that we discussed but tried to skirt around as much as possible. In 1987 we had dinner with a doctor and he talked about the test. I hadn't really heard much about the test. I didn't quite understand that you really could find out whether you were infected or not. I got turned on to this idea and decided that I wanted to do it. I wanted the two of us to do it together. We came to a conflict at that point in our relationship. It was a real turning point, because Brad didn't want to.

At that time they were saying that if you did test positive there wasn't really much you could do. That was his program. I, on the other hand, felt that regardless of what is going on in your body, the more you know about it, the more you know about ways to deal with it. So my feeling was, "Test, test, test." His was, "Not, not, not." Ultimately, the way we resolved the conflict was to do what was appropriate for ourselves independently. We weren't going to do this together as a team. This was one thing we were not going to "couple" on.

In late October of 1987, I had just turned 30, and I decided this was something I wanted to do. I didn't tell Brad. I didn't tell any of my friends. I didn't tell anybody. I just went to an anonymous testing site and took the test. I guess I'm a bit of a daredevil: I went into it blind. Maybe that's the only way I could do it. If I had known a lot of the stuff I know now about the epidemic, the prospect of testing would have been incredibly scary for me. The results came back favorably. I tested negative. I was very happy.

Then I went home and shared the information with Brad. He was a bit taken aback that I had done it. He was happy for me, but he was tense, because it clearly put the emphasis on him: "What are you going to do?" A couple of weeks went by and he decided he wanted to do it as well. He had a lot of fear about his past, but we had been together for over two years, and we had been monogamous, and he was feeling quite confident that since my test had come back negative, his would also come back negative.

So he made an appointment and he went. Because he was a gay-identified therapist in town, he didn't want to go to any of the local testing sites, for fear that if he were identified as HIV-positive or having AIDS, it would affect his practice. People would not want to come to see an infected therapist. So he went out to a middle-class suburb and got tested through the American Red Cross.

His test results were coming back the morning he was supposed to go home for Christmas, and he didn't want to spend his two weeks away in a state of anxiety. He set up an arrangement with his counselor to get the result over the phone. We had synchronized that I would be at his office between clients so we could be together when he called.

What compounded matters was that my grandfather had died the week before. I was driving back from Connecticut on that morning—I had just buried my grandfather—and there was a snowstorm and I was delayed. So I stopped at a pay phone to explain what had happened. He answered the phone and was hysterical. He was a mess because he had just called. He could not wait for me. The counselor had told him, "We think it would be good if you came back for another test." That was a code to say that the preliminary ELISA test had come back positive. I drove the rest of the way back here to Boston. I have never heard sounds come out of my body like they did that day. It was the beginning of what I would consider the worst period of my life.

❧

It was a situation that neither one of us was prepared for, and there was no place to go with it. There was very little counseling or support for people at that time. Brad didn't want to tell his friends. He didn't want me to tell my friends. I told my closest friend about my test result. But other than that I did not go around telling other people. My test result was overshadowed by his test result. We knew the natural question would be, "Well, what about Brad?" People were going to want to know that.

Brad went through a phase where he wasn't going to go for the final result of a confirmatory Western-Blot test. He decided it would be best for him not to find out, that it would be better to go through life functioning on the pretense that it was a false positive.

I should have abided by his decisions and judgments, but I didn't. I couldn't. There was a voice inside of me that was telling me to push, and I did. I felt it would be better for him to know. He understood intellectually, but in his heart he was full of fear. I think he resented me for pushing him. Subconsciously he resented my negative status, and that played itself out over the course of the next couple of years.

So I pushed. We waited six weeks. We went back and he got the final result and it was positive. During that six weeks, we read as much as we could, we talked to different people, we read about how AZT was being helpful, and other treatments. That presented a whole host of questions that needed to be addressed, with very few answers. We had all this information: the Chinese herb specialist, the acupuncturist, the chiropractor, AZT, pentamidine, holistic therapies, all of these things. What do you do?

Four months after getting the test result came the decision of whether to get T-cell counts. He didn't want to do that. He wasn't going to pursue any kind of treatment. I had to nudge. I became a nagging housewife. He went and got the T-cell count and he only had 187 T-cells, which was not good.

T-cells became the next huge thing. You had to protect T-cells.

There was an enormous amount of stress surrounding all of this. But by the same token, you weren't supposed to have stress, because stress could destroy your T-cells. If you destroy your T-cells, then you could go from being HIV-positive to being sick. So you had to try to smile living in a pressure cooker.

I came up with something we used in our house right away. If you've got a negative situation in life, you think of something positive about it. So I took the symbols "H.I.V." and instead of "Human Immunodeficiency Virus," I gave them a different meaning: "Hope Is Victory." We started a major campaign for hope, and we lived our lives around it. When his T-cell counts came back and they were escalating, we would make big poster-sized numbers and put them up in the bathroom as a visualization tool.

This changed both of our lives. He then was very good about treating his HIV. He went so heavily into creative visualization that he set for himself a real shoot-for-the-moon goal: he was going to seroconvert back to being HIV-negative. He had read somewhere that there had been maybe seven documented cases where men had done that. He decided that that is what was going to happen to him: he could control the HIV and change his health back to being HIV-negative.

So he put on his blinders and that is what he went for. That became his end-all and be-all in life. And that was a big adjustment for me, because in the beginning of our relationship, *I* was the end-all and be-all of his life. Nobody ever made me feel as good as he did. It was a big loss for me. I hadn't lost him to AIDS, but I had lost him.

I can remember what a horrible feeling it was to realize that it was *never* going to go away. That was a catharsis for me as far as accepting limitations in life. I always thought pretty much anything was surmountable. Given a challenge, I can overcome just about anything. But this was like a big monster that came in and took everything out of our cupboards and just threw it all around and said, "Fuck you. I'm here to stay. Learn to live around it."

ᔥ

A year after we did the testing, things like discordant-couples groups started to crop up. We enrolled in a study program for discordant couples at the Fenway Community Health Center. A new group for HIV-negative partners of positive men was just starting at the Fenway. I guess we were pioneers back then. There was an unspoken presumption: "Oh, well, he's negative, so he's fine. What does he have to worry about?" That was probably something I said to myself a lot too: "Any feelings that you might have *pale* in comparison to what your loved one is going through, so don't even think about it." This feeling was prevalent in the community and I think it still largely exists for negative men.

It sounds kind of weird, but in a way it was worse having Brad test positive than if I had tested positive. A lot of my feeling was wrapped up more in him than in myself. I didn't have a good source of support in my life at that time. I internalized a lot. I started to abuse drugs and alcohol and created my own little monster with that. I took most anything that would numb me. My doctor had given me an open prescription for Valium. Nyquil was another thing I liked to rely on. I was drinking too much alcohol as well. I felt this was what I needed to do in order to be supportive: to put down whatever I might be experiencing.

When I realized that, it was two years after he had gotten his result. He had been successfully taking AZT for about a year. His pentamidine treatments were working. As a result of doing a lot of creative visualization and our being very positive about his situation, his T-cells went from 187 to about 380 and they were climbing. So things were going good. They were saying, "You don't have to come for the pentamidine every ten days. You can come every three weeks or every month." His condition appeared to have stabilized. We were feeling really great about that.

I decided that I could take some time and address my issues. So on Memorial Day weekend four years ago, I decided that I was going to try to live for one year chemically free, meaning no alcohol, no marijuana, no Valium, and no Nyquil. Not knowing much about addiction and what happens when somebody puts down substances that he has become dependent on, I just put down everything completely.

I did not believe I was alcoholic. I did not believe I needed Alcoholics Anonymous. This was just something that had happened to me as a result of the situations in my life. I lived excessively to run from my pain. My solution was just to eliminate those substances. And so I did that. It put me on a path I really wasn't prepared for. Looking back on it, I think my expectations of Brad were unrealistic and my neediness was overwhelming for him. It was too much stress for the relationship to withstand.

We decided that summer to do a trial separation. I wanted space from him. I was experiencing tremendous amounts of rage and anger, and I didn't know what it was about. I attributed it to the loss of alcohol. I couldn't live with the fear of what my emotions were going to do to his now-healthy T-cell count. I felt that if we had a separation for a couple of months, it would give me time to get this out of my system. I wouldn't have to feel guilty about potentially destroying a couple of his T-cells as a result of an emotional outburst. It seemed like the sensible thing to do.

Brad agreed, but he prefaced that most of the time separations don't work, that people end up breaking up. I remember looking him square in the eye and saying, "We won't do this if you really believe that." And he said, "No. I think you're right. We should try it." Well, he didn't really hold up his end of the bargain. Once I was not in the apartment, he became more distant. My plan backfired on me.

In the fall, we talked about a reconciliation and made a plan that I would move back in. Then he changed his mind. I didn't know until four months later that he had met somebody else. He did with me what he had done with his lover before me, which was to drop me like a hot potato, like I didn't exist any more. It was overwhelming. We had done everything we could to create the symbols of a marriage. We had given each other legal power of attorney. That's why I felt confident with a temporary separation: there was a deep structure in place to work from. But I also knew him: he did have a fickle component in his personality.

The dissolution was very tense, because he had this other person in the wings and wanted to get on with his new life. And my expectations had been so totally different. He was unreasonable about trying to negotiate finances, living situations. We owned a three-family house together, and he wanted to stay in the unit that we had remodeled and was our home. I proposed that I take the first floor but he wouldn't hear of it. He was very all-or-nothing in that regard.

I felt cornered like a rat, incredibly angry, and betrayed. It created a very messy, ugly divorce. Very painful. We both really cut each other up. Not the type of thing that somebody should be going through during the first year of sobriety. It was a very passionate beginning and a very passionate ending. Sometimes I think that's what we both needed to do to destroy the feeling that was there. That was in 1990 and 1991.

That relationship, from beginning to end, was only five years long but it felt a lot longer and it took a lot out of me. I'm not as willing to gamble and take that risk. And it is a risk, when you let down your guard for somebody else. I don't rule it out as a possibility, getting involved with somebody. But it's not top on my list of priorities.

፨

A couple of years after Brad and I broke up, those few people I did date, I would somehow manage to find out their HIV status, and it would influence my decision about whether I spent time with them. I did date somebody for about six months and he didn't want to test. Then he did test, because I said, "I really don't want to go any further with this, because I don't want to end up in the same situation that I've been in before. I couldn't live through it again."

I haven't had the experience of finding out that somebody I

had a crush on was positive and then had to make a decision about whether to date him or not. I haven't been in that position, so I don't know how I'd respond. I'm always relieved when I hear that people are negative. It's easier.

But then this past spring I had a crush on a guy, and I didn't know his status, and I went along dating him for about a month without knowing his status. I liked him a lot, and I consciously didn't inquire about his status, because I didn't want that to influence my decision. I am a different person now. I probably could be involved again with somebody who is HIV-positive. I wouldn't put it real high on my list of priorities.

Although I was unhappy with the changes in my life, they did force me to confront demons that had been a part of my soul since childhood. Maybe something else would have happened that would have forced me to do that, but it was this HIV crisis that did. The imbalance and uncertainty that the testing process can create in your life, no amount of counseling and preparation is going to do anything with that. No matter how much understanding you have, the bottom line is that it's going to be a catalyst for change in your life. It forced me to look at some extremely scary territory and come to grips with it. That's what I consider my miracle from it. Early medical intervention I believe saved Brad's life and has put him in line to receive the miracle drug when it comes. I think that's a miracle and that's a happy story.

7

Getting Tested

"There are two ways to find out," said the outside of the envelope I received in the mail one day in 1988. "You can get tested. Or you can get sick."

Even though AIDS was not mentioned, I knew right away what this cryptic message meant. I was startled. The message was like an assault, challenging me to rethink my attitude about HIV testing.

What the envelope tapped into were my growing convictions that not knowing my HIV status was filling me with dread, that I might be forced to learn my HIV status by becoming sick, and that recent medical advances made it more logical to get tested. Wouldn't it be better, the envelope suggested, to take control of both my mental anxiety and my physical health by getting tested?

When I opened the envelope, I discovered it was from Project Inform, a San Francisco–based AIDS information clearinghouse that advocated early testing so people could consider early medical interventions and experimental therapies. Project Inform's provocative envelope pointed out that learning I was infected with HIV might be better for me than remaining ignorant. Had this envelope arrived in my mailbox a year earlier, I would probably have dismissed it. But in 1988 my attitudes about the value of HIV testing, like many gay men's, were changing.

CHANGING ATTITUDES TOWARD TESTING

By 1988, medical advances in the treatment and prevention of opportunistic infections meant that you stood a better chance of living if you learned you were HIV-positive rather than waiting until you got sick to find out. Aerosolized pentamidine, for instance, had been found effective not only in treating AIDS-related pneumonia but in preventing its occurrence. Azidothymidine (AZT), the first retroviral drug approved by the federal government to combat HIV, appeared to curb the decline of T-cells that leads to immune deficiency.

When reports suggested that AZT might delay the progression to AIDS even in asymptomatic HIV-positive people, it suddenly seemed there was something you could do if you were HIV-positive besides "wait to get sick." Encouraged by these medical advances, AIDS service organizations that had previously been officially neutral about testing, such as the AIDS Action Committee in Boston, changed their policies to a more pro-testing stance.

Alan, who in chapter 5 voiced skepticism about the purpose of HIV testing, remembered how the change in attitude toward testing was the result of work done by scientists and activists:

> Through hard work, some good science, and the magic of queer activism, the situation changed. Committed scientists did a lot of important technical work. Activists were out on the street, constantly demanding the impossible and once in a while getting it. I admire the people who had the creativity, the gumption, and the willingness to work hard to actually change the situation.
>
> We appropriated HIV testing, which had undeniably been a tool of oppression, as something that we could use as a tool of liberation, something that could be valuable to us in our lives. There is something magical about that. It took time and imagination to reconceptualize HIV testing. But lots of people's lives have been improved by that activism. I don't want us to ever diminish that in our minds.

When I asked the men I interviewed what led them to get tested, many—like Robert in chapter 4—cited advances in medical knowledge as one impetus. But there were many other reasons for getting tested as well.

REASONS FOR GETTING TESTED

Some men I interviewed got tested because of sexual encounters they felt might have put them at risk. Others tested because they were experiencing symptoms of illness and wanted to rule out HIV as a cause. Some tested because a former or current partner had tested HIV-positive or had been diagnosed with AIDS. "Ex got AIDS," was the stark sentence one person used. In these cases, people often expressed feeling an urgency about getting tested because of the closeness with which AIDS had hit home.

Having sexual partners or friends test HIV-negative was also a reason for getting tested. Watching others test negative helped some people gain the courage to get tested themselves.

Other reasons for getting tested involved a desire to plan for the future. These included getting tested to determine if conceiving a child was a possibility, getting tested before embarking on a graduate degree program or other career change, and getting tested before assuming a mortgage on a house. "I was tired of worrying, and I wanted to get on with my life," said Audrey, a 32-year-old bisexual manager from Troy, Michigan, voicing what I heard from many men as well. "If I wasn't HIV-positive, it was time to do some important stuff, like taking better care of my health and saving for retirement."

The ability to envision a future and plan for it was one of the casualties early in the epidemic. For those who didn't know their HIV status and assumed they might be HIV-infected, it was natural to live in the present and not give much thought to the future. Testing negative was one way of reclaiming a future.

Many men described the state of not knowing their HIV status as a kind of limbo—in which they had to continually imagine they might be infected—and mentioned that this was psychologically tiring. Taking an HIV test for them was a way of moving beyond that limbo. "Generally, I want to know if something is wrong. So not knowing if I was HIV-positive or not was unpleasant," said Harold, a 28-year-old computer scientist from Frederiksberg, Denmark. Scott, 24, who in chapter 3 described his alarm at finding an ink splotch on his skin and thinking it was Kaposi's sarcoma, recalled a phrase that characterized for him the nagging nature of wondering whether he was HIV-positive: "If there's a hornet in the room," he said, "I want to see where it is."

GOING FOR THE TEST

A few of the men I interviewed told me that once they had decided to get tested, the procedure itself went without much trouble. They had little anxiety going for the test or waiting for the results. But this was not the case for most of the men I interviewed. When I asked what it was like to get tested for HIV, I often heard stories of great personal courage as people described facing intimidating anxiety and yet mastering it.

Todd, a 26-year-old composer and pianist, was typical in not telling many people that he was going for an HIV test. He told a close friend, he told his guitar instructor, and he told his mother:

> Those were the only three people I told, the fear being that if I was positive I didn't want a lot of people knowing about it. I told only people that I knew I could trust. Testing was probably the scariest thing I have ever been through. It was such a nerve-wracking experience for me that I needed the support during the six weeks I waited for the results. I went to the Red Cross in Baltimore and it was a six-week wait.

By not telling many others that he was getting tested, Todd was unable to learn from anyone who had been tested what the procedure was like. As a result, he went into the test not quite knowing what to expect:

> I was very naive. I knew nothing. I always assumed that if you go to have your blood taken, you don't eat. So I

didn't eat anything all morning. I was terribly nervous, I went and got my blood drawn, and then I passed out from lack of blood sugar. The woman who was taking my blood thought I was a drug user having a flashback. It was a nightmare. I woke up on the floor with all these people standing over me. Thank God the needle was out of my arm.

Todd's experience illustrates that getting tested, because it can be so anxiety-producing, often leaves testers in an emotionally vulnerable state. Not every testing experience is as traumatic as the one Todd described. Sometimes, humor is allowed to penetrate what would otherwise be a daunting event. Nathaniel, 34, whose narrative appears in chapter 20, gave me an example from his own experience.

Although he worked as an HIV educator and test counselor in an agency that offered anonymous HIV testing, Nathaniel chose not to get tested at his workplace. "I didn't want to deal with my coworkers," he said, "and I didn't want to go to some of the other places around town, because I knew counselors there too." Nathaniel decided to get tested in the suburban community he lived in north of Boston:

And was that a different experience. My counselor was a nurse, but she didn't know a whole lot about HIV. She was like a character from the *Bob Newhart Show:* fumbly, scattered, and cute. She said, "Oh, you probably know a lot more than I do about this." And she was right.

It was so by the book that I kept laughing to myself. When she asked, "Do you have annual intercourse?" I said, "Goodness, no, we have sex much more often than that." I tried to keep a straight face. She looked at me and said, "Whaaat?" I wasn't trying to make fun of her. It was just very amusing.

Lying there as she was drawing my blood, I felt a little sick, because I hadn't had breakfast. She said, "Here, have a

Ding-Dong." And when I got up I blanched, so she said, "Ah, I'll make you a glass of Tang." I thought, "I'm almost glad this is happening, because I can laugh about it."

Although Nathaniel's counselor was doing her best to make him comfortable, the suburban testing experience was so different from Nathaniel's work in an urban agency that it provided a kind of comic relief for him, defusing the tension around testing.

WAITING FOR THE RESULTS

Waiting for the results of an HIV test, which can take anywhere from a few days to a number of weeks to be processed, depending on the testing site, was almost uniformly described by the men I interviewed as a nerve-wracking experience.

Anxiety during the waiting period is not necessarily related to whether the person tests HIV-negative or HIV-positive. Both Sandro in chapter 2 and Paul's partner Brad in chapter 6, for example, experienced anxiety waiting for their test results, even though one later learned he was HIV-negative and the other that he was HIV-positive. Perhaps this is because most people anticipate that they will be HIV-positive.

"I thought I was going to die. Literally. I had my funeral planned out," said Blake, 33, a library clerk from Portland, Oregon. "It's morbid, I know, but I wanted it to be right, especially the music. I did this because I felt that when I walked into the office for the results I wanted to be ready to fight the HIV and not think about dying. I even came out to my parents, because if I was positive I didn't want to tell them at the same time that I was gay and HIV-positive."

Alice, 40, the HIV-test coordinator who in chapter 3 discussed how AIDS anxiety manifests itself in physical symptoms, told me that the waiting period often encourages people to think about their mortality. "Some people go further than others. They start writing their will, planning who should take care of their children, getting their travel brochures out, all that kind of stuff." She went on:

Then there are the people who say they've never noticed it before but suddenly everything is HIV-focused wherever they turn. That's all they can see, and that's all they think about the whole week. They feel it's a bad omen and that there's going to be a bad answer when they come in.

Alice told me this ominous thinking was most problematic for people who did not have support from friends during the testing process. "When people have support from friends during testing," she said, "their attitude is that no matter what happens, whether they are positive or negative, there's going to be someone to care for them. They're going to have help from someone." For those individuals who have thought about testing for several years on their own, never having spoken to anyone about it at all, Alice said, testing is very difficult: "Without the support, I don't see them feeling a lot of hope."

Many people are able to pass the waiting period without much anxiety, until the time to get their results approaches. "The anxiety comes in when it's time to make the phone call to find out if the test result is ready," said Alice. "When we say their result is ready, that's the start of it. The heart starts pounding, all the anxiety comes back between then and the time they show up. They say driving down the road that connects to our buildings is really bad. Some people have said to me that they've sat in the parking lot and then gone back home. They just could not come into the building. That was the worst part of it."

8

A Snake in Your Pocket

Claude Dupont

I DON'T THINK gay men are doomed. I think the majority will survive AIDS. But I don't think I will survive it.

At the time I was most sexually active, I had maybe 20 or 25 partners in a month, maybe 150 partners in a year. This was in the late seventies and early eighties, first in Haiti and then in Boston.

I know some of my partners were HIV-positive, because a lot of them have died since. Occasionally I would hear that somebody had died, or I would read it in the paper, and of course I had not seen them in many years, and I would think, "Oh, my God. I went out with that person for a month or a few weeks."

I wasn't engaging in activities that would be considered terribly unsafe. Today they might be considered marginally unsafe. Definitely no anal intercourse. I didn't like that so I never really got into that. Oral sex mostly. It was more the numbers than what I was actually doing. No one can play around that much and not have his hand slapped.

&.

I worked myself into a state of such anxiety that I was ill. I would wake up in the middle of the night, for example, and my heart would be racing and I would be sweating. I would not be able to go back to sleep, looking at the clock until six when I had to get up. I would get up in the morning feeling sick and thinking,

"That's it. This is really it." Throughout the day I would work myself into a frantic state of anxiety where I was convinced that I was definitely HIV-positive. I'd feel exhausted during the day. I couldn't really concentrate and I couldn't work because I was so tired from not getting enough rest. I was convinced that all these things were symptoms of my HIV-positive status. Looking back, the symptoms I was experiencing were not HIV-related.

I didn't actually think about testing until 1987 or 1988. I thought I was probably HIV-positive and I needed to know. But I couldn't quite make that step. I wanted to know on one hand, but then I was afraid to actually confront the reality of an HIV-positive test. I thought, "What am I going to do if it is positive?" I didn't talk about it with my friends. I was afraid that they would say, "Well, why don't you go get tested?" I was not really ready to hear the results. This went on for about three or four years.

Finally a friend of mine got tested and his results were negative. We talked about it after he got his results. He said, "You should get tested, just for your peace of mind." So I decided that I was going to close my eyes and go ahead and do it. I got tested in the beginning of 1991. It was hell, waiting for the results. I wasn't sleeping. I wasn't eating at all. I had a knot in my stomach.

I felt an incredible weight being lifted from me when I learned I was HIV-negative, but in reality it didn't last long. It lasted maybe a month or two. And then I started to convince myself that the results weren't quite right and that even though at that particular time I was probably HIV-negative, eventually I would turn seropositive. It was just a matter of time. It's not really very rational. I would think, "I could turn seropositive overnight. Out of nowhere." But when I think about it, I could not turn seropositive in my sleep. Logically it's unlikely that I would turn seropositive five or ten years later. But I would go through this process of thinking, "Eventually I will turn seropositive."

❧

I think I carry a little bit of guilt. I was very sexually active in my late teens and twenties. Looking back, I wondered, "How could I do all this and still be HIV-negative?" It was like some day there would be something that I would have to pay for. The day would come when I would turn seropositive because of all the things that I did.

I was raised Catholic. My parents stopped going to church when I was very young, but I went to Jesuit schools all my life. I grew up with a lot of guilt. You learn how to feel guilty. You learn how to be good at guilt. AIDS is like a punishment. I feel that eventually I will be punished. Maybe not. Maybe the punishment will never come. It's this lingering thing.

I often think that not very many men did what I did, whether straight or gay. I mean, slept with that many people. Why did I do it? How could I possibly sleep with so many men and do other things in life? My anxiety acts like a magnifying glass: I imagine sex took up more of my time than it really did. I feel guilty that I had so many partners. I think it's too many. There are some people who had fewer partners and they're dead now.

I've been in a relationship with a lover for the last ten years. He's negative also. We engage in oral sex without condoms, no anal sex. My partner doesn't ejaculate in my mouth. But I'm still afraid. My partner would probably like to explore more, but I'm not really willing to. I'm just too afraid. He seems willing to accept that.

Philosophically I don't see anything that could be damaging if two men are both negative and are in a relationship for many years and are exclusive. They could have "unsafe" sex if they wanted to, because they probably won't be HIV-positive. If they don't have the virus then they just don't have it. But for me that wouldn't work. If I think that eventually I'll come down with HIV out of the blue, in my sleep one day, it's not going to work for me.

I got tested about six months later. It was again negative. And the same thing happened. The issue died for about a month or two and it started to resurface again.

The problem for me is not the test. I realize now that I could have the test every six months and keep at it for 20 years. I realize that's total nonsense. Why should I go to the doctor every six months? It's something that I have to work out in my own mind. And stop going to take those tests. It doesn't really answer the question. I think the question is in my head. I have to deal with the fact that I can't be thinking that much about it. I spend time thinking about being ill all the time. I just have to live and stop fretting it.

I have anxiety problems anyway, regardless of AIDS. I'm a very anxious person. I'm constantly fretting things. That's just one thing. I'm anxious about work. I'm anxious about traveling. I'm anxious about everything. I recognize that about myself. HIV is just another issue.

I'm not sure that my partner is aware of my anxiety. I don't tell him all of it. He's not aware of the magnitude of the issue. I think he knows that I'm basically an anxious person, but he doesn't know really how anxious I am. I'm not sure that he would particularly understand it. It feels a little bit silly to burden somebody with this. The anxiety is not a rational anxiety. How do you make somebody understand that? I don't even understand it myself, so how can I communicate it? I keep it away from him.

As frightening as AIDS can be, I think there's an element of the population that think they need to belong. They need a sense of belonging to a part of the gay community, and to really belong they need to become HIV-positive. I think it's fairly rare, but I think there are people that actively go out and have unsafe sex to become HIV-positive. There could be a feeling of isolation there. They may look at the HIV community as more of a community than the gay community. In order to belong you have to join this group that is HIV-positive. It's frightening, just thinking of somebody who gets infected so that they can belong.

I have been tempted to have sex I feel is unsafe. I'm just tempted. I don't have it. I fret it. I break into a cold sweat, but I don't do it. I might come close, and then I'll stop.

I've thought about counseling. If I think I have a problem about something, I try to work it out myself first. If I realize I cannot, then I would go see a professional. How many years will it take me? I don't know. I can get by reasonably well. Of course, there are ups and downs. It's day by day. Some days it's just awful. Some days it's good. Some days it's in-between.

I exercise: I do aerobics. That helps keep my anxiety in check. My anxiety does go up, but the exercise helps it go down again. Intense physical output helps me be a little bit calmer.

I don't know why I went to the HIV-Negative Support Group. Maybe to hear some other people's concerns, whether they were like mine. Whether people experience anxiety over becoming HIV-positive without having unsafe sex. Whether people thought that even though their status was negative on paper, eventually they would turn seropositive. I actually didn't find that. Most people there were pretty comfortable with their results. They didn't think that eventually they'd come down with it. I think most people are able to manage anxiety better than I am.

I look back at the numbers of sexual partners I had and it becomes frightening. How could I escape? It's almost like you're being thrown into a pit that has 500,000 snakes in it and you manage to escape. But you know that somewhere in your pants there is a little snake that you didn't quite shake out—that eventually is going to bite you.

Have you seen the *Indiana Jones* movies? There was a pit in one of them with hundreds of snakes down there. You can't escape that, you know. If you're thrown in there, eventually a snake is going to kill you. Even if you sort of manage to escape, there's a snake in your pocket.

9

Reactions to Testing Negative

"Shit," thought Stuart, a 37-year-old software engineer, when he found out he was HIV-negative. "I've got to go to work tomorrow after all."

Gay men spend a lot of time and energy during the HIV testing process anticipating a positive test result. When considering testing and during pretest counseling, they commonly imagine how their lives might change if they learn they are HIV-positive. Test counselors often ask potential testers, "How will learning you are HIV-positive affect your mental health? How will it affect your sexual behavior? Who will you tell? What reactions do you anticipate?" These hypothetical questions help testers assess whether they are ready to learn they are HIV-positive.

Test counselors might just as well ask these questions about testing HIV-negative, yet few do. In fact, gay men spend much less time and energy during the testing process anticipating a negative result and considering its significance. Perhaps this is because they tacitly assume that being HIV-negative is desirable and that learning about being uninfected is a good thing. Gay men frequently assume they will be relieved and happy when they hear they are uninfected. They expect that testing negative will somehow resolve all their issues, will magically "take care of AIDS."

Yet this is not the case. The individual who tests HIV-negative, although "reprieved" for a time, must continue to live in a world where the threat of HIV infection continues to exist, and where more gay men become infected each day. The individual who is HIV-negative still must contend with the fear of becoming infected and cope with the illness and deaths of others. Yet the belief that a negative test result will somehow magically "fix" everything is common. Perhaps the distress and uncertainty of not knowing about HIV status leads us to assume that testing negative will take care of things.

Few people consider in advance the complicated emotional reactions that sometimes follow a negative test result. Some of these reactions are expressed immediately during the posttest counseling session. These include relief, elation, feeling lucky, disbelief, and doubt. Other reactions may follow later, surfacing days, weeks, or even months after a negative result. These include survivor's guilt, reluctance to disclose negative results, isolation, disappointment, despair, depression, and—not least important—acceptance.

I hope this chapter helps gay men who test HIV-negative see that they are not alone when they have complex emotional reactions to a negative result. I hope too that it will encourage HIV-test counselors to look carefully at the messages they convey. Do counselors unconsciously suggest that a positive test result is more "important" than a negative test result—that being infected is better than being uninfected—when they spend most of the counseling session discussing the consequences of a positive test result? If counselors do not wish to give this impression, perhaps they should not focus exclusively on preparing their clients for positive test results.

RELIEF

Relief is understandably the most common immediate reaction to testing HIV-negative. "I breathed a sigh of relief," said Derek, a 25-year-old graduate student from Muncie, Indiana, about his negative test result. "For once I was glad I failed a test," Derek added, referring to the irony that a negative result was a positive outcome.

What is a negative test result a "relief" from? It can be relief from the anxiety of not knowing whether you have a life-threatening illness. It can be relief from the stigma of being HIV-positive in our society. It can be relief from concern about whether your past sexual encounters infected you or your partners with HIV.

These various anxieties and concerns are sometimes so repressed from conscious thought that relief is expressed by bursting into tears. This unmediated emotional response is one way of expressing the degree to which anxieties and concerns have been pent up. Joshua, a 52-year-old hospital worker, recalled, "I just cried for about an hour. It was such relief. I don't think I have ever known that kind of relief. And then I realized how scared I had been."

Edward, 39, who in chapter 3 discussed being afraid his nieces and nephews might become ill from spending time around him, told me this:

> I remember feeling an enormous sense of relief when my test came back negative, like a huge weight had been lifted off my shoulders. I didn't know what to do with those feelings, because I didn't realize where that weight was coming from. I had never really known I was carrying it around to that degree.

Men frequently used this metaphor of a burden suddenly being lifted from their shoulders to describe their relief, expressing the degree to which anxieties and pressures were bearing down on them.

ELATION

Relief is sometimes followed by a kind of elation. Todd, 26, the composer who fainted during his HIV test, described the concert he performed the day he learned of his negative test result:

I was absolutely euphoric when I found out I was negative. I had a concert that evening and I played blithely. It really was like I was celebrating something: I was celebrating life. I felt I had a second chance. I speak like someone who had had a great deal of unsafe sex. Now that I think back, it seems terribly irrational, because I hadn't really done anything very risky.

Elation upon learning about being HIV-negative can have drawbacks, however. When I learned I was HIV-negative in 1989, I sailed out of the testing site, elated at my good fortune in having escaped HIV. I walked right past an AIDS hot line coworker in the waiting area—with whom I had worked weekly for three years. He had gone for HIV testing the same day I had, without telling me, and had returned to get his result the same day I did. I did not see him or hear him call out my name. I wish my elation hadn't preoccupied me, because if I had heard him, I could have been nearby when he learned his test result. Instead, I walked on. He found out he was HIV-positive that day. He didn't tell me until six months later.

Another drawback of elation in response to a negative test result was mentioned to me by a couple of the men I interviewed. They reported going out and having unsafe sex after they learned they were HIV-negative. Perhaps the test result gave them a kind of permission to do this because it removed the fear that they might infect someone. Or perhaps this behavior reflects a more complex psychological discomfort about being HIV-negative, a kind of unwillingness to be a survivor. Then again it may simply have been a way to express elation and "celebrate" some good news. The irony is that this variety of celebration might have undermined the very HIV-negative status being celebrated.

FEELING LUCKY

HIV-negative gay men who had unprotected sex before the concept of "safe sex" arose often wonder why they were "lucky" enough to avoid HIV when their friends were not. This "feeling lucky" is common among men with high-risk pasts, who wonder at the capriciousness of fate that left them uninfected.

One of the tasks that survivors of traumatic events frequently undertake is to explain why they have survived. In trying to explain why they remained uninfected while peers with similar sexual histories became infected, some gay men toy with the idea that there is something unique about their immune systems that makes them less likely to become infected. Some men feel "charmed" when they get a negative result, believing it is a sign that they cannot become infected. I suspect, however, that most gay men recognize they are not invulnerable to HIV just because they have tested negative.

Others have tried to read a larger meaning into their good fortune. Jimmy, a 47-year-old psychology doctoral student from Kentucky, said testing negative had influenced his decision to change careers: "I do not believe in coincidences. I took it as a sign that I was meant to do something with my life. I chose AIDS-related work when I changed careers, and some part of that process has been my own negative status. I feel a responsibility to those who have not been so lucky. Luck had everything to do with my being negative. It is up to us, the healthy, to care for those who were not so fortunate. There, but for luck and perhaps a little education, go we."

The British writer Simon Watney, noting that luck played a large role in who became infected and who did not in the early years of the epidemic, argues in an essay about AIDS and gay identity that the uninfected have a responsibility to their infected peers.

> ... I believe that the single, central factor of greatest significance for all gay men should be the recognition that the current HIV-antibody status of everyone who had unprotected sex in the long years before the virus was discovered is a matter of *sheer coincidence*. ... Every gay man who had the good fortune to remain uninfected in the decade or so before the emergence of safer sex should meditate most

profoundly on the whim of fate that spared him, but not others. This is why HIV disease is, and will always remain, an issue for *all* gay men, regardless of our known or perceived antibody status. Those of us who chance to be seronegative have *an absolute and unconditional responsibility* for the welfare of sero-positive gay men.[1]

Watney makes this statement to argue that the uninfected must not judge themselves superior to the infected nor dismiss AIDS as an issue of concern only to the infected. His assertion that being HIV-negative was a matter of luck for many gay men is undeniable. But his claim that all HIV-negative gay men have an unconditional responsibility for the welfare of HIV-positive men—though morally compelling—does not follow logically. To me, Watney's sweeping conclusion sounds like a variation on the theme of "survivor's responsibility" described by Jimmy above. Must we atone for being HIV-negative by committing ourselves unsparingly to AIDS work and the welfare of the infected as a way of recognizing that our being uninfected is an unearned privilege?

I agree with Watney that some HIV-positive and HIV-negative men are not responsible for their HIV status, largely because of the caprice of fate. Certainly it is important to recognize the degree to which chance is responsible for HIV negativity. But we must not discount the ways in which gay men have consciously reduced their risks when they learned how to do so.

In the passage quoted above, Watney does not address those gay men who grew up and became sexually active in the age of AIDS. For them, being HIV-negative is not simply the result of luck but is often the result of deliberate decisions to stay uninfected by careful behavior. When these younger men voice "luck" as the reason they are uninfected—and they often do—are they not discounting their own activities, dismissing their own safer behavior, even though such behavior might well have saved them from HIV infection? If gay men believe the principal reason they have survived is that they are "lucky," might they also believe that one day their "luck" will run out? Attributing survival to "fate"—although attractive to older men seeking to explain their HIV negativity—has some drawbacks. Might it discourage some people from practicing safer sex? Could it lead them to imagine they have no agency in staying uninfected?

DISBELIEF AND DOUBT

Another common reaction to a negative test is disbelief. Some men honestly cannot believe that their negative result is correct. This is especially true of partners of HIV-positive men. They may express surprise or confusion at a negative result because they anticipated a positive result. Sandro, 23, whose narrative appears in chapter 2, expressed his disbelief by returning to the testing site to look at the paper on which his result was recorded. When he told me this, I remembered getting my own test result. Even though I had not to my knowledge had an HIV-positive sexual partner before I got tested, I too needed to see the result myself, as if viewing it printed on a piece of paper would somehow convince me of its accuracy.

Some men are doubtful about their test results for good reasons. They may have had very risky experiences in the past and be completely surprised at their negative results. Or they may have gotten tested too soon after an exposure to HIV to be certain about interpreting the result.[2]

Other men express doubt about their test results even when there is little reason to. They may ask to be tested repeatedly before they can accept the results. Even then, they may insist that there is some error[3] in their test results, or they may conclude that they do not create antibodies in response to HIV infection and so reconcile their belief about being infected with their negative results to the tests currently in use. Claude, 34, whose narrative appears in chapter 8, provides an example of this doubt. Unable to shake the conviction that he was infected, he wondered if he would "become positive" in his sleep.

For some people, expressing doubt about their test results is not related to an irrational conviction about being infected; rather, it is a way of ascertaining how to behave in the future. I frequently got calls on the AIDS hot line in Massachusetts from people who had recently tested negative wondering if they could trust their results. They sometimes expressed this by asking, "How accurate is the test?" Usually this was because they wanted to know if they could "throw away the condoms" and have sex without the fear of infecting a partner. Because I am not prescient, I was unable to assure HIV-negative callers that their test results were an indication of their actual HIV status at that moment. This often left callers frustrated and disappointed.

For HIV-negative gay men in particular, disbelief or doubt about negative test results may be an expression of the difficulty they have in accepting that they have been spared when so many of their peers were not. By maintaining that they have not really "escaped" HIV, gay men who disbelieve their HIV-test results are able to cement a link between themselves and the HIV-positive, returning to what I described in chapter 5 as the sometimes more comfortable position of being undifferentiated from HIV-positive peers.

SURVIVOR'S GUILT

Among those who believe their test results, relief and elation at getting a negative test result are often quickly curbed by a sobering realization that the result might have "gone the other way." Many men told me that they did not immediately tell others about their negative test result. In the face of the immense suffering and loss caused by AIDS, celebrating one's HIV-negative status is seen as crass. I believe this is a manifestation of a kind of survivor's guilt.

The term "survivor's guilt" was first used in the literature about survivors of the Nazi Holocaust, and it was later applied to veterans who returned from Vietnam. Nowadays the term is used in a wide variety of situations to recognize that anyone who has lived through trauma is likely to grapple with existential questions about having survived: "Why me? Why was I spared?" Similar questions confront many HIV-negative gay men: "Why was I spared from HIV when so many of my friends were not? Why should I be uninfected when I exposed myself to the same risks that infected others? Do I deserve to be uninfected?"

Like Holocaust survivors or Vietnam veterans, HIV-negative gay men sometimes have difficulty coming to terms with having survived. Often they attempt to explain why they have survived, attributing their survival to simple luck or natural immunity to HIV. Still others, troubled at having survived, take on an unrelenting commitment to AIDS work as a way of atoning for their survival, or of punishing themselves for having survived. Finally, many men seek to tell stories about the epidemic's impact on their lives as a way of "witnessing the epidemic." I suspect that one of the principal reasons men were eager to be interviewed for this book was that it offered them an opportunity for this kind of "sense-making" about surviving.

When gay men wonder if they "deserve" to be uninfected, I believe they are expressing ambivalence not only about surviving, but about being gay. Some gay men feel unworthy of surviving because they believe their past sexual behavior deserves punishment. During the Holocaust, Jews naturally wondered why they were being persecuted unjustly, and some of them could not help feeling that there must be some reason for the persecution. Gay men too sometimes internalize society's persecution of them and imagine that they must somehow "deserve" HIV. In this way, sexual guilt and internalized homophobia are linked to survivor's guilt.

Survivors feel that they must explain why they have escaped persecution or horror, why they have not experienced it fully. Jews who survived the Holocaust sometimes wondered why they were not killed. Was being killed a mark of the true Jew? Are those who survived somehow less than fully Jewish? These questions sound ridiculous, and yet many gay men feel that by being HIV-negative, they are not "truly gay," they have not experienced the complete gay identity.

Damien, a 38-year-old journalist, spoke about the complex identification between gayness and AIDS:

I think people who are HIV-negative feel that we are left out, that our gayness is lessened. The gay community has adopted AIDS, for obvious reasons, as its cause. For the past few years, AIDS has overshadowed every other aspect of the gay community. It seems as though AIDS is such a big thing that if you don't have AIDS, or you don't have a lover that has died of AIDS, you are not part of the dominant factor.

A great danger in identifying with a persecuted minority is that you are tempted to equate yourself with being persecuted, and then to experience shame or guilt if persecution is not carried out to fatal extremes. Could this shame or guilt ever be so great as to encourage someone to become infected with HIV in order to "belong"? In chapter 8, Claude speculated about this; in chapter 18, Frank discusses it explicitly.

Not all the men I interviewed felt guilty about being HIV-negative. Some of those who attributed their HIV negativity to luck told me that they did not feel "guilty" about being HIV-negative because they could not honestly claim responsibility for it. Others did not feel "guilty" that some men were HIV-positive because they did not do anything to cause that to happen. They did not think they had abandoned their HIV-positive peers simply by not being infected. As a result, they did not feel a need to atone for being HIV-negative, or that being HIV-negative was shameful. Finally, some men refused to discuss "survivor's guilt" at all, because the AIDS crisis is not over and they were not sure that they would survive the epidemic.

RELUCTANCE TO DISCLOSE NEGATIVE RESULTS

Discussions about disclosing HIV-test results usually focus on disclosing HIV-positive results. Because being HIV-positive is seen as a stigma, and because it raises the possibility of irrational fear, avoidance, and discrimination, disclosing one's HIV-positive status to family, friends, lovers, and colleagues is fraught with danger. The difficulties in disclosing HIV-negative status are rarely discussed. And yet, surprising as it may seem, many HIV-negative men are reluctant to tell others around them that they are uninfected, as if they are ashamed of being HIV-negative.

This reluctance is based on many factors. In the first place, the act of getting tested for HIV is for many a very private decision. Fearing that the result might be positive, some men get tested without telling anyone because they are afraid that seeking support from friends would mean they would have to announce their results to those friends. When the result comes back negative, it may be difficult to announce because of the lack of preparation.

It is also hard to talk about the fear and anxiety of the testing process with friends and family when the test result comes back negative. Listeners often dismiss the tester's agonizing experience of getting tested, concentrating instead on the test result, especially when the result is "good." They expect the person who has tested negative to be happy and may be perplexed or impatient if he is not.

It is perhaps most awkward to talk about being HIV-negative with HIV-positive friends. Some men are reticent about their negative status because they do not want to appear smug, boastful, or condescending. Underlying this reticence may be a belief that it is insensitive to speak of one's HIV-negative status with those who are HIV-positive. In fact, many HIV-positive men rejoice on hearing of others' negative status because it seems to offer proof that the epidemic will not take all gay men. Other HIV-positive men, occupied with their own issues, find it difficult to muster much enthusiasm about someone having tested negative. It may not seem a compelling topic.

ISOLATION

The reluctance to tell others around them that they are uninfected leads to feelings of isolation in many HIV-negative gay men. Aaron, a 46-year-old management consultant, said this:

I would like to know what other people are feeling who are HIV-negative, what other people's experiences are. It's something I don't talk about much with my close friends. Maybe going to a support group would help me feel less isolated. It sounds strange: I am caught in the epicenter of the epidemic and yet I feel isolated.

Some men I interviewed felt they were in a minority because they had tested negative. In reality, the majority of people who get tested in the United States test negative, and the majority of people in the world—both tested and untested—are uninfected. So being HIV-negative does not mean being in a statistical minority.[4] Men who talk of isolation are describing instead a kind of psychic minority status that is based on the prominence of AIDS in urban gay communities.

It may be that this psychic minority status is related to the visibility of services and support for HIV-positive people and the lack of services and support for the HIV-negative. In urban centers in the United States with well-developed gay communities, when a gay man learns he is HIV-positive he knows he is not alone. He knows there are support groups, social events, and medical services that he can take advantage of. He knows there are community activists, social workers, and medical professionals who can help him. A kind of culture has developed around being HIV-positive, a culture based on grassroots organizing, advocacy by people with AIDS, and the dedication of health-care providers, clergy, and volunteers. Is there a way in which this culture unwittingly tells uninfected men that in order to be taken care of they need to be infected?

People with AIDS formed the acronym PWA to describe themselves, but—to put it bluntly—there is no such thing as a PWoA. When a gay man learns he is HIV-negative, there is no culture in place to support him in staying HIV-negative and in coming to terms with being a survivor. Only in a handful of cities in the United States are there support groups for people to discuss the psychological impact of the epidemic. In most cities, even proposing that such support groups be formed is met with accusations that this would funnel scarce resources away from already underfunded services for the HIV-positive. In December 1994, for example, a man who identified himself only as an "HIV victim" disrupted a meeting of the Boston HIV-Negative Support Group and handed out leaflets criticizing two AIDS service organizations for funding the group. The leaflets featured a drawing of a house with rain outside and an open umbrella inside.

Curiously, it is not the HIV-positive who most frequently object to the provision of support services for the HIV-negative, but the HIV-negative themselves. Perhaps because of survivor's guilt, HIV-negative men are often ashamed to admit that they have concerns, fears, or needs regarding the epidemic. An HIV-negative support group leader in San Diego told me, for example, that even in 1994 none of the men in his group had told their friends that they were attending a support group.

I am convinced that this shame among the HIV-negative is one of the reasons that creating support services for HIV-negative gay men has been so difficult. We do not want to prioritize our concerns over those of the HIV-positive, which we deem more important. We are ready to disregard our own mental-health needs in the face of the challenges that HIV infection poses to our friends and lovers who are infected. We justify neglecting ourselves by believing we are unworthy of attention.

DISAPPOINTMENT, DESPAIR, AND DEPRESSION

Accustomed as we are to viewing being HIV-negative as a good thing, it may be difficult at first to understand why some people are not happy when they receive a negative test result.

One man I spoke with talked about a kind of disappointment, related to his expectations about testing: "I was convinced that I was HIV-positive," he said. "When I got my result back and it was negative, I expected to be euphoric, but there was really no such change in my life. Why don't I feel different because of this gift?" Not only was he "disappointed" by not being positive as he had expected, but he was disappointed that he did not experience a feeling of elation as a result of learning he was not infected.

Walt Odets, a psychotherapist in Berkeley, California, reports this story of a 37-year-old client whose reaction to a negative result perplexed a test counselor:

> When I went in, I knew I was positive, and I'd psyched myself up for two weeks about how I was going to deal with it. . . . But when the nurse gave me the [negative] results, I was really shocked—I had just not even given this possibility a thought. And for a minute I just didn't react, and then I thought to myself, "Oh my God, what am I going to tell all my positive friends? They're going to be very mad at me. . . . I have no right to be negative because I've done all the things they did." All of this went through my mind . . . and I started crying and the nurse kept saying, "I don't think you understand—*negative* is *good*." She just kept saying that over and over again, and I just kept crying.[5]

Disappointment can be acute in HIV-negative gay men who are in relationships with HIV-positive partners. Peter, a 26-year-old teacher from Toronto, told me that he was "not happy" when he learned he was HIV-negative. He had mixed feelings: he felt guilty for being spared, relieved at not being infected, and apprehensive about what would become of his relationship with an HIV-positive partner. It is common for such men to feel confused by learning they are HIV-negative, and to wonder if difference in HIV status will be a form of distance.

For some men, a negative result means that they are likely to observe more deaths as the epidemic rages on. Having to watch peers die is horrible, and anticipating having to do this for the remainder of one's life can lead to despair. David, 35, a software writer from San Francisco, wrote to me about the despair and depression he experienced shortly after his initial euphoria upon learning he was HIV-negative:

> More difficult to explain is the depression that followed, a darkness that has proven, if less dense than my old fears, even more pervasive. A friend explained it as similar to the depression that a survivor of a plane crash experiences, that

it is impossible to be in such close proximity to catastrophe and not be a part of it, even if you are left standing once the catastrophe passes.

The analogy my friend made was not quite correct. My situation is more like that of a person on a plane doomed to crash, with the knowledge that many of those around him will perish but that he will likely survive.

After one of the big jet disasters, I heard that dying in a jet crash is not instantaneous. You have about 45 seconds from the time the plane goes out of control to impact, lots of time to realize what is happening while being thrown around inside the spinning aircraft. In my mind's eye I see the gay community spinning in the 45 seconds of chaos, out of control, the final wreck to happen at some future moment, a tangle of bodies and lives I will likely live to see.

In extreme cases, despair and depression can lead to self-destructive actions. Marshall Forstein, in an essay about suicide and HIV, discusses a case example of a 24-year-old man, Mr. B, who had lost four friends and lovers in a short period of time and was convinced that he was HIV-positive:

> After the death of his last friend, Mr. B went to his physician for HIV testing so that he could find out his CD4 count and begin to prepare for his own illness and death. When his test came back negative, he assumed it was wrong and proceeded to be retested several times, always with the same result. Increasingly distraught, Mr. B became convinced that the whole medical system was intent on keeping the truth from him. When he finally allowed for the possibility that he had indeed escaped infection, he became profoundly angry and depressed, as he had had the same risk factors as his dead friends. In the midst of his own grief and despair that he would remain alive, he overdosed on a potentially lethal medication. Waking up in the intensive care unit, he was enraged that he had survived.[6]

Not everyone is as overwhelmed by the news of their negative HIV status as Mr. B was, luckily. No discussion of the reactions to testing negative would be complete without acknowledging that many gay men are able to accept their HIV-negative test results and move on.

ACCEPTANCE

Some men easily accept the news about being HIV-negative because they did not have great anxiety before the test. Whether because they had been tested previously or their sexual behavior had not been highly risky, some men told me that a negative test result was often merely a confirmation of what they had suspected. Arthur, a 30-year-old bisexual computer programmer from Evanston, Illinois, said, "It was what I had hoped for but wasn't sure of. I was saying to myself, rationally, 'That's about what I expected,' at the same time as I was saying to myself, emotionally, 'What great news!'"

For others, the acceptance of the test result is a celebration, in a way, that safer-sex precautions really work. Alan, 31, who spoke about shifting attitudes toward HIV testing in chapters 5 and 7, was involved with an HIV-positive man when he went for his first test. "I felt really lucky and happy about my test results," he said. "I felt great. I had put a lot of energy into changing my sex life to prevent transmission either to me or from me, and it was good to know that it hadn't been in vain, especially considering that my partner was positive. It was good to know that what I was doing was working."

For Edward, 39, accepting that he was HIV-negative caused him to make a commitment to protecting himself, a commitment that he felt had not been as strong before he knew his HIV status:

> I had always been careful of someone else's risk. I never would put someone else at risk. But in terms of my own risk, particularly in terms of getting fucked, I was more willing to play with that before I got tested. There were times when I had the temptation to throw caution to the

wind, going on the assumption that I was already infected and what difference would it make?

Testing negative made me feel more committed to safe sex, to be honest. Safe sex was not something I was doing just because I had to do it. I was doing it out of self-preservation: there was something in it for me.

Austin, 36, who in chapter 5 described not knowing his HIV status as like being a time bomb, told me that when he tested negative he didn't share the disappointment or confusion that he saw among some members of the Boston HIV-Negative Support Group:

> Some people in the support group have been tested several times and their reactions were, "Yeah, so, I got my results and I still have no zest for life. I thought this was going to make some change, but there's no thrill in finding out." My perspective is different. My reaction to testing negative was, "Yes! Yes!" I felt like a minority.

I asked Austin what it was that helped him maintain his optimistic attitude. "I realize I have an incredible network of people who support me and things I'm involved in, that keep me motivated," he said. My question was not a new one for him. "People ask me, 'How did you get where you are? How do you maintain it?'" Austin continued, "I had to find a balance. I had to work to find it. It's a journey, always getting there. But it can be done."

10

A Mark of Intimacy

Sam Pappadopoulos

BEING IN THE CLOSET may have saved me. Because I had heard a little bit about AIDS in 1981, there was a baseline fear that I put into practice: I didn't engage in a lot of anal sex, but I swallowed semen. I had maybe two instances of unprotected anal inter-course, insertive and receptive. It was experimentation. I didn't have many sexual partners.

I wasn't very sexually active because I wasn't very comfortable with myself as a gay man. I was struggling with being gay and felt I had no support. I wasn't connected to the gay community. I was living in my hometown on the South Shore near Boston, where I grew up. I was 20.

The amount of emotional turmoil I was experiencing was sig-nificant. I could have gone the other way dealing with this tur-moil. Had I been more comfortable with myself, I would have been much more sexually active than I was. Had I been more sex-ually active in 1982 and 1983, I might not be here today, because I would have let people fuck me without a condom.

❧

In 1984, a friend I had had sex with in 1983 was diagnosed with AIDS. I told only one person about this. I told him because I trust-ed him and knew he wouldn't reject me. There was a lot of dis-crimination and rejection going on in the gay community. My fear was that if I told someone I had had sex with someone who had AIDS, I would not be a desirable partner. I would be marked: "Don't do anything with him because he's a potential carrier." I thought I was an okay guy, but other people—just because I had done this—would mark me.

I practiced safer sex. I did not fuck at all for several years, or get fucked, and when I gave or received oral sex, there was no exchange of semen. I usually did not use a condom for oral sex.

I got pneumonia once and that terrified me. I remember feeling, "This is it. Finally the end is here." I felt this is what I deserved. I would characterize it as a time of terror. I was terrified I was infected, and terrified of finding out the results. There wasn't a whole lot to be done in terms of treatment, so why find out some devastating information that could be harmful to me emotionally? Why dig any deeper emotionally if I didn't have to? I was in an incredible amount of denial. I didn't want to know.

&

I first tested in 1988, when the person I had been dating got diagnosed with AIDS. My partner, Michael, was 32 at the time, a lawyer. He was diagnosed on April eighth, and on the tenth he went into the hospital. I was at Northeastern University then, and I was at the hospital with him every night for two weeks. I hid this all from my roommate. That is the level to which I was isolated. I wasn't going to tell anyone I was going through this.

Suddenly I was very close to HIV again. That led me to the point of saying, "Okay, I've got to get tested. I have to find out." I was extremely anxious. I got an appointment at Boston City Hospital. I talked to the counselor explicitly about the sexual activity Michael and I had engaged in. I tried to narrow in on any potential risk of infection. We had always used condoms every time we had anal intercourse. During oral sex, he never came in my mouth, and I never came in his. I never sensed precum from him.

I didn't mind the wait, but I almost didn't show up to get my test results. I called the test site from a pay phone in the lobby of a university building and told the counselor, "I'm too scared to come in. I can't get my results." I wanted to get a sense, over the phone, of what the results were. Instead, the counselor talked to me about how I was feeling and presented a lot of options. I chose to go and get the results.

The test counselor said he was glad to see me. I was extremely nervous. I had my little yellow sheet with my number. He matched the numbers, I saw it was negative, and I was relieved. I felt saved. I felt lucky. I felt guilty. Saved: that we had used condoms. Lucky: that I could go on with my life. And guilty: that I could have been infected and was not. I was doing what everyone else was doing. Part of me felt I deserved to be infected.

I didn't tell Michael right away that I had tested negative. First of all, I wasn't sure my test was valid. We had had sex just a couple of weeks before I got tested. So I was cautious because of the uncertainty of the window period. Also, I felt I couldn't tell him because I had joy about testing negative, and he was going through a horrible time. I felt guilty about my joy. When I finally told Michael I was negative, he said he was relieved. Relieved that he didn't infect me and that he didn't have to wonder about that.

Michael and I broke up around this time, but it was not directly related to his diagnosis. In fact, we broke up a week before his diagnosis. Michael had been in a relationship with someone else for a few years prior to meeting me, and he had decided to reestablish that relationship. When he made that decision, I had to make a decision too, and what I did was to end the relationship and become friends. Even though there was a change in our relationship, we still maintained a fundamental bond, an intimate language. We continued to use the nicknames we had developed with each other as lovers. Going through my papers the other day, I found a note from him that reminded me of that.

Michael did end up reestablishing a relationship with his former lover. Their relationship was a deeply emotional one, but to my knowledge it was no longer a sexual one. The two of them lived together as roommates until Michael died, in March of 1992.

*

What terrifies me sometimes is that the first time I had sex with Michael, he was insisting on using a condom, and I almost wasn't, because I liked him. That could have been a time where I could have been infected, because I wasn't insisting. I thought he was handsome and I wanted to be his partner. By not asking that he use a condom I was showing him that I trusted him, that I liked him a lot, and that I wanted to be with him.

At that period of my life I was willing to sacrifice safety for a hunk. I wanted to let him know that because I really liked him I was going to let him do this, and he was the only one. I wasn't going to let anyone else fuck me without a condom, but with him I was. It was a mark of intimacy. That was the intention.

Finding out that Michael was positive was a pivotal point for me. I feel I came really close to death. Back then I didn't feel good about myself as a gay person. Now, five years later, I feel like a survivor, and I want to maintain my negative status. It's important to me. I think I have more wits about me now: more experience, more age, and more capacity to handle complexity in my life. I've had more opportunities to think about how to reduce a lot of my fears about HIV. AIDS has given me the opportunity to do that.

How do I feel now about unprotected sex? I'm tempted to say that now I would insist on a partner using a condom, regardless of my feelings. But that's not entirely true. The truth is that it's really hot to get fucked without a condom and have someone you like come up your ass. Who wouldn't want to get fucked? If you like anal intercourse, whether it's receptive or insertive, who wouldn't want to do that with someone they love or care about, without a condom? We don't talk about this in our community, because it's a taboo. We're not supposed to want to do that anymore. It's not being "responsible."

I think it's important to acknowledge that it *is* exciting, because that's the motivation behind a lot of risk taking. Once that's acknowledged, it gives people a little more freedom and open-ness to have a discussion about safer sex.

ɞ

Someone has wanted to have unprotected sex with me very recently. He wanted me to fuck him and come, without a condom. He didn't seem to question it; he just wanted me to do it. I didn't consider it safe at all. I'll tell you what I did: I asked him to get a condom and some lube, and we went ahead. We talked about it afterwards.

He said he knew I was negative. We talked about that. I explained that my fucking him with a condom even though I was negative was to protect both of us, bottom line. I haven't had unsafe sex for a long time. I've trained myself to have safer sex. To have unprotected sex would be reversing all of that behavior modification, all of that change. I wasn't having sex with him because I wanted to model safe sex; I was having sex because we both wanted to. Yet I felt in a sense I *was* modeling for him: this was how I could show him how to take care of himself.

We talked about how he was feeling about things in his life. He revealed that he had been hurt by a past relationship, and he missed his lover. He missed getting fucked by his old boyfriend, and he longed for it.

I was really concerned about him, wondering if he had been wanting other people to fuck him and come without a condom. We didn't do it, so I don't know if he would have, but there was something about his actions and words that made me believe he really wanted me to. He was willing. It made me really sad. I'm sad talking about it now.

It's very sad to insist on using condoms. Sometimes the way someone could hear that is, "I don't trust you. I don't love you. I'll keep you at bay a little bit longer until I am sure about you." That can be unwelcome in a dating situation, or even in a tricking situation.

ɞ

A year and a half ago, I did something I wouldn't have done had I known my partner was positive. This person knew his status was negative. I knew this person's status was negative. We were outside, at the Arnold Arboretum. I gave him oral sex and he came in my mouth. Boy, was that a trip! I had not done that in just about ten years.

I didn't know I was going to do it. He didn't know we were going to do it. Things were leading up to it, though. As I was blowing him, there was a moment when I decided to do it, and there was a moment when he decided to do it too. It was really one of the most exciting experiences I've ever had.

I wouldn't have done that with someone I didn't know or knew was positive. I just wouldn't. But I knew this person was negative, and I did. I took a risk. I guess I'm really across the board on this particular question. I have a certain set thing I'll do with people. I know what my bottom line is. But in this situation, I did much more than that. I'm smiling because you're the second person I've told. I don't tell people because I do AIDS-related work.

I felt some remorse afterwards: "I put myself at risk. How could I have done something like that?" I was telling myself what I have heard other people say: "You should have known better." And then I thought, "I based my decision on some information. Sure, you never know. But based on who he is and the information he told me, I trust him." He's still negative. He's been tested after we did what we did, and he disclosed that to me.

It taught me a lot. I learned that I'm vulnerable just like everybody else. And that I missed being able to do that with people I care about. And that I felt a lot of loss that we can't do that. That's a rule for me: I don't swallow cum. Have I done it since? No. Is it a temptation? Yes.

I would love to do that with someone in a relationship. I look forward to the day when I can swallow cum again. Someday I might fuck or be fucked without a condom, too, if there's information that my partner is negative over time. There would be lots of discussion and ground rules around this. If my partner did something outside the relationship, there would have to be some discussion. If he got fucked or was fucking someone without a condom, or if he swallowed someone else's cum, then we'd go back to using rubbers until he got retested. I'm confident that if I have a negative partner, we'll work something out. And if my partner is positive, we'll work something else out.

෴

People have to be comfortable with all aspects of a relationship, and I think in the 1990s HIV status is an aspect of gay and bisexual male relationships. I don't think it should be the only factor in selecting a partner. I just think it *is* a factor for some people. This is really hard stuff to talk about.

Sometimes I don't like the thought of getting into a relationship and having my partner get sick and having to take care of him. I learned something from my relationship with Michael before he died. Even though we were no longer lovers, I was very connected with him. In some ways, I felt we were still in a relationship for a while. It was taxing. I didn't like seeing him change in the way that he changed. But feelings are feelings, and I cared about him.

What I mean is that if you feel something towards someone, and that person is positive, why deny yourself the beauty of getting to know that person in the time you have? But I had difficulty with that. I thought, "I'm too young for this." I saw what it took, and it was a lot. This sounds so insensitive. I don't like talking about it.

I find myself reluctant to talk about wanting a negative partner. I feel very private about it. When I'm dating, I think I operate from that principle, but I'm not honest about it. I want a negative partner, but I'm not going to tell anyone that. I'm just going to go about finding it. It's pretty easy to figure out other people's HIV status. If I don't ask, it usually comes out. Maybe other people are also secretly operating on the same principle. Maybe they want to find a negative partner too, even though they might not say it.

There are some positive men who only want to date positive

men, and there are some negative men who only want to date negative men, and there are some men who don't care what their partner's status is. It's all okay. If somebody only wants to date negative men, that really is okay. It's being honest and telling the truth. Let's stop treating each other poorly and just go for what we feel we want.

The second time I got tested was to test the window period, in July of 1988. That was more anxiety-provoking than my first test. I had a lesbian counselor at Somerville Hospital. When I saw her come down the hall, I thought, "Oh, God, what does this lesbian know about gay men being infected with HIV?" But she was extraordinarily effective with me. She taught me to accept what my status was. I wanted it to be negative, and I didn't want anyone to tell me otherwise. I was terrified this was going to be the one that was going to show up positive.

We had discussions on the phone about getting the results. The counselor provided me with an opportunity to look at what the issue was for me. The issue was: If I was positive, who was going to want me? Until I was able to accept that I could be positive, I wasn't able to get my results. I didn't go back for the results until a year later. It took a year.

If I were to seroconvert to being HIV-positive now, I might feel I had betrayed myself, because I have made a commitment to stay uninfected. It would shake people up at work, because I work as an AIDS educator. I fear people saying, "How can an AIDS educator, who is supposed to be knowledgeable about safer sex, possibly seroconvert?"

I had a discussion with a straight friend last week about this very issue. He was shocked when he found out that a gay man he worked with had seroconverted. He was perplexed. How could that happen? We had an hour-long discussion about it. Basically the discussion was around being human.

Later I found myself resenting my friend's attitude. He is married and is probably not practicing safer sex with his wife. And yet he displayed a lack of understanding about why gay men might have unprotected sex. I found myself wanting to say, "Who are you to say that he should have known better? Is it just based on the fact that he is a member of a community highly affected by AIDS?" I resent that expectations are placed on the gay community that are not placed on the heterosexual mainstream. We are under heightened scrutiny. If we identify with the gay community, we are expected to have protected sex 100 percent of the time.

One of the most disturbing aspects of the AIDS epidemic has been the attempt to modify gay male sexuality. Noncompliance with traditional sexual mores—such as sexual monogamy—is singled out as the source of disease. Buzzwords like "sexual compulsion" and "sex addiction" have become vogue. The moral judgments placed upon our lives have all the attributes of a medieval inquisition. We're instructed through insensitive educational activities that the value we once placed on our sexuality must now change and we had better conform and learn to live "like everyone else." That implies we have not been living like everyone else and that there is some superior form of human relationship and sexual conduct of which we are not aware. Even our own community has sought to rehabilitate our sexual behavior through behavior modification in order to enforce new sexual norms.

ﻬ

Current AIDS prevention campaigns don't really give room for the reality of people's lives. The messages they deliver are absolutes like "Always use a condom, all the time, for everyone." Those messages do not take into account reality.

In my work as an AIDS educator, I experience a covert pressure to give a clear, concise message, and to damn well practice what I preach. If there's any discrepancy between what I say and what I do myself, I fear people will judge me as irresponsible or hypocritical. Putting myself to that standard is superhuman.

Remember my question: "Who wouldn't want to get fucked without a condom?" That has been something I don't want to say very much, because of the work I do. I have thoughts about saying that in a public forum and people thinking, "Oh my God, this guy's an HIV educator. What's he talking about?"

But until we're able to address the stuff we're not talking about, people are going to internalize it in a negative way. People are going to think they had better not say anything about their real-life difficulties with safer sex: "There's something wrong with me. I don't match up to the other men here." I worry about the kinds of risks people take based on that interpretation: "I must be stupid. Why should I bother taking precautions?"

We need a forum where people get a chance to tell the truth, to get rid of the heavy baggage people are carrying around, like I was. People need peer support and community support.

Sometimes I think we've forgotten to have fun. So much of our celebrations are focused on AIDS: the AIDS walk, the fund-raising dinners and dances. I need some diversity. I might want to celebrate some things that aren't about AIDS.

We have to learn again how to live. Doing gardening, restoring furniture, and some of the other domestic things I do are ways I've been able to reclaim simplicity, to reclaim growth. It's a way for me to see and revive life.

I'm tired of hearing about the transmission of HIV. I don't need that kind of information anymore. I know what to do to protect myself, what will and will not transmit the virus. That's not the issue. I need to address how I feel about myself: my work, my family, my significant relationships. I want to know how I can meet someone and be intimate with him, how I can enhance my life. Those are the things I need to talk about, because when those things are in balance, I am less likely to put myself at risk.

11

Division by HIV Status

The first time I went country-western dancing in Boston, I danced with HIV. Or rather, I danced with a man named Jack, who was HIV-positive. It was at the Boston Living Center, a service center for people affected by AIDS. Jack and I were both new to this kind of dancing—and strangers to each other—so we were awkward in each other's arms.

Dancing with Jack made me nervous, not just because we were strangers, but because I knew he had AIDS. Burgundy lesions from Kaposi's sarcoma spilled across his face. I did not fear touching him, but I did not like seeing his lesions. I wanted to look through them, to see the person beneath the pox. But I could not ignore the visible signs of the virus ravaging him. His lesions marked him as someone with AIDS and therefore marked our difference. I had just learned that I was HIV-negative.

Two-step dancing etiquette encouraged us to remain slightly apart, a legacy of the time when women wore petticoats and men held themselves an arm's length away to make room. When Jack and I two-stepped together, both of us in blue jeans, this formal distance carved out a space between our bodies, a nearly palpable column of air.

I think of this moment when I consider the divisions between HIV-positive and HIV-negative gay men. We are dancing the same dance and we are dancing it together, but we are separated by a distance. A space intervenes, a self-imposed barrier to close-ness. At any moment, if I wished, I could have moved closer to my dance partner. That I didn't was a sign that I preferred to maintain my distance. Dancing with Jack, I wondered silently to myself, "What if he likes me? What if he is interested in more than just a dance together?" I didn't want to get closer. I preferred to hold HIV at arm's length.

AIDS AS OTHER

That I wanted to avoid getting close to Jack because I knew he had AIDS left me feeling ashamed. I believed it was wrong to dis-criminate against people based on their HIV status. Indeed, I had looked with horror and indignation at the ways some people had reacted to AIDS with avoidance, scapegoating, and violence: fear-ful neighbors burned a family in Florida out of their home, for instance, because one child had AIDS. As a gay man in a commu-nity enlightened about AIDS, I imagined I could never behave in such an ignorant or irrational manner.

I understood the foundation of such prejudices, though. Early in the epidemic, I too was tempted to define AIDS as "other." Like many gay men, I denied the threat of the epidemic by imagining that it was something that happened to other men, in other cities—to men who were older, more promiscuous, less educated, more reckless—to anyone, in short, but someone like me. As the epidemic persisted, it began to hit closer to home. Soon it was no longer a matter of a few reports from New York or San Francisco. As I met people in Boston with AIDS, my denial began to erode.

As I admitted my own vulnerability to HIV, I became more committed to reacting without prejudice toward people with AIDS. My commitment was based not only on community soli-darity but also on a kind of self-interest: I would not want others to shun me if I learned I was infected. In this way, not knowing my HIV status in the early years of the epidemic helped me avoid discriminating against those with AIDS.

Testing changed that. Learning I was HIV-negative caused me

to think differently about AIDS than I had before. Suddenly, I could not so easily presume that I was HIV-positive. I began to feel more vulnerable to HIV than I had before and wanted to protect my HIV-negative status. To my dismay, learning I was HIV-negative unleashed a kind of thinking that I thought I had conquered: AIDS once again became "other."

The most damaging aspect of defining AIDS as "other" is that it encourages us to view people with HIV as if they are nothing more than HIV itself. When I wrote above that "I danced with HIV" and "I preferred to hold HIV at arm's length," I illustrated the trap of identifying Jack with a virus, of equating him with HIV and thereby dehumanizing him. Several of the men I interviewed fell into this trap, using the phrase "people who are HIV" when they meant "people who are HIV-positive." This slip of the tongue reveals how readily we dehumanize those who we believe threaten our health. Because HIV is infectious, HIV-positive people can seem more threatening to the HIV-negative than they would if they had other disabilities or diseases. After all, we don't say "people who are blindness" or "people who are cancer."

THE MEANINGS OF HIV STATUS

HIV testing reveals an objective difference among gay men: It divides us into those who are infected and those who are not. This objective difference, however, is overlaid with many subjective meanings that heighten the divisions gay men experience based on HIV status. When I learned I was HIV-negative, some of these meanings about HIV positivity and HIV negativity resurfaced, even though I believed I had discarded them long before as stereotypical thinking:

HIV-positive	HIV-negative
infected	uninfected
infectious	susceptible
sick	healthy
dangerous	vulnerable

unlucky	lucky
victim	survivor
guilty	innocent
punished	spared
tainted	pure
marked	unmarked
dirty	clean
promiscuous	chaste
slut	virgin
reckless	cautious
unsafe	safe

As much as I tried to banish these simplistic polarities from my thinking, they were hard to repress, and they continue to influence my attitudes about HIV-positive and HIV-negative gay men. How many of these terms crossed my mind unbidden as I danced with Jack?

In the above table of paired terms, perhaps only the first few pairs are neutral. The rest undeniably damn the HIV-positive and laud the HIV-negative. The left column demonizes the HIV-positive as dangerous and morally corrupt, while the right column portrays the HIV-negative as vulnerable and morally upright. This is no accident. It reveals how easy it is for the HIV-negative to moralize about the HIV-positive. Indeed, the table shows how HIV testing—ostensibly a scientific assay—can become a surrogate for moral evaluation.

The term "HIV status" itself holds a couple of competing meanings evident in the above table. In one sense, the word "status" implies a rigid social or moral hierarchy, like caste. In the table, HIV-negative status is portrayed as better than—rather than merely different from—HIV-positive status. In another sense, the word "status" implies a state of being that is mutable, like a status report. When HIV-negative gay men think about the possibility of becoming HIV-positive, they realize their HIV status is something that could change, that is precarious, and that they may wish to protect.

The table of meanings of HIV status suggests at least two ways of interpreting my desire to avoid getting close to Jack after I learned I was HIV-negative. The left column suggests one interpretation, that I feared Jack, an HIV-positive man, because he represented a threatening "other." The right column suggests a different interpretation, that my reaction may have been an expression of a desire to preserve my HIV-negative status as something valuable. Both interpretations are important to consider when looking at the ways in which HIV status causes divisions among gay men.

HIV NEGATIVITY AS REVIRGINIZATION

In chapter 4, Robert discussed receiving an HIV-negative test result and feeling that being HIV-negative was "something tremendously valuable." He felt it was something precious and desirable, something that needed to be protected and guarded. Robert's sexual experience with an HIV-positive friend in Provincetown was traumatic for him precisely because it seemed to him to threaten his HIV status, although his friend did not consider the encounter particularly unsafe.

Because being HIV-negative is highly valued, and because it is something that can be threatened by sexual intercourse, I liken it to virginity. Testing HIV-negative is a kind of "revirginization" for many gay men. It seems to offer "another chance" to those of us who have had sex we fear might have been unsafe. Testing HIV-negative tells us that we are "good," that we are clean, that we are saved, redeemed, absolved. "Go," we imagine the test counselor telling us, "and be unsafe no more."

Could a heightened sense of vulnerability and related feelings of "revirginization" be responsible for the fear of intimacy that engulfs some gay men after they receive a negative test result? Could a heightened sense of being infectious and related feelings of being "dangerous" be responsible for similar fears among gay men who learn they are HIV-positive? Could these feelings lead to reluctance to form new friendships, especially with those whose HIV status is different?

HIV-NEGATIVE SEEKS SAME

"I avoid people who admit they are HIV-positive and would not consider any sexual contact with them, even contact considered safe," said Buzz, a 37-year-old real estate investor from San Diego, California. "It may be considered cold by some, but in my book, someone who is HIV-positive is a dead man. Sex with him would be on par with putting a gun to my head."

With those words Buzz expressed in raw form a feeling present among many of the men I interviewed: a reluctance to become sexually involved with HIV-positive gay men if at all possible. In describing a hypothetical HIV-positive partner as both "a dead man" and "a gun," Buzz brought out two distinct ways in which relationships with HIV-positive men are difficult for HIV-negative gay men: They involve becoming close to someone who is likely to fall ill, become disabled, and die; and they involve a risk—if the relationship includes a sexual component—of HIV infection. For some HIV-negative gay men, these risks are too great, and as a result they seek only HIV-negative partners.

When I asked how learning his HIV status influenced his sexual behavior, Doug, a 37-year-old computer programmer, also from San Diego, told me how he tries to avoid having sex with people who are HIV-positive. "My friends are all HIV-negative, I believe," he said. "I also have tended to stay with certain people longer rather than risk what someone new might bring. Further, folks who I used to play with I avoid just because of where they live: San Francisco, L.A., Berkeley, Boston. And finally, I find myself with much younger guys, ones that have had no previous experience." Through these strategies, Doug hopes to reduce the chance of becoming involved sexually with someone who might infect him with HIV.

Although fear of infection is probably the greatest motivator for discrimination against the HIV-positive, the men I interviewed also mentioned other reasons. One of the chief ones was that such relationships do not seem to offer permanence. "I'm afraid of being attracted to someone who might die soon," said one man. "I fear the anxiety that I might die as a result of the relationship, but I also experience a fear of being left behind, of being left alone. I want to be able to envision myself with my partner ten years from now, even if at any time one of us could be hit by a bus."

Another man, recognizing that he often becomes involved in relationships in response to neediness in his partners, told me this: "I recognize that it might be dangerous for me to be involved with an HIV-positive man. Not because I fear infection with the virus, but because I know that I very easily slip into a routine of accepting other people's dependence on me. It is very attractive to be needed by someone else."

Kevin, 46, who in chapter 5 described postponing getting an HIV test because he didn't want to feel distant from his partner with AIDS, told me that he did not want to watch another partner die from AIDS. "I have to ask myself, 'Could I do this again, have a positive partner?'" he said. "And when I'm really honest with myself, I say no. I feel uncomfortable about that, because my life has been built around nondiscrimination, yet I'm saying, 'Please don't be HIV-positive in my bed.' It's a form of discrimination, like saying, 'No fats, no femmes, no HIV-positives, please.'"

It is sometimes difficult for HIV-negative gay men to admit publicly that they discriminate against the HIV-positive when looking for a sexual partner or relationship, because discrimination is so painful for gay men. Sam, 30, whose narrative appears in chapter 10, admitted that he wants an HIV-negative partner but is reluctant to talk about this and is not forthright about it when dating.

Because of HIV-negative gay men's reluctance to appear discriminatory, personal ads in gay newspapers only rarely specify that someone is seeking an HIV-negative partner. Occasionally I have seen ads in which a man discloses that he is HIV-negative or is seeking someone who is HIV-negative. More often I have seen the word "healthy," sometimes used as a code word to imply "HIV-negative."

In contrast, I have quite often seen ads in which men disclose that they are HIV-positive or are seeking an HIV-positive partner. Indeed, some newspapers have established separate sections in the personal ads specifically for HIV-positive people, a visible example of the way in which the HIV-positive are "divided" from the HIV-negative. Why is it acceptable—indeed encouraged by gay newspapers—for HIV-positive men to seek HIV-positive partners, but not acceptable for HIV-negative men to seek HIV-negative partners?

HIV-POSITIVE SEEKS SAME

It could be argued that the existence of separate sections in the personals for the HIV-positive is simply a consequence of widespread rejection of the HIV-positive by the HIV-negative. But HIV-negative gay men are not solely responsible for divisions among gay men based on HIV status. Positive gay men too sometimes discriminate against HIV-negative gay men, seeking relationships only with other HIV-positive men.

HIV-positive men who seek HIV-positive partners do so for a variety of reasons. Some say that even though they practice safer sex, having an HIV-positive partner eliminates the concern that they might infect an uninfected partner.

Others find that being HIV-positive means they experience life in a way that they imagine HIV-negative men cannot fully appreciate. "There may be many reasons why HIV-positive men would want to date other men with the same HIV status," said one man I spoke with. "Some of them might not even have anything to do with infection. Perhaps the experience of being HIV-positive changes your life in such profound ways—in terms of your immediate and long-term plans—that you want to be with someone with similar experiences."

Ross, a 37-year-old human resources counselor for a university, learned he was HIV-negative after he found out that his lover, John, was HIV-positive. Together he and John walked along the shore of Lake Ontario, talking about the difference in their HIV status and the distance it seemed to impose on their relationship:

John was disappointed by my negative status. What he said was, "Well, that changes everything." It was like, "You can't understand. You're different from me. It's just not the same." It makes me angry when people who are positive say, "Well, you're negative, so you don't know." I find that very frustrating. I can't say I know what it feels like, but I can understand my experience of it, what it means to me.

HIV is fucking my life up too. It has caused me pain. No, it's not the same, but my life isn't a bed of roses just because I'm not HIV-positive. I don't have the disease physically in me, but it's emotionally and mentally in me. I'm not infected by it, but I am affected by it.

Because John was living in Rochester and Ross was in Boston, their relationship suffered from physical distance as well as the emotional distance John felt. Ross told me that although he still loves John, the sexual aspect of their relationship has ended.

Another reason HIV-positive men might seek HIV-positive partners is that HIV-negative men encourage them to. "I've found myself trying to convince HIV-positive friends of mine to date other people who are HIV-positive," said one man I spoke with. "I find myself hoping that my HIV-positive friends might match up."

AIDS APARTHEID

Because of the division that HIV status poses to gay men, and because of the many forces that encourage gay men—both HIV-negative and HIV-positive—to develop sexual relationships with partners of the same HIV status, it was only a matter of time before the word "apartheid" was used to describe social and sexual segregation based on HIV status.

I first saw this term in a 1991 article by Charles Barber in *NYQ*, a now-defunct weekly magazine. In the article, titled "AIDS Apartheid," Barber voices frustration at the ways in which HIV-negative and HIV-positive gay men have erected barriers among themselves:

In gay male communities, walls have gone up, and lines have been drawn; some of us are in, and some of us are out. ... Prospective sexual partners are screened for their HIV status. ... Many HIV-positive men report blanket rejection. Many couples in which one partner is HIV-positive and the other HIV-negative have completely shut down their sexual lives. ...

... Have people with HIV and PWAs withdrawn into lonely spaces, seeing themselves as poisonous and therefore to be kept apart (apartheid literally means "apart-hood")? Do HIV-negative people have a right, in pursuit of "risk-reduction," to discriminate in their choice of sexual partners. . . ?[1]

According to Barber, the fact that HIV-negative men sometimes shun HIV-positive men as sexual partners has created a "rigorous climate of sexual apartheid, a climate so rigorous that several friends of mine have been quizzed on their HIV status *on the telephone* before someone they'd met would agree to even a first date."[2] Barber suggests that the attempt by HIV-negative men to screen out HIV-positive partners betrays an irrational fear of infection, and possibly more: "Is it HIV itself that negatives are afraid of contracting," he asks, "or is it a fear of getting close to illness, and possible death?"[3]

The discrimination that Barber described is a real phenomenon, but is "sexual apartheid" the most useful term to describe it? Those who use the term do so because they know it is an emotionally charged word. After all, it is difficult to argue in favor of apartheid of any kind. The term appeals to HIV-positive men who feel they need its emotional charge to adequately describe the magnitude of the hurt they experience when they are rejected because of their HIV status.

There are several ways in which the term "apartheid" is misleading when discussing discrimination in the gay community based on HIV status. First, it calls to mind the racial segregation formerly in place in South Africa. Although prejudice may be at the root of both racial apartheid and discrimination based on HIV status, it is unfair to compare state-imposed segregation to individuals' acts of discrimination. Discrimination based on HIV status is not mandatory, nor is it universal: many HIV-negative men have partners they know are HIV-positive.

Second, sexual "apartheid" is not sponsored solely by one group at the expense of another, as was the disenfranchisement of nonwhites in South Africa. HIV-negative men are not the only ones who choose sexual partners of the same HIV status; HIV-positive men do too, although the reasons are sometimes different.

Third, sexual "apartheid" depends on the participation of HIV-positive men in order to function. To disrupt it, HIV-positive men need merely refuse to disclose their status. This was not the case with South African apartheid, which was based on the visible characteristic of race.

Barber describes how rejection by the HIV-negative depends on disclosure by the HIV-positive. He mentions a workshop he attended for HIV-positive men during which he watched a videotape by David Wojnarowicz and Phil Zwickler. The videotape, called *Fear of Disclosure,* features a telephone conversation between two men:

> They get hot and prepare to meet for action until one reveals that he has the virus, at which point the other promptly rejects him and hangs up. . . .
>
> . . . One of the first lessons many men with HIV/AIDS learn is the price of telling the truth: Once we clearly state to a partner who is HIV-negative or who hasn't been tested that we're HIV-positive, suddenly safer sex is no longer seen as safe. Condoms develop a curious tendency to be likely to break only when one partner is openly HIV-positive. In this instance, as throughout our cultures, silence and deception are rewarded; truth-telling is punished. As Vito Russo once remarked to me, "Safer sex is something that HIV-negative people do together."[4]

The irony here is that the fear that leads some HIV-negative men to act in a discriminatory way may actually encourage HIV-positive men to be quiet or dishonest about their HIV status, a consequence that HIV-negative men may not have anticipated and that undermines the purpose of their discrimination. Barber, Wojnarowicz, and Zwickler do not suggest that HIV-positive men should disguise their HIV positivity or decline to disclose it. They simply point out the irrational stance that HIV-negative gay men take when they are willing to behave one way sexually with someone of unknown HIV status, but an entirely different way once they learn someone is HIV-positive.

THE PRICE OF DIVISION

In one important respect, the term "apartheid" fails to illuminate one of the most painful aspects of discrimination based on HIV status: that it occurs voluntarily among men within a community, rather than being legislated by one community against another.

Early in the epidemic, gay men fought against those who suggested that people with AIDS should be sequestered or quarantined. We prided ourselves on our ability to educate people about HIV and to counter the myths that led people to distance themselves from the HIV-positive. That the HIV-negative might themselves seek distance from the HIV-positive is disturbing because it suggests hypocrisy: although we denounce discrimination, we may ourselves be practicing it in our most intimate relationships. Not only do we betray HIV-positive gay men by abandoning them, but we betray the gay community by abandoning its commitment to nondiscrimination.

Besides the political price, gay men who divide themselves from others because of HIV status also pay another, more personal price, because they cut themselves off from others. In a 1994 GQ article titled "When Negative Meets Positive," Dudley Clendinen describes his dilemma as an HIV-negative gay man when he finds out that someone he is interested in developing a relationship with is HIV-positive. "What are we to do?" he writes. "If I am to grow in love and humanity, do I decline to take risks, refuse to make myself vulnerable, cut myself off from anyone who threatens me with the possibility of intimacy, love and death? Isn't that what any investment of real feeling is about? Risk?"[5]

Clendinen resents the way that HIV has caused people to seem hazardous and suggests that divisions between HIV-positive and HIV-negative gay men damage us all:

> I don't want to think of people as I now think of cigarettes and alcohol. As toxic. I don't want, having given up tobacco and whiskey and wine, to think that now I have to give up people, too. If we all begin to recoil from one another, it will be not just the protection of our lives that we ensure but also the death of our souls.[6]

Clendinen is unwilling to recoil in this way. Near the end of his essay, he describes how he might answer an HIV-positive man who asks whether they will see each other again: "I would breathe, and with what now seems an effort of will say again what I have come to believe I believe. That we all live with the virus now. We all are affected. Some of us have it and some of us don't, and both kinds of us have to decide whether we are going to draw a line between us. I have decided that I will not, because the person I love could be on the other side."[7]

THE DESIRE TO ESCAPE

Just as the HIV-positive must accept that we cannot eradicate HIV from the physical body, so too must those of us who are HIV-negative accept that we cannot eradicate the HIV-positive from the social body.[8] And yet the desire to escape from AIDS by running away from the HIV-positive is a compelling one, even if it is not practical. Woody, a 52-year-old HIV-negative support group leader in San Francisco, told me about this fantasy:

> Occasionally I find myself thinking, "I wonder if I could just go away somewhere, someplace where people are just living normal lives?" In this fantasy, everything is simple and straightforward again. The men in my HIV-negative

support group talked about this fantasy over and over, the desire to run away from it all. Some men actually claimed that they were going to try to run away. Others would ask, "Where are you going to go?"

James, 44, whose narrative appears in chapter 22, told me that he struggles to hide his rage when he hears men express this desire to run away, and yet he has also found a way of viewing this desire in a more forgiving light. Wanting to run away, James suggests, may be just a way of expressing our fatigue with the epidemic, and our desire to avoid the HIV-positive may be just a way of expressing our desire to return to a time when there was no AIDS, to live in a world without AIDS. Is there anything wrong with that, aside from its impossibility?

12

I See Blue Real Blue

Matthew Lasalle

I CAME OUT IN GAY BARS. Alcohol took the inhibitions away, gave me that little glow, made me more apt to talk to people, took the edge off stress at work—all the things that alcohol is supposed to do. With the alcohol would come cocaine, and with the cocaine would come sex.

When I was using—drinking or drugging—I would have unsafe sex, that is, going to a peep show and having someone suck me off. I've contracted gonorrhea that way. Going to the Fens, an outdoor cruising area. I never did that until I started drinking. Having unsafe anal sex, where I've penetrated someone else without a condom. Why would I take the risk? Why would they let me unless they were positive? I never thought about that until after I stopped drinking.

I moved to New York City in 1985. I did the Fire Island scene, partied a lot, did a lot of drugs. I was smoking two packs of cigarettes a day. In 1986 I was experiencing night sweats, loss of weight, diarrhea, shortness of breath, all those things. I thought I was infected. I had friends in the design industry who were getting sick and dying. After a relationship broke up, I moved back here to Boston in 1988 and wanted a fresh start. I got tested and it came back negative.

I was going out every night after work. I'd end up tricking every night. It was, to my understanding, safe. Sure, I had anal penetration without a condom, but that was all right if the person was a married man. My awareness just wasn't there as it is today. If I was penetrating, I wasn't using condoms. If I was being penetrated I would, which wasn't that often, maybe four or five men. From an oral sex standpoint, I only swallowed four men in my life. However, I would let anyone and his brother suck me off.

My sexual patterns also changed as I went to different places. I commuted to Amsterdam for a while. In Amsterdam, the bars still have back rooms. If I was fucked up, I had unsafe insertive anal sex in back rooms of bars there. On the flip side, if I met someone and I was in his bed, it would be safe. Very strange.

I knew I was drinking too much. At the end of my drinking, I saw nothing in the mirror. There wasn't anything to hate; there wasn't anything to love; there was just nothing there. That body drank, drugged, abused his body—and other people's bodies—having unsafe sex. The day I stopped drinking, I buried someone. I buried an evil, nonfeeling, abusive person who had died. It's a cliché: I was sick and tired of feeling sick and tired.

If you're not in recovery, you really can't relate to what I am going to say: on a Tuesday I went to my first meeting, Thursday saw my first shrink, and the following Wednesday got tested for HIV, because I was going to fix everything and be fine in two weeks. I realized it wasn't going to happen that way later on down the road.

When I got tested in June of 1992, I was a week sober without a drug or anything in my system. That two-week waiting period was the hardest two weeks of my life. I hoped I would be positive, so it would give me an excuse to go back out and drink and drug. I was scared to get a negative result because it would force me to get sober. I hoped it would be positive, so I wouldn't have to deal with the other disease. But the test came back negative.

I went back in January to be retested, just to be sure. At that point I was hoping it was negative. Because I was in a recovery group and because I was seeing a therapist at the time, I had my support network set up. When I went in for my test results, the counselor asked if I had brought someone with me. My immediate response was, "Why? Should I have?" And she said, "Oh, no. I should have told you: it's good to have someone with you." It *is* good to have someone with you for support, whatever the result may be.

&.

Recovering from my addictions, I started meeting people who were HIV-positive who were in recovery. I started seeing people in advanced stages of AIDS who were in recovery. I isolated myself to get away from them. If I found out they were HIV-positive, I would be more distant to them, because I didn't want to develop a friendship and then suffer the loss. In my recovery I was just starting to learn how to be myself and how to be with people who were doing the same thing. I wasn't ready to suffer that kind of loss.

When I got sober and started meeting people who were HIV-positive, I started having feelings like, "Oh, my God, why am I negative? What did he do that I didn't do? What did I do that he didn't do? I can't count how many men I've slept with. Why am I negative?"

A lot of people assume that I'm positive. Someone I befriended had seen me at the Fenway Community Health Center. I was there for counseling rather than HIV-related treatment. At a recovery meeting, he came up to me and said, "Matthew, my name is David. You know, they have recovery groups for people who have just found out they are HIV-positive." I had to look at him and say, "I'm negative." That was hard. I almost wanted to say, "Oh, thanks a lot. I'm glad you told me," and pretend I was positive, so I wouldn't have to see the look on his face. Part of me wanted to cry, and part of me just wanted to walk away. David died in January.

I have a friend in New Hampshire I hadn't seen in a few years. A lot of our friends have died. I was at his restaurant and he said, "Matthew, how many do you have left? I have four."

He was referring to his T-cell count.

I had to look at him and tell him, "Over a thousand, I guess. I'm still negative." That was the hardest thing for me, to look at him and say, "I'm still negative."

I told a friend I was going to an HIV-negative support group. He said, "Why the hell do you need that? I'd be jumping for joy." I don't think he's been tested. He was convinced there wasn't a need to know. And when the time came that he needed to know, then he'd go and get tested. Well, I *am* glad I'm negative, but there's still the "Why me?" question. I went to the group to explore the core issues facing HIV-negative men. To say, "I have these feelings too. I'm scared of getting infected," or, "I'm afraid to develop a close relationship because I don't want to lose people." And I have. In my first year of recovery, I have seen nine people I have met die.

Then I started to date Frank, and that's where things changed. We had dated twice, slept together once, without the question of HIV status coming up. The second time we had sex, we were lying in bed after sex, and I just asked him, "Is there a plus or minus sign next to your name?" And he said, "I'm positive. I take it you're negative."

It didn't make things any easier, but it laid everything out on the line. The next day he was going away on vacation with his family. Walking back to my apartment, he said, "You know, Matthew, I want you to think real hard while I'm gone. And if you don't want to continue this, if you want to walk away, I won't think you're a jerk. I'll understand."

The last relationship Frank was in, he hadn't disclosed his status right up front. They were together a couple of months before that came up. His partner was negative and shut the door, slammed it in his face, humiliated him: "How dare you. How dare you risk infecting me. You knew all along and you never told me." I don't think Frank could have gone through that again.

My sister, a physician, made me say to her that I'm aware of the risk in entering a relationship with someone who I know has a terminal, infectious disease: "Why are you entering into a relationship with someone that you know will eventually become ill, who will die over a long period of time?"

I told my mother I was going to be interviewed for this book. I told her I was negative but my partner wasn't. The first thing she said was, "Oh, you're being safe?" And then she said, "Isn't it going to be hard?" I said, "Well, he's fine today. I don't know when he's going to get sick." She was supportive: "If you need me, call on me. If something happens and you need us, we'll come right down." My mother is a very loving, open, accepting parent of a gay child. I think there's a lot of caring in my family.

ُ

Currently I will deep-kiss my HIV-positive partner. My definition of unsafe sex is unprotected anal sex and the exchange of semen or blood. There was one incident early on in our dating. Frank had a cold sore that had scabbed on his lip. I scratched it with my beard—my shadow—and it started bleeding. I didn't realize he was bleeding. We were kissing when I did it. I got blood in my mouth, and Frank tasted it himself. "Honey," he said, "I'm bleeding. Go to the bathroom." So I rinsed my mouth out with hydrogen peroxide. Hope that did it. And Frank broke down crying, because the disease reared its ugly head and was right there.

Recently we've experienced night sweats—where he has soaked the bed—and I'll lie there and try to comfort him. This week, he sweated one night and got up and changed the sheet, and I stayed in bed. Last night, he asked me if I wanted to stay over, and I did. He started sweating really bad and changed the bed once. Then he asked me, "Honey, should you sleep on the couch?" He gave me the option. I didn't, because I didn't want to. This morning, I wondered, "Maybe I should have, because I have a scratch on my hand." That never seemed risky to me before. If he's crying, to wipe a tear away from him doesn't bother me.

What I perceive as risky behavior is an exchange of semen. I will not take his ejaculate in my mouth. He is very dry up to orgasm, so I have not tasted any precum or seen any precum, so I feel comfortable with that. He will pull me away if he thinks he's precumming. His orgasms are violent; they are not something that would happen without you knowing about it. My lover will eat my ejaculate because he likes the taste. I come near his mouth, jacking off in his face. He feels, "I have nothing to lose, and you're negative."

&

I have to accept the risk that I took by entering this relationship, knowing there is a chance for me to convert. I can't change that without abstinence. Abstinence just isn't me. I can't be abstinent. Part of me says, "Oh, it won't happen to you. Everything's fine. You're safe. It can't happen." Which is very stupid, because I know it can. I think there's an element of denial, that it won't happen as long as I'm consciously aware and know what's going on.

I know the risk is there. I know there is a transmittable virus in the partner I am having sex with. I'm more aware of my bodily functions and my partner's, by knowing. I know that if I have a cut on my hand, I'm not going to jack him off. Or if I've nicked my chest shaving, I'm not going to lay in his ejaculate when it's on his stomach or his chest. I just won't do that.

There's a more intimate bond, because there are no secrets. I don't think it would be as intimate, not knowing his status. It would be just mutual masturbation and that's about it. In terms of risk, there's more risk not knowing, in my eyes. There's no hidden knowledge, and there's no guessing: "Is he? Or isn't he? How can I really make love to this person, be close to him, if I don't even know if he's positive or negative?" If somebody said he was negative, I don't know if I would trust whether he was telling the truth or not. But I would trust somebody if he told me he was positive. Oh, God, that doesn't make any sense at all, does it?

&

My sex with other men prior to Frank was strictly the act of sex. The sex I'm having with Frank is making love. It hasn't just been

"Slam, bam, thank you ma'am." It's intimate. There is talking, there is communication, there is foreplay. There are other arenas that I have not explored with anyone else, and I think partly because of his status. There's more of him with me than just his body. I've gotten to know him, what he's talked about, his emotions about the disease and the whole process.

As I develop a relationship, I tend to get more comfortable with my partner's body: knowing when my partner is going to come, sensing when he is going to come. There is a chance that I may, because I am so comfortable with it, subconsciously or consciously, take his cum in a fit of mad passion. I see myself getting more comfortable.

Would it be easier if I was infected, in the long run? That's a question I'm asking myself. It would mean a common bond that's not there now: "Will you take care of me or will I take care of you?" Now, the question is: Do you want me to take care of you? Which is a very different question. And will you let me take care of you? Is my partner going to give me the opportunity to? Or is he going to shut me out: "Get away. I don't want you to see me like this"? Is he going to take his life? Is he going to be fine on Monday, when I go to work, and then decide, "Now it's time, because I don't want to get sick," and I'll come home and find he's dead?

Today, I know I'm negative. I'll get retested in June. And although I said my test in getting sober was the hardest because I wanted it to be positive so I could go back and drink and drug, this June I don't know how I'll feel about the test. If I have converted from negative to positive, I don't know if I'll tell Frank, because of the guilt in that seroconversion. I would want to protect him from knowing I had converted in the relationship. That might last a month. I wouldn't be able to not tell him; he would know. He'll feel that he infected me: "I told you this would happen. It wasn't a good idea. Now I've killed you." I can hear him saying that. And I don't know how I would feel.

Maybe I'll ask him to come with me. I think for me to be retested with him, I will need to ask him to get involved in a discordant-couple group, or to see a therapist prior to my testing and at the time the results are given. I've asked him to start going to a group-therapy session with me.

&

I've got to talk about the positive part of this relationship, and that's the day-to-day. Frank's not sick today. He's asymptomatic. He's living healthy with HIV. We work out. We live like a normal couple would live. So if I have a year of that, if I have three years of that, or if I have ten years, for me it's better to have the quality of time with Frank than never to have had it at all. That's what I have to look at. And that's how I have to live, every day.

I have a disease that will kill me if I don't control it: alcoholism. I have the luxury of keeping my disease in remission by not drinking or drugging. Frank has a terminal illness that he had no choice in getting. He got it. I did not choose to become an alcoholic, but I am one. We have very different diseases, but the outcome will be the same if I pick up. The difference is he doesn't have a choice. Eventually he will die.

What I've learned with him is that he makes the best of every day because he doesn't know if tomorrow is going to be as good as today. I live every day just for one day because I'm only sober for one day. I need to keep that common bond: the way that I perceive life on a daily basis. And that's why I think we are a very good couple. We get support from each other.

Two people meet; they fall in love; they're going to build a house and live happily ever after. Entering into a relationship with someone who is HIV-positive—when you are negative—kind of puts a damper on that. It's hard to plan. You know that eventually something is going to change. That's the negative side.

On the good side of this relationship? I smell flowers with him. I see things that I've never seen. I take the time to see the beauty in people and the beauty in things. I take the time, even in snowstorms. We held hands and walked down Berkeley Street recently, tasting the snow as it was coming down. When I was drinking, I would be bitching, "Oh, this goddamn slush." It was really beautiful. I see a lot of things through him. On the blue days, I see blue real blue.

The disease isn't there 80 percent of the time. It's there when it has to be. And when it comes up unexpectedly, it's not as big a deal. It's manageable. Last night, we reupholstered a chair, which I had never done in my life, and neither had Frank. So the two of us sat there and experimented and reupholstered this chair. It took seven hours, and it came out beautifully. It was a project we did together, something that a normal couple would do. The disease wasn't there when it was being done—until I stepped on a tack and he stepped on a tack. Then Frank said, "Matthew, put your shoes on." And I said, "No, why don't you?"

13

Positive-Negative Couples

NOT THE KRAMDENS

When I mentioned this book to an HIV-positive friend with an HIV-negative partner, he was curious to know what term I would use to describe the kind of couple he was in. "Ralph and Alice Kramden of *The Honeymooners* are a discordant couple," he said. "My partner and I are not."

My friend objected to the use of the term "discordant" by social scientists to describe relationships between people of mixed HIV status. He felt the term implies that such couples are incompatible. The related term for relationships between people of identical HIV status—"concordant"—suggests that those couples are naturally harmonious. Is there not an ideological bias in these terms, he suggested, one that encourages people to develop same-status relationships and avoid opposite-status ones?

Researchers wishing to avoid these connotations sometimes use the unwieldy terms "serodiscordant" and "seroconcordant" instead, focusing on the fact that disagreement exists in the couple's blood, not in their temperaments. Another term I have heard used to describe couples with mixed HIV status is "magnetic." This reverses the polarity of "discordant," turning the partners' difference in HIV status into an asset, since "magnetic" describes something attractive. Yet this term overstates the case in the other direction, suggesting that such couples are likely to bond naturally, as the positive and negative poles of magnets cling to one another. It also suggests that couples with identical HIV status are unlikely to bond in this way. What term would we use for those couples? Repellent? Repulsive? I shudder at the thought.

I use the term "positive-negative" to describe couples of mixed HIV status, not only because it is neutral, but because it allows me to use the related terms "negative-negative" and "positive-positive" to describe other couples.

If HIV status is capable of dividing gay men in many ways, as I suggested in chapter 11, then positive-negative couples are one of the places where such division is bridged. If we use the term "apartheid" to describe relations between the HIV-positive and the HIV-negative, then this term certainly fails when we apply it to positive-negative couples. They combat such simplistic terminology by their very existence, challenging us to reexamine the relationship between the HIV-positive and HIV-negative in intimate terms.

LEARNING OF MIXED HIV STATUS

One of the fears in couples who go for HIV testing is that their results may be different. The shock and surprise that this yields can throw a couple into a precarious position.

Keith, a 40-year-old dividends specialist for an insurance company, spoke to me about getting tested with Mark, his partner of nearly 14 years. Mark was in recovery from drug addiction when he decided he wanted to get tested. "In the first year, your concentration is on being drug-free," said Keith. "When Mark celebrated his first year of being clean, I thought, 'Gee, everything's going good. He's been clean a year.' He decided to get tested, because when he was using drugs he was also promiscuous."

Keith and Mark began to get nervous when they called to learn whether their test results were in:

> When I called, I was told that my results were in. Mark called the same day and was told his results weren't in yet, which got him worried. He said, "I'm positive." I said, "They could have done mine as the last test of the day and

yours the first test of the next day. Yours may be in tomorrow." His results *were* in the next day.

When we went in, the counselor said, "Who wants to go first?" I gave him my blue slip with my number and he looked it up and said, "Okay, you're negative." Mark gave him his blue slip, and he looked at me, looked at the result, looked at Mark, and said, "You're positive." Then he left the room. Mark was stunned.

I started crying, immediate tears. I had Mark dead and buried and myself in black. Then the counselor came back. He said, "Let me double-check those numbers. I want to make sure I didn't get them mixed up. It could be the other way around." He did double-check the numbers, but it stayed the same: I was negative and Mark was positive.

Keith was emotionally overcome by the news. "For about two weeks after that, even at the gay pride parade, I would break out in tears at the slightest thing," he said. "I couldn't concentrate at work. The fact that I was negative bothered me a lot because Mark and I were finally at the stage where we thought our relationship was going to work right."

Ross, 37, who in chapter 11 discussed being alienated from his partner, John, because of the difference in their HIV status, told me about the conflicting emotions he felt when he tested negative after John tested positive:

I had mixed feelings about testing negative. I was definitely happy I wasn't positive, but I felt almost disappointed. I expected I was going to be positive, because John had tested positive and I had been sexual with him for six years. I didn't get fucked that much, but I swallowed a lot. I think we assumed that we would both be positive and that we would deal with it together as positive guys. Then it turned out that one of us was positive and one was negative.

I felt bad for John. I felt good for me. I felt anger about John's test. When I met John, I wanted to be in a relationship, and I would have been monogamous. There was an angry part of me thinking, "If you had done that, then you could have avoided this."

Learning about mixed HIV status is not always unwelcome, especially to a partner who knows he is positive. Dudley, a 42-year-old public relations marketer, told me that his lover Michael was relieved when Dudley tested negative. "I think he was relieved he hadn't infected me," Dudley said. Because Michael's former partner had died of AIDS, Michael was also relieved that he could count on Dudley. "He felt good: at least I would be around to take care of him if he needed it," Dudley said. "Michael didn't want somebody to get sick on him again. He wanted to work very hard to keep my status negative."

TELLING OTHERS

When Keith learned that his partner, Mark, was infected, he was unsure whom to tell. "I didn't want to come out and tell anybody about it," he said. "Eventually I did start telling my family, because I've always been honest with my brothers and sisters. They know I'm gay. They know that Mark and I are lovers." When Keith told his family, everything went well. Encouraged by this, he was able to tell others. "Little by little I started telling certain friends, and from there it just got easier to tell other people."

Dudley faced the question of telling his young son, Alex, about Michael's illness. Before Michael's diagnosis, Dudley had talked with Alex about AIDS, but only abstractly. They had gone to see the NAMES quilt, and Alex knew that Michael's former partner had died of AIDS. "A couple of years ago, when Alex was in fourth grade, he had to do a science project. He picked HIV and AIDS as his project. We asked, 'Why did you pick this?' He said, 'Because nobody else in my school will, and I know you know all the answers, so I'll be able to do a good job.' So we talked about it then, but it was an abstract discussion. I don't think we told Alex at that time that Michael was positive."

It was not until a few years later, while Alex was at summer camp, that Michael experienced his first AIDS-related hospitalization. "When he became hospitalized," Dudley said, "Michael went from 'being HIV-positive' to 'having AIDS,' because he got pneumocystis pneumonia. We decided to tell Alex on the way home from camp. By then, Michael was out of the hospital. So we did, and Alex was upset and cried. We certainly told him at that time that I was negative. We talked about transmission. We told him we don't do anything that would cause me to become positive." Since then, Alex has not talked much about AIDS, but when I interviewed Dudley, the family had recently been thinking about it again. "A few weeks ago, our church had a healing service dedicated to AIDS," Dudley said, "and Alex and Michael and Michael's family attended. The whole thing was about AIDS, so Alex was sitting there, thinking about it again."

For some negative partners in positive-negative couples, the decision to tell family members is a complicated one. Cathy, a 27-year-old social work graduate student who had done a lot of volunteer work in AIDS service organizations, was unsure how much to tell her family about Louie, her partner with AIDS. "I met Louie in August," she said. "I didn't tell a lot of people about it until October. Christmas was coming up and I was going home to Texas to visit my family. The big question among my friends and Louie was, 'What do I tell my parents?' My parents knew I was seeing him. They knew something about his history, meaning jail and his drug and alcohol use. The question was, 'Do I tell them his HIV status? Do I tell them he has AIDS?'"

Some of Cathy's friends urged her not to tell her parents, especially not at Christmas. "You can tell them if and when it's necessary," they advised. But Cathy spoke with her mother every week on the phone, so she figured her mother should know:

> I figured I might as well tell them. They came to pick me up at the Dallas–Fort Worth airport, and we were driving out of the airport. I was sitting in the back seat. My mother looked at me in the rearview mirror and asked, "Does he have AIDS?" My mouth dropped. We were just getting over

the "Gosh, it's hot here." We hadn't even hit the tollbooth where you give the parking ticket. I was hoping we'd at least make it home.

I didn't say anything, and she said, "Well, I'll take that as an affirmative." I don't remember talking about Louie's health that much. Maybe she put two and two together.

Cathy's mother was concerned about Louie's health and Cathy's health. She hoped they were "being safe," but she didn't ask specific questions. Her mother was also concerned about Cathy's psychological health, wondering if she would be able to handle having a partner with AIDS. She knew that Cathy had a supportive group of friends, and that she had already lived through the AIDS-related deaths of a "buddy" and a neighbor. "I think my mother was okay with it by the time I left," Cathy said. Her father, though, didn't say much. "My father doesn't say much in general," she added.

Cathy's situation was particularly dramatic because Louie was her first sexual partner. Her younger sister had difficulty accepting Cathy's decision. "My sister was really upset," Cathy said. "She was upset about the whole concept of me being in love with—having sex with—someone who has AIDS. She was very concerned about the health side, even though she's way more sexually active than I am. Was I just going to call home one day and say that I had AIDS? Why was I doing this? Of anyone in the world, why would I choose somebody with AIDS? Why didn't I just find somebody who didn't have AIDS?"

HAVING SEX

When I asked HIV-negative partners in positive-negative couples about their sexual behavior, I got a wide range of responses. Some do not have sex with their partners, some have sex that does not involve penetration, and some have sex with penetration using condoms.

In chapter 11, Charles Barber suggested that some positive-negative couples completely shut down their sexual lives, and I found this to be the case with one of the men I interviewed. Keith told me that when he tries to have sex with Mark, both of them have problems maintaining erections. "I think it's his fear of transmitting the disease to me, and my fear of getting the disease from him," Keith said. "It's in the back of our heads and it kills the whole mood. We still consider ourselves lovers, but our sex life has died totally."

Complicating Keith's situation is the fact that Mark doesn't sleep in the same bed with him. "He hasn't slept in the same bed with me since he found out he was positive. He has slept with me a few times, but he doesn't stay in the bed all night." Keith could not attribute Mark's behavior solely to a fear of being intimate. "Mark doesn't even sleep in his own bed," Keith said. "He has slept on the couch for the past year and a half. I don't know why. He doesn't know why. I've asked him. He doesn't have an answer." Clearly, learning he was HIV-positive disturbed Mark in complex ways.

Many men with HIV-positive partners have sex that does not involve penetration. Edward, 39, who in chapter 9 discussed how testing HIV-negative encouraged him to practice safer sex out of self-interest, told me that he remembered "the old days of unprotected screwing" and missed them, but that other forms of sexual play were just as satisfying. He described sex with a former lover, Chuck, who was HIV-positive:

> Chuck and I always kissed very deeply. For us, jerking off was very satisfying, and we were both totally involved in each other's nipples. I used to be able to play his body like an instrument. That's what it felt like to me. He would ripple under my touch. As I got to know him, sex just kept getting better and better. It was just fine.

Seth, a 35-year-old engineer, found nonpenetrative sex appealing even before he met his HIV-positive partner, Jerry. "I was never attracted to activities that would be potentially unsafe, even before HIV," Seth said. "I didn't find them to be within my realm of sexual tastes. It so happens that Jerry has a similar set of tastes and sexual behaviors. It's a matter of preference, just as there are certain foods we don't like."

Because Seth and Jerry are compatible in this way, they did not have to make major changes in their sexual repertoire. "There is simply no sharing of bodily fluids between us at all: no anal penetration, no oral sex, no deep kissing," Seth said. "We have a very vanilla sort of sexual life, but it's very satisfying for us."

Among those whose sexual activity includes penetrative sex, using condoms—and also withdrawal—is prevalent. "The 'safer sex' stuff is just always there," said Cathy. "I was a virgin until I met Louie, so I've never had sex without a condom. He's never come in me. We don't do oral sex without a condom, which is a big bummer." Dudley told me that practicing safer sex was not a problem for him and Michael. "I'm convinced that the virus is hard to get, that the only real transmission is through semen or blood contact, and that is pretty easy to prevent," Dudley said. "For the most part, when we have anal intercourse, we seldom come in each other, even though we use a rubber. It has happened, but rarely. And with other partners—because we're not monogamous—we do the same thing."

FEELING SAFE WITH A POSITIVE PARTNER

One of the unexpected things I learned from HIV-negative partners of HIV-positive men is that they sometimes feel safer with an HIV-positive partner than with an HIV-negative partner. Because the risk of HIV infection is clear in a positive-negative couple, it may be easier to adopt and maintain safer-sex practices with an HIV-positive partner than with an HIV-negative partner. But this is not usually what the men were talking about. Rather, they revealed that there is something uniquely comforting about the *certainty* of an HIV-positive partner's status that makes intimacy easier. The uncertainty of an HIV-negative partner's status, on the other hand, raises issues of trust that do not plague positive-negative couples.

Matthew reflected upon this feeling of safety in chapter 12, when he mentioned that there was "more risk not knowing" a sexual partner's HIV status. For him, an HIV-negative partner would be difficult to trust, but an HIV-positive partner would not. Seth also spoke to me about this idea. "Interestingly enough," Seth said, "in some ways I feel safer with a positive person than a negative person. I know up front what I am dealing with, whereas with a negative person there would always be a sense of not being sure, first of all, that he was telling the truth, and second of all, whether his status had changed since the last time he had taken the test." Seth emphasized that he did not think having an HIV-negative partner would encourage him to discard safer sex practices, but rather that it would simply make him more anxious:

> My sexual behavior would be the same, but my anxiety level would be different. Even if my behavior were relatively safe, my anxiety would be greater with a negative person than a positive person because I wouldn't know what I was dealing with. It's the uncertainty of not knowing what the status of the person is, of assuming the person is negative but potentially positive. The actual risk is greater with a positive partner, but the anxiety is less.

Alan, 31, who in chapter 9 said that testing negative reassured him that safer sex actually worked, told me that the comfort he feels about sex with his HIV-positive partner, George, arises from the fact that George knows him well and therefore respects his decisions about safer sex. With an anonymous partner, whether HIV-positive or HIV-negative, Alan feels less secure:

> With someone I know and trust, I know that if I give some signal, some cue—"No, this is not what I want to be doing"—there's an immediate reaction. When I'm having an anonymous encounter, I don't know if people are going to get it when I try to get across to them that I don't want to do something. I make it sound so technical, but in the big picture it's true in a million little ways.
>
> I am more adventuresome with George, who I know is

HIV-positive, than I am with a stranger. I know what's going to happen when I'm having sex with George. I know that I have two people's judgment working full force. He's not going to do anything that's going to be dangerous for me or for him. We're taking care of each other. It sounds so sweet.

It surprised me that being in a couple where HIV is known to be present in one partner could be more comfortable than being in one where it is not. But as the above remarks demonstrate, psychological comfort about sexual behavior in a couple may depend less on the actual risk of HIV transmission than on levels of trust and intimacy. This idea is developed further in chapter 15, where I explore the ways in which sex in negative-negative couples is not always easy, even when the risk of HIV transmission is low.

THINKING ABOUT SEROCONVERTING

When I spoke with Keith about the reasons that uninfected men have unsafe sex, he mentioned that in the back of some men's minds may be an unconscious desire to become HIV-positive. "Maybe subconsciously they want to catch it," he said. "There was a point after Mark found out he was positive when I was contemplating having unsafe sex with Mark to get myself infected," Keith admitted. "I thought it would make things between us easier if we were both positive. But after a little bit of rational thinking, that idea changed very quickly."

Cathy had also thought about seroconversion. "I don't *want* to be positive," she said emphatically. "Louie doesn't want me to be positive. It's sort of set. I'd love to be closer to him, but there's no way I'd want to be positive. That does not compute." Because she was on the board of directors of an AIDS service organization, Cathy found herself morbidly imagining what she might do if she seroconverted: "We were talking about what we were lacking on the board. I was imagining calling the director and saying, 'Guess what? You do have a positive woman on your board.'"

Cathy told me she would feel extremely guilty if she seroconverted: "I would feel judged. I would feel it was my fault. It's not like I got it during the seventies or eighties when nobody knew anything. As many times as I have told people that AIDS is not punishment, I think I'd probably feel that way. That goes back to what my sister was saying: 'How can you knowingly put yourself at risk? How would you explain it to us if you did test positive?' Those are big questions that we're starting to have to deal with."

MANAGING A PARTNER'S ILLNESS

To combat feelings of helplessness, HIV-negative partners of HIV-positive people sometimes adopt a "caretaker" role, becoming advocates for their loved ones in health-care settings, and seeking to "manage" their partners' therapeutic regimens.

Edward told me that finding out Chuck was HIV-positive had "forced" him to make a commitment to their relationship that he later felt was premature. They had known each other for only four months, but Edward soon found himself ready to make a commitment like a marriage: "in sickness and in health, until death us do part." Edward described the way he sought to help Chuck:

> I went into my shepherd-caretaker mode. I know how to work systems. I know how to network. I lined up practically free health care for him, taking advantage of a program for HIV-positive people in which the federal government reimbursed 90 percent of his health costs. It was a great program for a while; it has since ended. He got on that. I freaked out, worried about him, so I did that stuff. I also worried that I was getting a little overbearing, not letting him deal with it, making it out to be a bigger deal than he wanted it to be.

Cathy too told me that she worries about being overbearing in caring for Louie. Although she supports Louie's regimen of alternative therapies—Chinese herbs, acupuncture, tai chi, and candle magic—she also wants him to seek traditional medical care. "When Louie's ears are ringing and it hurts," she said, "I want him to go to the doctor. He doesn't believe in doctors. He thinks the medical profession is out to make money and kill people. I want him to do it my way. I find it difficult for him not to have his disease the way I want him to have it. I'm finding it really hard to step back."

Cathy's urge to be a caretaker sometimes leads to misunderstandings. One night, for instance, Louie was sore and achy, and she sat on the couch with him rubbing his feet. He told her to stop. "I was feeling bad because nothing I was doing was right," Cathy said. "Every time I touched him, I hurt him. And so I jokingly said, 'Okay, I won't touch you.' He flipped. That's the one thing he's always feared: that people won't touch him." In this instance, Cathy's desire to be helpful backfired.

LIVING IN THE PRESENT

In professional chess games, two clocks in a single case tick off the time allotted to the players. If the players take different amounts of time to make their moves, the two clocks get out of synchronization. One player ends up with less time left than the other. As a result, the pace of his later moves must be quickened. Positive-negative couples can be like those chess players. Time ticks away for both partners at equal rates, but the significance of the time that remains for each is different.

HIV-negative men I spoke with told me that their HIV-positive partners live with an energy and urgency that arise from not knowing how much time they have left. Their example sometimes influences HIV-negative partners to live at the same pace, just as the speedy moves by a chess player with less time on his clock may cause an opponent to quicken his pace. Keith, for instance, told me that one thing he has learned from living with Mark is to live one day at a time. "I've learned to just live for today," he said. "That is the best way to live. You don't know what's going to happen down the road. You can still have your future goals and dreams, but don't put so much emphasis on them. Concentrate on the present."

The sense of urgency felt by an HIV-positive partner can

destroy a relationship with an HIV-negative partner. Edward told me that his partner, Chuck, evaluated his life goals as a visual artist when he learned he was HIV-positive and became more committed to his creative work than to his relationship with Edward:

> He started figuring out what his priorities were, what he wanted to do with his work, and what role—if any—I had in that picture. What I saw was an intense commitment to getting as much of his work out as possible and a serious- ness about his work as an artist that wasn't there before. Which, of course, is a very healthy response.

As a result of his soul-searching, Chuck left Edward and moved to Paris, so that he could prepare work for a show and then return to establish himself in New York. Chuck's commit- ment to his work shut Edward out emotionally. "Instead of seeing the relationship as something that enhanced his ability to do his work," Edward said, "he felt that it was a drain on his emotional energy, and that if he was going to get his work done, he needed to not have me in his life. I think it ultimately led to our breakup." When Chuck returned to the United States after a successful dis- play of a new series of works, he settled in New York on his own and distanced himself from Edward. Edward tried to see him sev- eral times, but Chuck avoided him. Musing about the dissolution of their relationship, Edward said, "I presume I take an emotional toll on him I just don't understand."

Sometimes the dramatically altered expectations about life that characterize an HIV-positive person's first reactions to his HIV status change over time, as he realizes that he may be healthy for a long time. Dudley told me that when he first met Michael, Michael believed he was going to die soon. Michael's belief was strengthened by the fact that his former lover had died within 18 months of finding out he was HIV-positive. "Michael got quite depressed and didn't foresee much longevity," Dudley said. With very little advance planning, Michael went on a trip to China, spending about $15,000. "After a while, he realized that life was going to go on. He wasn't symptomatic, so he really didn't have AIDS. He was just HIV-positive."

Since then, Michael and Dudley have been more optimistic about the future. "What we always do is plan, so there's something to look forward to. We're going to Palm Springs for Thanksgiving. That's not so far in the future," Dudley said. "The major difficulty in planning is the uncertainty, because the disease is progressive and you don't know how fast it progresses. But it's no more uncertain, I suppose, than any type of terminal illness."

In the face of this uncertainty, Dudley's approach is pragmatic: he is ready to handle crises as they occur, but he doesn't spend time anticipating them. When a loved one becomes ill or needs to be hospitalized, Dudley said, at that point your life becomes different: "You stop what you're doing, your normal routine, and you rise to the crisis, whatever the crisis may be. It's like knowing your kid is fine until he falls off his bike and breaks his leg. Then you leave work and take him to the hospital. Your life changes when you have a crisis, but you can't live in a crisis. So we don't live in a crisis."

14

Pillars of Monogamy

Don Willet

I HAVE ONE OF THOSE *Longtime Companion* stories. I was 22 in 1981 and I remember being with a former lover, having a party in his backyard, when a bunch of friends from Los Angeles brought over the first *Advocate* that had an article about the "gay cancer" in it. We had a lengthy discussion about it. Then we smoked some pot and forgot about it. It's ominous: that man has since died, and his partner of 20 years has also died. I was freaked out when I found out he had died of AIDS-related complications. We had had very risky sex. He was the only person other than my present lover that I've had anal intercourse with.

I came down with a case of hepatitis B in 1983 and was convinced that it was HIV-related. I was doing street outreach work and was involved with some people's body fluids, so I may have gotten it that way. Also, I did have a very minor casual sexual encounter; I don't think I could have gotten hepatitis from that. Whatever the case, it was worrisome for me to get sick at that point. There was an early connection made to hepatitis B: people were saying AIDS seemed to be transmitted the same way. It was troublesome not knowing my HIV status. It's hard to say whether I believed I was infected. In some ways I believed I was infected. In other ways I was afraid of becoming infected.

I was suffering from acute anxiety attacks for about a year before I got tested. It was a fear of danger lurking around the next corner. Not a paranoia, just that I felt my life was constantly in danger. First, it manifested itself in fear of dropping dead of this disease. I didn't understand how long it took or what happened. I was convinced I would wake up one day and have purple spots all over my body or have pneumonia and then be dead in a few days.

The anxiety became almost debilitating as time went on. I would break out in sweats and not be able to sleep at night, or I would wake up very early and begin worrying about it all day. I was one of the "worried well," although I didn't know I was well. I was convinced I wasn't well.

The anxiety attacks were my immediate prompt to get tested. My lover, Ben, felt they were paralyzing me. He said, "Don't you think maybe we should be tested, just to put it to an end?" Also, I was beginning doctoral work, and I decided I didn't want to do the doctoral work if I tested positive. I didn't want to spend my time that way. That was the other piece.

My lover and I were tested together in the winter of 1987. We went on vacation to California for a couple of weeks to visit my sister and take our minds off things. The vacation was fine. Even though I didn't have the results yet, I felt a great sense of peace just having been tested, just having had the blood drawn. Taking control of the situation brought a certain amount of peace. Part of me thought, "Now somebody knows what my HIV status is. Even if I'm not ready for it, somebody knows." There was some kind of control over the virus in that.

When I was sitting waiting for the results I was a wreck. I didn't know whether I was actually going to be able to hear the results. I didn't know if I could take it. Ben and I went together. We went up to the room, and the counselor started going through the papers. She checked the numbers once, and checked the numbers twice, and checked the numbers a third time. I thought I was going to pass out. She said, "I'm happy to say that you're both negative. I want to be sure you understand what that means." After that, I just heard her talking at the mouth. She gave us a long talk about how we should be practicing safer sex, even as lovers, which we didn't really take to heart.

I remember both of us commenting that it was like an enormous weight taken off of us. I realized at that point how much pressure not knowing my HIV status had put on me. It was only after the test that I began to realize that. My perspective changed, the anxiety decreased, I was less depressed. I think I was easier to live with afterwards.

It was still in the early days of testing. Nobody knew what the window period was. We had heard talk about false negatives. I really believed that some day I might seroconvert. I thought, "I'm going to be in that small percentage of people who may not seroconvert for years and years." I worried about that. Or I worried that I would never develop antibodies and that my partner would develop antibodies, so we would be discordant. Even though we were both really positive, I might not test positive.

My anxiety started to creep up again, and I was tested a second time in the fall of 1990. Actually, what happened was that my lover had gone to the doctor, and the doctor suggested that he be tested again, so my lover went through the testing process without telling me until he got the results back. He tested negative again and told me afterwards. In fact, he told me right after we had had sex. I remember that distinctly.

I was furious about that, because it was something I felt we should have done together. If he had some kind of fear or anxiety or some reason to believe something wasn't right, then I should have been included in that process. He shouldn't have gone through it alone. His reason for not including me was that my anxiety was too high and he didn't want to add to that.

Ben and I have a generally monogamous relationship, although there is an occasional jack-off session with somebody outside the relationship. We have an agreement that we don't engage in any risky behavior—what we've defined as risky behavior—with anyone outside the relationship. We have unprotected sex with each other, based on that agreement and our testing history as well.

And yet, I would feel incredible anxiety after I jerked off with somebody else. Even that kind of contact, which I knew intellectually didn't pose any great risk to me, would cause great anxiety. Fear crept back, very closely related to guilt in my mind: if Ben got sick, I couldn't live with myself. I would be the guilty partner. This anxiety did not discourage me from having encounters outside the relationship; it just made me feel guilty.

I felt that Ben and I hadn't talked about our explicit understanding of the relationship regarding sexual fidelity. We had talked about it years before, but we hadn't revisited it. I was concerned that maybe I understood our agreement differently than he. Sometimes he would say things that would lead me to think, "Maybe he expects a different kind of fidelity than I am giving him." I felt he would judge me for having sex outside the relationship, even though he was okay about my jerking off with somebody.

As close as we are, and as deep companions as we are, Ben and I don't always talk about sex very easily with each other. It's not one of the things we are on the same wavelength about. That's something for us to deal with over the course of our relationship.

But we've come beyond that point. We're more comfortable with the agreement now. Ben and I agree that there's no oral sex outside of our relationship, meaning that I don't go down on anybody and nobody goes down on me, and the same with him. And there's certainly no anal sex, even protected. We also have agreed not to deep-kiss anyone else. We err on the side of safety. "We have each other's life in our hands" is how we put it.

The other night we were joking about the Boston Jacks events, the jack-off parties that go on around town. I've never been to one, but many people I know go. We were with some close friends and I said, "Well, Ben of course would never let me go to one of those things." And he said, "That's not true. You can go if you want." It was explicit license to go ahead if that's what I needed.

❧

I met Ben in 1982. I basically grew up with him. It was a different era, in some ways. I don't know what it would be like to meet somebody since 1985 and have a long-term relationship. I would imagine—this is a fantasy for me—that I wouldn't have any trouble insisting on condom use with a new partner now, because I would have no background. I know I would need to protect myself, because there wouldn't be a foundation of trust built.

For me, it's unrealistic to imagine having protected sex with Ben. Ben and I have never had protected sex, never in our lives. It would have been a major change to start having protected sex. And to do that now would be a psychological shift for us, a symbolic one. It would symbolize a kind of distrust of each other, I think. I trust Ben completely. He's an incredibly trustworthy person. I decided at one point that I trusted him more than I loved my own life, if those two things can be weighed together.

Reactions from our peers have always been affirming. We've never been challenged. Ben and I are often viewed by our friends as pillars of monogamy and stability. To a degree, that's true. To a degree, we're very monogamous. And when an outside thing happens, it really is incredibly safe. There is no contact with any kind of body fluid, on my part. I have to say that part of my trust of Ben is built on my trust of myself in those situations.

Both of our families, I think, see our relationship as a marriage. I think they assume we are not having protected sex. They don't assume that marriage has any openness to it. If it does, it's a breach of that marriage contract. That's how they see it. In reality, many marriages breach that contract all the time.

❧

Many couples I know of, my situation included, often ask, "Is part of the reason we're still together because of the epidemic?

Was it safe for us to stay together?" We identified ourselves as an isolated couple, insular: nothing was going to get in. We could stay with each other and have a relationship that was emotionally and sexually fulfilling, but maybe not as exciting as having a new partner.

Ben and I hit our lowest at about the seven-year or eight-year mark, when it was very difficult to stay together. One of the reasons we both stayed with each other was because it was safe. I asked Ben point-blank once if that were the case. He said, "I couldn't imagine putting myself in a sexual situation with anyone else, because of AIDS." He just couldn't imagine it. He's very disease-phobic. When we talk about safer sex, he is incredibly conscious of disease and the potential of transmitting disease.

Ben was working in New Haven when I moved to Germany on a Fulbright scholarship and met a wonderful person. We had an affair, an emotional affair. I didn't have oral sex with the guy, nor anal sex, and there was no deep kissing, but there was a lot of physical contact. He had never been tested. He was in a circle of friends who were very hard-hit by the epidemic. I knew when I was getting into the whole thing that this was risky. At the same time I was very emotionally drawn to him. But I never crossed a certain line, even though at times I was tempted to. It was my relationship with Ben, perhaps, that kept me from that and—this is interesting—not my feelings about myself.

I felt the affair put me at enough risk to tell Ben this had happened before we came back together, to give him the opportunity to make a choice: "I realize you might want to use protection. Or you may not want to have sex with me." It was all very explicit.

In fact, Ben and I were abstinent until the time we got tested again, five or six months later. I was mandatorily tested in Germany and came back negative. The guy I had the affair with was tested last year and he also tested negative. It's interesting that that was a real relief. I hadn't even realized that was a pressure in the back of my mind. Even though I had tested negative, it was a relief to hear that he had tested negative as well.

That affair turned out to be important for Ben and me, emotionally. At that point we had been ten years into the relationship. We were at a real juncture. It became a cementing experience.

Now that I've been with my partner for so long, there's such a companionship that I couldn't imagine my life without him. Our sex life has changed significantly over the years. We still have sex together, but it's not nearly as frequent, nor as experimental, nor as exciting as it once was. And that's okay for me.

❧

I believe I am HIV-negative, generally, although there are moments when I believe that I'm positive, in a way. I don't know if it's a question of empathy, or what, but there are sometimes moments when I think, "You know, I'm probably positive." I don't know where that comes from, but it's there.

I think we HIV-negative men often think of ourselves as positive. We identify, I think, as potentially positive. It's not because safer-sex education told us we should think of ourselves as positive, but because we heard and assimilated the messages that we got throughout the epidemic: that being gay equals AIDS. For those of us in our early thirties, much of our early twenties—when we were coming to terms with dating and having sex—we were absolutely surrounded by messages saying, "If you're gay, you have AIDS." I imagine it's worse for even younger people.

What the identity is, when I think of myself as an HIV-negative person, has changed over time. I used to think of myself as one of the "spared" people. Then there was a period when I thought, "I guess I'm kind of milquetoast. I haven't really been around." Then I thought I was lucky: having had risky behavior with a person who I believe was infected at the time, and somehow not getting infected. Now that I'm doing AIDS work full time, there's a kind of guilt that comes along with being negative which I haven't quite come to terms with. It's a question of credibility. When I'm with people who are HIV-infected and who are doing AIDS work, I somehow think their messages are more credible than mine. I'm somehow less authentic.

When I was a high-school sexuality educator, I would often

start a class by saying, "If I stood here in front of you and told you I was HIV-infected, what would be the first questions that go through your mind?" I never disclosed whether I was infected or not. Playing that role, I would play it as an infected person. I used to feel identified as that positive person. And in that fantasy I would often feel a certain self-righteousness.

❧

I have a friend who knows he's HIV-infected. He goes to public-sex areas and has unprotected intercourse with people. He's very learned in AIDS issues, very much an AIDS political activist. His feeling is that people need to take responsibility for themselves, and if they allow him to have unprotected anal intercourse with them, then that's their problem.

I decided I can't be a friend with someone like that. I simply can't. I can't condone that behavior. I can't make believe it doesn't bother me, because it does. I think sex is always mutual. Even if it's the most anonymous sex, it's a mutual thing. There's a certain level of taking responsibility for your partner in it.

Do I think my acquaintance should be held accountable? I don't think he should be put in jail for the rest of his life. But he heard from me how much I disagreed with him. And as a result, when I do HIV education, I always talk about the mutual responsibility of sex partners.

❧

I understand some of the studies that are showing that older gay men are now becoming infected at an increased rate. They find themselves alone, most of their friends are gone, and it doesn't matter anymore. They'll have unprotected intercourse because they want to enjoy themselves, and because they want to give up. In some ways it's slightly suicidal, but also slightly life-positive. You just want to give in and live to the fullest whatever time you have left. Even though part of me knows the tragedy of that situation, there's another part of me that understands it. Even though anal sex hasn't been taken away from me—and that's true, it hasn't been taken away—there is something about freedom of choice that has been taken away.

Gay men take risks for a number of reasons. Something about growing up as a gay male in our society held me down and made me feel inferior for a very long time. I can imagine a response to that being "I'm going to be somebody who will take the lead. I can make my own decisions, and I can feel confident in that." Part of taking risks may be wanting to be identified as a leader, as a maverick.

When we talk about HIV in communities of color, it becomes clear that it is a question of relative risk: How do you talk about a disease that might kill people 5, 10, or 15 years from now, when they're worried about walking home from school and being shot? Likewise, we don't always understand the violence that gay people experience. If they have gone through life feeling violated for being gay, the risk of dying ten years from now doesn't seem so horrible. It's easier to think there will be a cure in ten years: "I can take risks, and I can start living a full life. Even if there's not a cure, I'll still have lived a full life."

I think the ACT-UP sign—"The AIDS Crisis Is Not Over"—is important. I think many of us believe it *is* over for gay people, that other populations are going to be hit. We feel we've gotten some control over the epidemic. That is not true.

&

Sometimes I do sense divisions between HIV-positive and HIV-negative people, especially in AIDS work and activism. Larry Kramer says that you have to be HIV-infected to scream loud and use really effective language, that HIV-negative people don't do that. They lack a sense of urgency, so they're all playing bureaucratic games. Sometimes people like him make me feel guilty. Here I am, working in a state agency, and things move slowly. They plod along. Maybe it *is* because there isn't so much at stake for me. I do question that.

I remember one day I was working on a project at the AIDS Action Committee with someone and he was completely stressed out by the project. I said, "You need to go home and relax. Just put it away for a couple of days." He said to me, "We're in the midst of an epidemic. We can't put this away." I assume he was HIV-infected. I remember feeling very guilty about that.

૬

I think HIV-negative people bring longevity to the work against the epidemic. We provide continuity for the future. In my own work, I think of that all the time. I want to be able to see policies fully implemented 20 years from now, and to make sure that they are. It's a responsibility. It's part of the commitment that I personally—and secretly—have made to my HIV-infected friends.

When I think of this, I think of one dear friend. He was sexually molested as a child, then went through a severe drug problem, and found out he was HIV-infected right when he started getting a handle on his drug problem. Although he thought he was newly infected, it turns out he's actually in the later stages of the disease. He's so vulnerable, it's incredible. I think about him a lot when I think about the continuity I can provide to the future. He's worried about all kinds of things, including health-care policies that keep him from accessing care. And he's not going to live to see those policies change. I feel that I can.

I talk about the future with my HIV-infected friends, but it's usually about their future. It's very rarely about my future. They don't very often ask about my future, and their future is much more important right now. I'm willing to defer to that.

I get blown away thinking I will probably outlive all the people that I know are HIV-infected. I imagine, sometimes, a rather sad future: being an old person sitting and thinking back on the epidemic, remembering the people who have gone, who never had the opportunity to reach old age. That plays on something in me I haven't quite dealt with, something spiritual. I'm not a religious person, but it touches something I haven't quite come to terms with. It's not completely bleak. When I imagine sitting on my porch, it's usually in a nice rocking chair on a beautiful sunny day, reminiscing with someone. But certainly it will be a retrospective on an incredible tragedy.

When I saw the ending of *Longtime Companion*, where they all came back together on the beach, I thought it was too sappy. I think that when death happens, there's nothing after that. That's why the epidemic is such a tragedy. It wouldn't be such a tragedy if there was a great reunion. It's a tragedy because there's not.

15

Negative-Negative Couples

FIND A NICE NEGATIVE BOY

"Why don't you just find an HIV-negative man and settle down?" was the question that a psychotherapist posed to one HIV-negative man I interviewed whose lover had died of AIDS. I imagine the therapist's tone was that of a Jewish mother chiding her daughter to "find a nice Jewish boy."

When I told my mother that this book would discuss positive-negative couples, she reacted as if the very idea that such couples existed was incomprehensible. "Why would anybody be in such a couple?" she asked. Perhaps she assumed that HIV-negative gay men would only consider relationships with other HIV-negative men.

A devout Christian coworker of mine who read the interview-based chapters of this book noted that anxiety about becoming infected was prevalent among those I interviewed. He asked me why abstinence or monogamy with an uninfected partner was not more often considered as a way to reduce this anxiety.

All three of these people—the therapist, my mother, and my coworker—expressed a common idea: that HIV-negative people should be able to manage their anxieties about HIV by becoming sexually involved only with other HIV-negative people. Not only does this idea ignore the divisiveness of discrimination based on HIV status among gay men, but it also implicitly assumes that negative-negative couples have unprotected sex without worrying about HIV. I found the latter was seldom true among the men I interviewed. Anxiety about HIV is not absent from gay men who are in negative-negative couples. HIV is not a "nonissue" for them, and therefore decisions about whether to have protected or unprotected sex are not trivial.

VIRTUAL HIV

It is easy to see how the actual presence of HIV in one or both partners can affect a couple. Positive-positive couples often find themselves wondering who is going to become sick first and whether one partner will be well enough to take care of the other. Positive-negative couples experience other stresses: not only must they anticipate and adapt to changes in the health of the infected partner, but they must also acknowledge and reduce the risk of transmitting HIV to the uninfected partner.

When HIV makes its presence felt in these couples, whether because of declining health or the threat of infection, couples may feel that HIV demands their attention, drains their energies, and blocks intimacy. It is common for men in such couples to mention that HIV is like a third party in the relationship: "You and me and HIV makes three."

It seems logical that negative-negative couples would not experience HIV as a presence in this way. And yet HIV has so infiltrated the consciousness of gay men that it has a virtual presence even in the lives of the uninfected. For negative-negative couples, virtual HIV can be a third party, an unwanted intrusion, even though HIV is not physically present in either of the partners. Virtual HIV influences the sexual behavior and mental health of couples where neither partner is infected.

A simple example of the influence of virtual HIV was mentioned by Cal, 42, of Rochester, New York. One of the reasons Cal got retested for HIV was to reassure a new boyfriend that he was HIV-negative. "He's negative himself, and I want him to feel safe with me," Cal said. "The other night he got a little precum in his mouth and spit it out. I, on the other hand, want him to feel safe to come in my mouth. I want our sex to be as natural as it can be. But he pushes me away when he becomes too aroused." This is virtual HIV in action.

PROTECTED SEX IN NEGATIVE-NEGATIVE COUPLES

Many of the HIV-negative gay men I interviewed reported using condoms or avoiding penetrative sex even with long-term partners they believed were HIV-negative. Why is it difficult for gay men to have unprotected sex in negative-negative couples?

As I mentioned in chapter 9, some HIV-negative gay men do not believe their test results. Common reasons for this disbelief are uncertainty about the validity of the test, unresolved sexual guilt, and homophobic equations of being gay with getting AIDS. Claude, 34, whose narrative appears in chapter 8, has protected sex with his HIV-negative partner of ten years because he is unable to shake the idea that his early sexual behavior in Haiti infected him. Despite a series of HIV tests indicating he is uninfected, Claude remains convinced that he will seroconvert "out of the blue," perhaps even in his sleep. For Claude, practicing safer sex is a way of protecting his partner in case he really is HIV-infected.

Part of Claude's difficulty in accepting that he is HIV-negative stems from the fact that several of his former sexual partners have died of AIDS. Having been "touched" so closely by AIDS makes it hard for him to believe he is uninfected. Aaron, 46, told me that he and his partner, Max, feel similarly "touched." Even though they have both tested HIV-negative, doubts linger in their minds. "We still wonder if we can trust our results," Aaron said, "because Walter—Max's former lover of ten years—is HIV-positive." These doubts influence Aaron's sexual behavior with Max:

> We've both tested negative, and yet I still don't quite feel comfortable ingesting Max's precum, because of the lingering knowledge of Walter being positive. When I have oral sex using the "harmonica method" with Max, I am tempted to take his cock in my mouth, but the only way I can do that

and feel comfortable is with a condom. It's not the same thing, but it's better than not having oral sex.

Three years after we both tested negative, we're trying to be a little more flexible about what we define as safer sex. I would like to be able to come into contact with Max's pre-cum. I would love not to have to worry about safer sex. We have not yet reached the point where we feel comfortable with that. It's something we're struggling with. What we're doing is trying to accommodate our anxiety. The anxiety is more of a risk than getting HIV is. When can we both really believe that we're negative?

Walter's HIV positivity has affected Max and—by extension—Aaron. Walter's influence is also apparent to Aaron because Max is still living with Walter as a housemate. "Max is living every day in the same house with Walter," Aaron said. "In many ways he is taking care of Walter. Emotionally this is a real obstacle in our relationship. What's going to happen to Walter? Who's going to take care of Walter if Max moves in with me?" Aaron guesses Walter "will remain a shadow in Max's life, probably for the rest of his life," just as Walter's HIV positivity remains a shadow in their sexual life.

Many gay male couples are not sexually exclusive, so some men in negative-negative couples practice protected sex because they are not certain that their outside sexual contacts are safe. For such men, insisting on practicing safer sex within the couple is a sign of their commitment to each other's health. "Safer sex is the ultimate form of caring," was the way Derek, a 25-year-old graduate student from Muncie, Indiana, put it. Another man in a sexually nonexclusive negative-negative couple told me, "We use condoms even though we both know we're shooting blanks." His metaphor reveals that although he hopes he is not packing a "loaded gun," he fears he or his partner might be.

Sometimes avoiding unprotected sex is the result of indoctrination by AIDS prevention efforts. Phillip, a 30-year-old high-school teacher, told me that when he began a relationship with

Dave, he had only nonpenetrative sex because he wanted to continue following the safer-sex guidelines he had adopted early in the epidemic:

> When I first became sexually involved with Dave, I was only interested in jerking off and kissing. That was what I was comfortable with, and I felt okay doing that with anyone, regardless of HIV status. In fact, I didn't usually ask anyone about HIV status, because I didn't want it to influence my behavior.
>
> I met Dave after I found out I was HIV-negative, and he was actually the first sexual partner who told me he was HIV-negative too. That threw me. All of a sudden I had to reexamine my safer-sex routine. Why shouldn't I swallow his cum if he was HIV-negative? Why shouldn't I let him fuck me if he was HIV-negative? If he wasn't HIV-positive, why should I treat him as if he was?

Finding out Dave was HIV-negative did not change Phillip's sexual behavior immediately. Social norms, he said, influenced him. Phillip was a volunteer on an AIDS hot line, and he thought it would be hypocritical to say one thing to callers on the phone and yet do something else in his personal life. It was difficult for Phillip to flout education campaigns that encouraged gay men to "use a condom every time with every partner."

But in addition to these social reasons, Phillip told me there was also a more personal reason for his reluctance to have unprotected sex. He was not ready to relinquish control over his HIV status to someone else:

> I wasn't sure I should trust Dave with my life. That's what unprotected sex amounted to. As long as I stayed with my safer-sex guidelines, I had complete control over my own HIV status. No one could change it. That made me feel secure.
>
> Sucking Dave off or getting fucked by him without a condom would have taken away some of my control over

my own HIV status. It would have meant relying on someone besides myself to keep me uninfected. Maybe avoiding
unprotected sex was a way of telling Dave that I wasn't sure
I could rely on him, that I wasn't ready to trust him fully, or
that I wasn't ready to give up the sense of absolute control I
had over my HIV status.

Phillip voices here an important truth about relationships in the
time of AIDS: Without trust, unprotected sex with an HIV-negative partner feels dangerous.

UNPROTECTED SEX IN
NEGATIVE-NEGATIVE COUPLES

Not all gay male couples use condoms for sex. An Australian
study reported in 1993 that among 82 gay men with regular partners, 41 never had sex without condoms, while 41 often or occasionally had sex without condoms. Among the 41 who did not
always use condoms with their regular partners, 30 were HIV-
negative, and of them, 26 had HIV-negative partners, 3 did not
know the status of their partners, and 1 knew his partner was
HIV-positive. These data suggest that HIV-negative men who
have unprotected sex with regular partners usually have it in the
context of negative-negative couples.[1]

The study authors suggested that the term "negotiated safety"
be used to describe unprotected sex in negative-negative couples,
because they found that the decision to have unprotected sex was
frequently linked to explicit agreements about whether sex outside the relationship was allowed and, if so, what kinds of sex
were defined as "safe." Several of the men I interviewed spoke
with me about this kind of "negotiated safety" and, in so doing,
revealed some of the ways they have managed to have unprotected sex without the anxiety reported by other men.

For Don, 33, whose narrative appears in chapter 14, unprotected sex with his partner, Ben, is something he has valued for a long
time. The two men have never had protected sex with each other
since they met in 1982. To do so now that they have both tested

HIV-negative, Don suggested, would be "a major change ... a psychological shift for us," one that would symbolize distrust. When Don had an affair overseas, he told Ben about it, and they decided to abstain from sex rather than use condoms while they waited for subsequent HIV test results.

Because Don and Ben had been practicing unprotected sex before they knew their HIV status, they faced the decision of whether to *continue* doing so. Younger gay men accustomed to practicing protected sex because they grew up in the age of AIDS—and others starting new relationships—face a different decision: whether to *initiate* unprotected sex when they are in a negative-negative couple. Greg, a 26-year-old medical student, spoke to me about the way he and his partner, Arthur, made this decision.

Greg and Arthur met as teenagers, but it was a long time before they had anal sex. "It was mostly just oral sex," Greg said, "and never to the point of taking semen in the mouth. We decided we wanted to get closer together emotionally before we started doing anal sex." When they did, they used condoms at first for safety reasons, because Arthur had had other sexual partners during the beginning of their relationship. Even with condoms, anal sex was not a major part of their sexual life; it was something they did perhaps once or twice a year.

Three years into their relationship, when Greg and Arthur realized they were staying together and wanted a monogamous relationship, Greg asked Arthur to be tested, so he could be confident they were both HIV-negative. Greg told me about the first time he and Arthur had anal sex without condoms, after they had both tested negative:

> One night, we were making love, and it happened: we had unprotected anal sex. We talked about it afterwards. I said, "What we just did was very dangerous. I want to feel confident that what we've talked about in the past year is where we really stand." He was honest with me and told me it was. "We can do this if we agree to do this," I said,

"but only if we're not fooling each other." And I added, "Arthur, if anything ever does happen, don't have unprotected anal intercourse with me. Start using condoms." So we agreed about that. We've had a monogamous relationship since then.

Greg is confident about his decision. "We have a really open dialogue about sex now," he said, "so I feel confident that if Arthur had sex with somebody else he would tell me. And if I was going to do that, I would be able to tell him. Yes, there's that one millionth of a chance that he could lie to me, but I know Arthur: he couldn't keep anything from me."

Because of the open communication in their relationship, Greg is not threatened by the idea that one of them might stray from sexual exclusivity. In fact, Greg recognizes that sexual exclusivity is probably not realistic:

> I doubt I will spend the next 60 years with Arthur without him ever having sex with someone else. It seems plain to me that the human animal is not the most monogamous thing created. We have a commitment to a monogamous relationship right now, but we realize that people are human beings.
>
> I don't *want* Arthur to go out and have sex with other people, but I don't want him to feel that if he makes a mistake he can't tell me about it. It would matter, but I don't think it would end our relationship.
>
> If we needed to alter the way we have sex, that would be fine. Maybe I would say, "If these things continue to happen, this is what I'm willing to do sexually." It would probably mean that if we had anal sex, it would be protected.

Phillip and Dave too were able to come to an agreement about having unprotected sex, based on a mutual understanding of what kind of sex would be considered "safe" outside the relationship.[2] "Because I was so afraid of HIV," Phillip said, "I asked Dave to agree that if either of us had sex outside the relationship, it would involve just kissing, touching, and mutual masturba-tion—no oral sex or anal sex." Agreeing to this allowed Phillip and Dave to have less restricted kinds of sex:

> It was something that happened gradually. First we started having oral sex without condoms but without com-ing in each other's mouths. Two years into the relationship, I decided I was ready to swallow his cum, and another year later, I let him fuck me. I resent the fact that it took me so long to feel comfortable with that. It shows how much the fear of AIDS has entered my consciousness.

For Phillip, having unprotected sex with Dave was an indication of his growing trust. This is evident in the way his attitude about being "in control" has changed. "Having unprotected sex with Dave means that in some ways I am no longer in control of my HIV status," Phillip said. "I used to worry about that. Now, strangely, I find it comforting to no longer feel I have to be in con-trol. Instead, I can share the responsibility for staying negative with my boyfriend. It feels good to be able to trust him this way."

CAUTIONS AGAINST UNPROTECTED SEX

Although many negative-negative couples don't use condoms for sex, their decisions are not widely supported, at least in AIDS education campaigns in the United States. By promoting a single course of action—use a condom—for all people, whether HIV-positive, HIV-negative, or untested, AIDS education efforts in the United States neglect negative-negative couples to whom such a strategy is unappealing, unnecessary, and unrealistic. Other countries, such as Australia and Canada, offer more fully elabo-rated AIDS education materials, which acknowledge that some negative-negative couples do not need to use condoms.[3]

Aside from the general tone of AIDS education, negative-neg-ative couples are also discouraged by HIV-positive people from deciding not to use condoms. One HIV-positive woman I knew who died recently used to speak about AIDS to high-school and college audiences. She said that one of the questions she frequently heard was from couples wondering, "When can we throw away the condoms?" She usually answered, "When sex is over." I'm sure her facetious answer got lots of laughs, but it dodged the issue.

At an HIV-prevention conference in Dallas in 1994, I attended a small-group discussion during which an HIV-negative man spoke about his decision to swallow his HIV-negative partner's semen during oral sex. He characterized his decision as "a major psychological and emotional step" in his relationship. Reactions from the group to this announcement were mixed. One participant—an HIV-negative AIDS prevention researcher—said that it sounded like an example of rational decision making about HIV. Another participant—an HIV-positive test counselor—cautioned against this decision by referring to an example from his work experience. Recently, he said, he had counseled a couple that were both initially HIV-negative, and later one of the two seroconverted as a result of outside sex. Because the couple was having unprotected sex, he said, the other partner seroconverted as well. He offered this story by way of warning.

The insistence by some HIV-positive individuals that everyone use condoms may simply be self-serving. After all, if everyone uses condoms every time with every partner, then there is no responsibility to disclose one's HIV-positive status and potentially suffer rejection as a result. Then again, insistence by the HIV-positive upon universal condom use may be more generously attributed to a desire that others not become infected. Eager to discourage others from their own fate, some HIV-positive people are Cassandras: they seek to warn people of imminent danger and at the same time despair that their warnings may go unheeded. Perhaps these feelings are what motivated the HIV-positive woman and man described above to caution people against unprotected sex.

In my interviews, the most poignant example of an HIV-positive gay man warning people against unprotected sex came from Saul, a 37-year-old administrative assistant from Los Angeles:

I learned the hard way that you have to take your health and life into your hands and not rely on sexual partners to tell you their status or to even tell you the truth.

I was dating a guy for five months last year. I was at fault for not putting two and two together. There were a lot of signs, but I didn't see them or didn't want to. I had talked with him about how lucky I was to be negative all this time. He agreed.

I didn't realize until we broke up—and a week later I got tested and was positive—that he was only agreeing that, yes, I was lucky to be negative. I assumed he meant that he too was glad to be negative. Well, he wasn't. I got it from him.

I was at fault too for not practicing safe sex, but I am damned pissed he didn't have the *balls* to tell me he had AIDS. It has taught me a lesson about people, even people who tell you they love you. Unfortunately, I didn't learn this lesson before I got HIV. *Treat every sexual situation as if the person has AIDS.* Unfortunately, that is now a way of life for us. There are honest people out there who will tell you the truth, but there are some who won't, so you have to take control of your life and health.

Saul's example shows the dramatic consequences of faulty assumptions and miscommunication about HIV. In addition, Saul expresses beliefs that are now common among many HIV-negative gay men, namely, that treating everyone as if they have AIDS is "now a way of life for us" and that because some gay men are dishonest, gay men should never trust each other. To have unprotected sex within a negative-negative couple is an expression of such trust, and the difficulty that some men have with such intimacy reflects their difficulty in trusting other gay men. That gay men feel they cannot trust each other shows how profoundly HIV has undermined their mental, emotional, and spiritual health even when it is not present in their bodies.

PROTECTED SEX AS WAR EFFORT

It would be misleading to suggest that men in negative-negative couples use condoms solely because HIV-positive people encourage them to, or because they fear infection from untrustworthy partners. It may be that something larger is being expressed by protected sex in negative-negative couples: a kind of community solidarity.

Having sex without condoms underlines a way in which HIV-negative men are different from HIV-positive men. By having sex with condoms instead, men in negative-negative couples identify themselves with the besieged community of HIV-positive gay men. If HIV-positive gay men can't have unprotected sex, these men seem to be saying, then we shouldn't either. Wearing condoms or avoiding penetrative sex does not really do anything to "protect" men from HIV if HIV is not present in either partner, but the activity may be viewed as part of a community effort to eradicate HIV.

Tucker, 31, who in chapter 3 described growing up with the "grim reaper" of AIDS at his bedside, spoke to me about the ethic of community participation that motivates some men in negative-negative couples to use condoms. "In the face of this immense frightful specter," Tucker said, "we have—predictably—manufactured new forms of behavior. Safer sex has become an ethical obligation." Tucker used a wartime analogy:

> During World War II, when there were shortages, government authorities would ask people to save certain things—bottlecaps or whatever—and then turn them in. Sometimes they didn't actually use these things. But it was a standard of behavior that gave people a sense that they were doing something positive to help the effort.

HIV-negative men may use condoms with other HIV-negative men, Tucker suggests, not because it keeps them free of HIV, but because it is part of the "war effort," something HIV-negative gay men can do to show that they are willing to make sacrifices in their sexual lives voluntarily, sacrifices that those "on the front"—the HIV-positive—have been forced to make.

Giving up unprotected sex is a bit harder than collecting bottlecaps, however. That so many gay men do so suggests that no sacrifice seems too much in the face of AIDS. Aaron, Max's partner, revealed to me how easy it is to dispense with important forms of sexual expression and to discount this loss. "I've been feeling the loss of unprotected sex for years," he said. "It's like mourning: it's a fact of life. Maybe at this point I'm so used to loss, having lost so many friends, that losing forms of sexual expression is just another loss. It's certainly nothing compared to having lost friends, so I feel I don't really deserve to mourn it too much." But gay men should not discount this loss. Aaron does deserve to mourn it.

16

Solid Foods Aren't Good for You

Ryan Joseph

AT A CERTAIN POINT I felt there were only two responses to make to AIDS in New York City: move or die. It was that big a phenomenon for us. The sad thing is that a lot of the guys who left New York at about the time I did are now dealing with AIDS in Los Angeles, San Francisco, the Midwest, and Washington, D.C.

I thought I was pretty definitely infected, because I lived in New York City from 1969 until 1981. As I was leaving, the acronym for AIDS was GRID: gay-related immunodeficiency. Having been sexually active in New York during the seventies—really joining the general sexual freedom going on that decade—I thought, "Why not? Why wouldn't it be something I have?" Especially around 1985 or 1986, when I started to get reports of HIV-positive test results from friends who had been in New York, and when I started to experience the first illnesses among friends, and shortly thereafter the first deaths.

There was a period when people in the medical profession were not recommending the test. I was stunned. Why would a doctor tell you not to get tested? At that time, doctors did not know what to do with that information. This is before treatments actually existed. It sounds like a light-year away, but that's what it was like in the mid-eighties, before AZT and any other drugs had been developed.

ও

I decided to get tested because of a combination of things. We were starting to hear about treatments, so testing became much more encouraged from the medical profession. Anonymous test sites were available; that certainly was an encouraging sign. Friends were getting sick; that became a clear example of the fact that this disease was out there. It wasn't just people I didn't know. It was people I knew. A few friends tested and found out they were negative; I suppose that was encouraging. The more that people in my friendship group got tested, the more comfortable I felt to do it. In 1988, a support group for people affected by HIV started at my university workplace. There was some encouragement in the group to find out what your status was, without requiring you to do it.

I shared that I was getting tested with close friends. I shared it with people I knew who had been tested. I was probably trying to find out from their experiences what it might be like. I was trying to change something unknown and scary into something I might know about, so I would be prepared for the ways I might react to it. The people I shared the news about testing with were people I could trust, people who would accept either result: they would be happy if I tested negative, and supportive in a broad range of ways if they found out I was positive.

In fact, I took someone with me to the first testing. For first-time testing, it's helpful to have someone there you can share the news with in a very immediate sense. Ironically and sadly, the person who came with me to my first testing was someone who had tested negative and since that time has converted. He has just had his first symptomatic diagnosis—a two-week hospitalization with pneumonia—and is now out of work on disability. His life has dramatically changed in the past three months.

Beyond the sadness I feel, he was a real example to me of the possibility that you can test negative and then—after time, with additional sexual behavior—you can find the result going the other way. You would think I would know that without needing a personal example. That has had a reverberating effect on me in my second and third testings.

೫

My sexual behavior has changed gradually over the last four or five years. Before testing, there was the awareness that something was out there, the beginning of discussion of safe-sex standards, and then a kind of denial: there were "those people" over there who were getting sick with their sexual behavior, and I was over here being well with my sexual behavior.

I think back on it now and wonder why I'm not positive. I don't know what I was doing differently than other people. There are maybe two or three things I can say. One is that I had no heavy drug use. A second thing would be that although I had an open sexual life, I did not have multiple partners to the extent that you hear among some men. And a third thing would be that in terms of anal sex, you could call me a top, the insertive partner. That's just a preference of mine. That might have been somewhat related to a reduction in risk.

There was a time before condom use became generally accepted and required, where—after great anal sex with someone where I was the active person and also the receptive person—I realized something that beautiful could in fact cause transmission of HIV. That wasn't a great feeling at all.

The use of condoms for anal sex certainly became a much more accepted standard of behavior. I'm sure it had a lot to do with the first free handouts. That was very impressive in the gay community: in bars and other places you literally had condoms given to you, with the encouragement to use them. They became a physical presence in my car, on my person, in my house, in the bathroom, by the bed. I wouldn't say I used them 100 percent of the time, but I started to be a more conscious user of condoms for insertive anal sex.

But there were parts of my behavior that didn't change at that time. Oral sex without a condom, all the way up to receiving cum in the mouth, did not change. Rimming prior to anal sex did not change.

During the last two years, I've certainly stopped receiving cum in any oral sex situation. Cum became something that was best kept out of my body. Anal sex without a condom is unthinkable. And rimming is something that people have generally moved away from. I have too. Have I given up oral sex prior to coming? That's a good question. I'm certainly moving in that direction, just to feel comfortable. Have I given it up totally? That's a question I have to answer for myself right now. It's a process.

My sexual activity is way, way reduced. My libido is not as driven and my looks are not as compelling as they were when I was younger. I have no control over that. I jokingly tell my friends that aging is one of the better safer-sex devices in my life.

I have a friend who told me, "If all I have to look forward to is vanilla sex for the rest of my life, I think I'm just going to give up sex." He was speaking humorously, but I know for a fact that he has gone through periods of three, six, maybe nine months where no man has slept in his bed. I can see how he feels. If sexuality goes back to the stuff we did as teenagers, hugging and kissing, mutual masturbation, I don't know how I'll feel. The giving up of the last few things is probably not as big a barrier as I thought it was earlier.

It comes with great sadness, I have to tell you. I don't know that the gay community is willing to admit what the loss of free and comfortable sexuality in our lives means, individually and collectively.

In an area in life where one of the purposes is to be uninhibited, we have had to bring inhibition. It's compounded by the fact that gay people have had to deal with conflicted feelings about sexuality from the get-go. From the moment you knew you were gay, you knew it was not a generally accepted norm of sexual behavior. Now you might be comfortable with your sexuality, but what you can do in bed has to be restricted.

To find a negative man you can fall in love with and not have to practice safer sex with sounds like a wishful, hopeful, dreamy kind of scenario. You have to have great faith in the person telling you truthfully what his HIV status is. And I'd have to have great faith in the test being absolutely perfect. I'm too cynical to believe either one of those right now. I'm sure it can happen. For the people that can find that, go for it. Do I think it will happen to me? I don't know. I don't think in those terms.

I don't ask anyone's HIV status. I've come to the point in the last few years where I think that everyone that I sleep with is potentially HIV-positive, whether they know it or not. It certainly cramps your sexual style, doesn't it?

❧

Why do people who are negative have unsafe sex? Because it feels good. There's just something about flesh on flesh. There's something primordial in human beings' need to have genital contact. I haven't read any anthropological reports on this, but I'm willing to bet that there's something so primal in our nature as to make that a requirement almost. The pain that the gay community is feeling right now, and anyone who is practicing safer sex, is the barrier between the genitals and the mouth or anus. We have to accept in our sexual lives a barrier to tactile sensations. That is very, very, very difficult. That's one reason why people who are negative practice unsafe sex.

The second reason for older guys could just be habit. We've had a number of years of unprotected sex. How do you go about changing that kind of behavior? It's like telling people, "There's something very dangerous about eating, so when you eat you have to do a certain amount through this kind of barrier, and a little bit more through that kind of barrier. And solid foods aren't good for you any longer, so everything is going to have to go through a blender." Eating and sexuality are among the three or four primary urges we have. And now we have health reasons to take one of those primary natural urges and say it has to be performed with a barrier against fluids that could carry disease. That was profoundly difficult for me to do, and it continues to be. I don't think I'm the only person who feels that way.

Third, some of my friends feel—and maybe I do to some

185

extent—that if you practice certain kinds of sexual behavior and you test negative, then that becomes a validation for your behavior. I'm moving away from that kind of thought: "What I'm doing must be okay, because I keep testing negative." I don't want to use the test to validate my behavior.

How can it be that—at my age and with my education—I could not just immediately change my behavior? I think the answer is that I could understand the concepts behind safe sex in an intellectual fashion, I could hear the messages and rationally understand them, but I could not turn them into behavior in a very short period of time. When I ask that question, I'm not beating myself up so much as I'm trying to figure out, "Why is that? Why did it take that period of time between when I knew this intellectually and rationally, and when I could incorporate it into my behavior comfortably and consistently?"

There have to be some lessons that we draw out of the epidemic, or we'd all be a little crazier than we are. In my friendships now, I try to be more of a passionate hugger, or hand-holder, or kisser. Genital sexuality is not the only way to be expressive about how you feel about someone else. If you have to put rubbers on part of your anatomy, then there are other parts of your anatomy that you don't have to cover up. I'm finding ways to express love that aren't genital. That may have something to do with age, too.

Other positive things are that you think more clearly about what it means to be involved in a sexual act. The seventies in New York were an incredible high of instantaneous meetings of people and situations that could become sexual. Some of them were wonderfully beautiful. Ten or fifteen years later, those kinds of spontaneous sexual meetings now have to be prefaced by some knowledge. That could be positive. That's not to say that those other experiences were negative. I would never want to take away from the kind of fun that sex was during that period. We have had to stop and think. And those who have been very affected have become more caring people. We've had to.

೩

The HIV support group at my workplace started more than four years ago. It meets once a week during lunch hour. It's facilitated by a social worker, Nan, who does not call it a therapy group because she doesn't think of it as ongoing therapy. She thinks of it as a safe and confidential place where anyone who is infected or affected by HIV can talk about it. Over the years, anywhere from eight to a dozen people will show up on a given Wednesday for the lunch hour. Half of them might be dealing with the infection. The other half might be friends of, mothers of, brothers of, daughters of, wives of the infected. Those are the kinds of people there who are HIV-negative.

We've talked about how we feel about each other's status. For example, when someone comes back to the group with an HIV-negative test, we usually say that to the group. And Nan, the facilitator, will say, "I'm glad to hear that. Could we talk about how people in the group feel about that?" Because we meet regularly, we have become pretty close friends. The guys who are positive will say, "I'm happy for you. I'm glad somebody is going to get out of this alive. But I'm also a little sad, I'm a little angry, I'm a little jealous. I can't make a big deal out of your HIV-negative status. I'm sorry. I've got too much to deal with here on my own."

HIV-negative people have said on occasions that they feel reticent about bringing their issues to the table until all of the positive people have had a chance to say something. A kind of hierarchy seems to overcome us. Why is that? I think it's because we have this human belief that the people with the greatest need merit the greatest attention. In an HIV support group, there are almost always those who are dealing with the infection and its ramifications: they are hospitalized that week; they've just gotten out of the hospital; they're trying a new medication; they've had a bad week; they've had a good week; they've had to talk to family or friends about this. All of those issues seem to have an urgency beyond what a negative person brings to the table.

We've talked quite openly in the group about how everyone's

concerns have a legitimacy that doesn't have to be hierarchical or prioritized. We know that. We're all intelligent enough. But even knowing that intellectually doesn't help you avoid thinking, "This is the person with the greater need."

When the first meeting of the HIV-negative group took place two years ago in Boston, the title was "It Can Be Hard to Be HIV-Negative." That caused a row at the group: "You think you have it hard? Try the other side." When I came to the first negative group, I remember somebody asked that we talk about it in a more neutral kind of way: "Why not just say it's a support group for people who have tested HIV-negative?" And that's the way it has gone.

Nan's point in trying to keep the group a mixed group that includes HIV-positive, HIV-negative, and untested people is this: "Doesn't it reflect the reality of life? Aren't we all in a social context that has some of this, some of that, some of these, some of those?" She's trying hard to hang on to that, and she has succeeded.

At some point, we just want someone who will listen to us. The group at my workplace comes back to that quite often. There are many days when we can't do anything for the person who brings bad news to the meeting. We can't do anything to make someone feel better. But sometimes people leave feeling better, just because they've come in and said, "Look at me today. Look at how I am. Look at how I feel." People come in wheelchairs sometimes. Sometimes they come from the hospital with oxygen, saying, "This is where I am today." We're just good listeners.

There are legitimate concerns that we have as HIV-negative people. They can't be put in the same realm as HIV-positive concerns, which are life-threatening, of course. We know they are. Ours are legitimate concerns, though. You just have to find the place to express them and not make them part of a competitive, hierarchical triage. You have to find a safe place to take your HIV news about yourself and share it where it won't be judged against some other piece of HIV news.

I have a very good friend—a straight woman—who is a great listener. She has gay male friends who are infected with the virus.

She is not so passionately caught up in it. That's a good thing to find. Try to find somebody who is not personally battling it right now, who can listen to your concerns. It can be someone else who is HIV-negative, or a family member, or a friend for whom HIV is not a primary concern. It has to be somebody who is not going to judge how you feel.

&

I think the first responsibility I acknowledge is a responsibility to myself. You have to truly believe that you deserve to survive this incredible scourge, that there is something personally valuable in yourself. That takes some doing for a lot of gay men. It takes some doing for myself. If you don't value yourself at that level, then you can say things to yourself like, "It doesn't really matter if I slip this time," or, "This guy is so cool. The fact that we don't have a condom around is immaterial. We'll probably get away with it this time." Those kinds of things become unacceptable if you accept responsibility for yourself at its highest and fullest level. Why did it take me years to figure that out? I don't know. You have to ask all sorts of questions about gay men and their valuing themselves. I've asked myself some of those questions.

I think I feel a keen responsibility for helping out people who are infected. There's a tremendous amount of volunteer time that a lot of us are giving. That certainly has permeated my life in the last four or five years. There are over a dozen people in Boston whom I have helped and continue to help.

As I get older and have no children of my own, I have started to feel the possibility of being a Big Brother. God, I'm old enough to be a father figure for many younger gay men. And maybe you can say mentor, too. All of those things are about modeling behavior for people and being supportive of them.

I think all of us respond best to personal, close interactions with people who model behavior for us in some way. If you want to become the perfect violinist, you have to know somebody pretty early in life who is a perfect violinist. So around the HIV topic, if we want to be good there, we probably ought to start on a personal level. This is the way HIV became real and vivid to me: from people who are infected, and through the friend I told you about who was HIV-negative and then tested HIV-positive.

How do you institutionalize that? I suppose some organizations have done that through their speakers bureaus, where one can talk and be an open example. I think the more openly we talk about it and can admit our HIV status in the workplace, in the family, and in our friendship groups, the better. I'm very comfortably out at work, and after I got my last HIV test I told my boss. I just wanted him to know that I'm okay. I think I wanted him to hear on a personal level how people deal with HIV issues.

What if I seroconverted? It's a possibility, isn't it? You can imagine what that news would feel like, but I think you would really have to have that news delivered to you to know what your reaction would be. I think that's one of the reasons my behavior is moving in the direction of the safest possible behavior, so that fear of seroconverting doesn't continue to be an anxiety or even a thought in the back of my mind.

Through all the volunteer work I've done in the last four or five years, I have acquired a lot of information about what some of the common illnesses symptomatically bring out, what medications are available, how quickly or aggressively one should seek treatment, what it means to your physical constitution. I've seen it all, from the first day after getting a positive test result to the day of someone's death. So I have some idea of what HIV disease could mean to me.

One time, some of the HIV support group members asked me why I have continued to come for so many years even though I am HIV-negative. "I want to know what we are involved with here," I told them. "I want to know the beast."

17

Deciding What's Unsafe

DOUBLE BAGGING

"I've decided that I'm not going to fuck or get fucked without two condoms," said Richard, a 31-year-old community activist. "But there have been times when I've deviated from my standard a little. There have been times when I've let one of the condoms go." Richard told me the times he had used only one condom were when he was embarrassed about letting a sexual partner know his safer-sex standards. "I felt it might be perceived as too weird, too reactionary, just like people used to worry about proposing one condom."

In chapter 15 I suggested that under some circumstances gay men decide that sex *without* a condom is not always "unsafe." Richard's statement suggests that for him sex *with* a condom is not always "safe." What this points out is that the terms "unsafe" and "safe" are subjective when they are used by gay men and largely useless when applied to sexual behaviors stripped of their context. Social science researchers, epidemiologists, and AIDS educational materials often discuss sexual behaviors—such as unprotected receptive anal intercourse—as if their "riskiness" were inherent. But gay men reveal through their actions and beliefs that whether behaviors are considered unsafe or safe depends on many factors, including HIV status and personal decisions about levels of acceptable risk.

LOOKING FOR EXPERTS

Sex among gay men would be simpler if we all agreed on what was "safe" and what was "unsafe," and in the early years of the epidemic we tried to pretend this was possible. Faced with a frightening new sexually transmitted disease, gay men were the first in the United States to develop educational materials that informed people about the sexual transmission of HIV. These materials frequently placed sexual behaviors along a "spectrum of risk," in which anal sex was considered "very risky," oral sex was considered "possibly risky" or "possibly safe," and mutual masturbation was considered "very safe."

The crudeness of this spectrum was largely due to the lack of reliable scientific evidence about transmission of HIV under various circumstances. The advantages of this spectrum were that it was simple, it proposed a convenient way for gay men to conceptualize risk, and it allowed us to hold out some hope that our sex lives would not be shut down entirely. It also offered a working definition of "safety" that let men say they practiced "safer sex" even though in reality that meant very different things to different people.

Gay men relied on the risk spectrum because there was nothing else available and our anxiety about sexual risk encouraged us to look for guidance to help us make sexual decisions. "Tell us what to do," we seemed to be saying. "How can we have sex in an epidemic?" In the face of uncertainties about risk, we looked for experts who could make decisions for us. This search for experts continues today, principally around the issue of how risky oral sex is. When I worked on an AIDS hot line in Massachusetts, this was the issue gay men asked about most frequently: "Is oral sex safe? Should I swallow cum or spit it out? What about precum?" We had very little data, so I ended up parroting simplistic answers like, "There may be some risk. You might want to avoid getting cum in your mouth or use a condom for oral sex." It was easy for me to parrot those answers because at the time I worked on the hot line I abided by the simplicity of the HIV-risk spectrum myself, avoiding oral and anal sex entirely for many years.

Interestingly, after I got tested for HIV and learned I was HIV-negative, I began to change my attitude about oral sex, and as I did so—especially after I started having unprotected oral sex with an HIV-negative partner—my answers to callers became more nuanced. Suddenly, I was better able to hear their concerns and speak with them about the complexities of making decisions about safer sex. At the same time, my hot-line coworker, who had learned he was HIV-positive, became more conservative and directive in his approach to questions from callers about oral sex. "You should avoid oral sex without condoms," he said. "You don't want to get this disease."

I raise my experience on the hot line to illustrate that even when gay men think they are getting "information" from "experts"—such as by calling an AIDS hot line—they are often getting no more than one person's view of the issues, a view that is likely to be colored by personal experiences. I also raise it to suggest that since the advent of HIV testing, sexual behaviors can no longer be viewed categorically as "safe" or "unsafe," because some people know their HIV status, and thus know whether they are capable of becoming infected or of infecting others.

THE MEANINGS OF UNSAFE SEX

The consequences of unsafe sex are radically different for people who are HIV-negative and HIV-positive. For the HIV-negative individual, unsafe sex with an infected partner involves the possibility of becoming infected. For the HIV-positive individual, unsafe sex with an uninfected partner involves the possibility of infecting another. In starkest terms, the difference has been compared to suicide and homicide. The analogy is not exact, of course, because HIV infection is not usually premeditated. However, I have heard unsafe sex after HIV testing described by different people, depending on their perspectives, as assisted suicide or murder with the consent of the victim.

The different consequences of unsafe sex for HIV-negative and HIV-positive men can be seen in our attitudes about why people have unsafe sex. When I asked people why they thought uninfected men might have unsafe sex, the answers often cast the HIV-negative as low in self-esteem, depressed, grieving—in short, possibly suicidal. When I asked people why they thought infected men might have unsafe sex, the answers often cast the HIV-positive as revengeful, demented, irresponsible—in short, possibly homicidal. Keith, 40, who in chapter 13 discussed his relationship with his HIV-positive partner, Mark, summed up the difference this way: "If you're negative and you're playing unsafe, you're taking a chance. You might as well take a gun and put a bullet in and play Russian roulette. If you're positive and having unsafe sex, you might as well just go out and take a six-shooter and shoot a few people dead."

And yet why should we imagine that the reasons uninfected and infected men engage in unsafe sex are so radically different? Perhaps we engage in unprotected sex because it feels better, seems more natural, connects us to our partners intimately, expresses our desire to share our semen with each other. It may not indicate either suicidal or murderous intention. Further, why should we assume that by becoming infected, people suddenly switch from being suicidal to being homicidal? And yet our culture, by painting the uninfected as "innocent bystanders" and the infected as "guilty perpetrators," reinforces this idea.

Considering the distinct meanings of unsafe sex for HIV-negative and HIV-positive men also allows us to better understand what it is like not to know one's HIV status. If you don't know your HIV status, then you cannot place an unequivocal meaning on unsafe sex. Is it unsafe for you or unsafe for your partner? As I discussed in chapter 3, the position of not knowing whether your sexual behavior is endangering yourself or others is quite familiar to gay men, especially those who had sex in the early 1980s, when testing for HIV was either unavailable or not encouraged.

The ability to simultaneously imagine danger to yourself and to others, so immanent in sexual encounters before HIV testing was available, is drastically reduced when you learn your HIV status. When you learn you are HIV-negative, you gain a heightened awareness of your vulnerability to infection. When you learn you are HIV-positive, you gain a heightened awareness of your infectiousness. What were previously equal concerns are no longer equal; one concern is heightened while the other is attenuated. I discussed this dichotomy in chapter 11, where I postulated that the "meanings of HIV status" are different for HIV-positive and HIV-negative people. I wonder what influence the different consequences of unsafe sex have on whether people who know their HIV status have unsafe sex.

REASONS FOR UNSAFE SEX

During my interviews, I found that getting gay men to talk about unsafe sex was difficult. Perhaps our community has made it intolerable to discuss unsafe sex because we wish to convey the impression that gay men practice safer sex consistently and enjoy doing so. I usually broached the subject by asking men, "Why do you think some uninfected men have unsafe sex?" I posed this question first because it was less threatening. Then I asked, "When have you had difficulty practicing safer sex?" This second question offered men a chance to discuss unsafe sex they had had or were tempted to have without suggesting they were bad. Interestingly, the answers I got to these two questions were quite different.

The reasons cited for why *other* people had unsafe sex were almost uniformly harsh. "Why do people smoke? Why do people drive without wearing a seat belt?" asked Scott, 24, a graduate student from Newark, Delaware. "I don't know why people flirt with disaster. I guess the reasons are that unsafe sex is more fun than safe sex—and irresponsibility." Jesse, a 29-year-old scientist from Philadelphia, suggested that uninfected men have unsafe sex because of "a false sense of security, a sense of abandonment, lack of knowledge, or just plain stupidity."

Anton, a 31-year-old graduate student from Pittsburgh, suggested that some men "really like getting fucked and just cannot resist the temptation." Reed, a 36-year-old computer engineer from Charlottesville, Virginia, concurred: "People just want sex sometimes badly enough to ignore the risk, don't we? We sure did when the risks were things like gonorrhea or hepatitis."

Others attributed unsafe sex to denial, low self-esteem, or feelings of despair. "It is tempting to deny the existence of the virus. Perhaps out of frustration or a feeling of immortality, some engage in unsafe sex," said Lenny, a 23-year-old student from East Lansing, Michigan. "Low self-esteem can also contribute to self-destructive behavior, of which unsafe sex is an example." Blake, 33, a library clerk from Portland, Oregon, said people have unsafe sex out of desperation: "When you have so many people dying around you the loss is awesome. I think some people are emotionally suicidal about it so their senses of reason are blurred." Buzz, a 37-year-old real estate investor from San Diego, said, "They no longer care. I don't think anyone feels immune. Clearly they feel it doesn't matter. A friend of mine used to say, 'There is a bullet out there somewhere for me, no use in trying to hide from it.' His bullet found him this summer."

The reasons cited for why my interviewees *themselves* had unsafe sex were more forgiving, sometimes suggesting that unsafe sex was the result of situational factors. "I was overwhelmed—literally—by a couple of guys in a gay sauna," said Harold, 28, of Frederiksberg, Denmark. "One of them kept me busy while the other simply placed himself on top of my cock. I was inside him before I had time to put anything on." Cal, 42, of Rochester, New York, said that "the difficulty is when my partner leads me on and gets me to really *want* to fuck and then plays the "I won't do that; it's not safe" card. I don't get angry at that point, but I am disappointed."

Drugs and alcohol were also mentioned as playing a role in unsafe sex. "When I get drunk and horny, all bets are off," said Brendan, 43, of Concord, California. "I am unable to say no when real horny, real attracted to a guy, or when drunk." Bart, a 39-year-old psychotherapist, said that when he broke up with a boyfriend who learned he was HIV-positive, the combination of loneliness and anxiety about whether he was infected led him to combine drugs and drinking:

My doctors had me on benzodiazepines because of anxiety. I started drinking a lot. The combination of the benzodiazepines and the alcohol lowered my inhibitional levels to the point that I didn't give a shit about whether I was having safe or unsafe sex. All I cared about was being with someone and not feeling lonely, so I picked up people on a regular basis every night of the week, trying to fill the void that Jack had left.

I'm sure that if I hadn't gotten sober, if I were still drinking and went out to meet people, I would possibly be so drunk that I could get fucked, not know if my partner used a condom, and not care.

Other men mentioned that they "slipped" from safer sex practices because of feelings of safety within a relationship. "In my last relationship, after the three-month mark it became hard to practice safer sex," said Derek, 25, a graduate student from Muncie, Indiana. "After six months, we slipped a few times. When you fall in love, a sense of invulnerability takes over. Stupid, yes, but it happens." Austin, 36, imagined what might make him "slip" and what he does to counter that: "The tempting thing is if you meet somebody and imagine a hot sexual encounter—the thought passes through your mind. If the temptation was there, and I didn't have the knowledge that I do today, that's when I would have a hard time with safer sex, thinking, 'Oh, I can do this just this one time.' All it takes is for that thought to enter my head, and there's enough knowledge in there to know that it only takes once to become infected. I might think about it, but I don't want to be dead."

It shouldn't have surprised me that the answers I got to my two questions about unsafe sex were different. Psychologists have developed something called "attribution theory" to describe how people evaluate their own and others' actions. "One finding of this theory," writes Robyn Dawes, "is the 'fundamental attribution error,' by which we attribute others' behavior largely to personality factors and our own behavior largely to situational factors to which we respond."[1]

It makes sense according to this theory that in "explaining" unsafe sex my interviewees should judge unsafe sex practiced by others as evidence of character flaws—irresponsibility, stupidity, sexual incontinence, low self-esteem, self-destructiveness—but judge unsafe sex practiced by themselves as largely influenced by circumstances—forced sex, intoxication, the influence of intimate relationships or "hot" partners. I may have unwittingly encouraged my interviewees to respond in this way by the way I phrased my questions. The first question asks "Why?"—eliciting responses that focus on character—and the second question asks "When?"—eliciting responses that focus on specific situations and events.

NEGOTIATING SAFER SEX

In chapters 13 and 15 I discussed positive-negative couples and negative-negative couples, each time assuming that the partners in these couples knew each other's HIV status. But lots of sex happens between men who don't know each other's HIV status, and therefore the need to "negotiate" safer sex is still very much with us. This chapter could have been titled "Unknown-Negative Couples" because a principal question facing gay men who are trying to decide what is "unsafe" and what is "safe" for themselves is this: What kind of sex should I have with a partner of unknown HIV status?

The common answer is to treat every sexual partner as if he is HIV-positive, and many of the men I interviewed operate in this way, especially with new partners. Some men told me that they would trust someone if he said he was HIV-positive, but they would not trust someone if he said he was HIV-negative. Believing someone who says he is HIV-negative was equated with believing that "the check is in the mail" by one man I spoke with. As a result, most of the men I interviewed were cautious about sex with people of unknown status and unwilling to acquiesce to a partner's definition of safer sex if it was less cautious than their own.

Many of the men I interviewed balked at the use of the word "negotiation" to describe decision-making about sexual behavior. Peter, 26, a teacher from Toronto, told me that his definition of safer sex was "non-negotiable" unless his partner's was more conservative. "Anything he's not comfortable with we won't do, but I won't compromise my standards." Brent, a 36-year-old software engineer from Los Angeles, agreed: "I don't feel you should have to negotiate. If you don't do anything your partner doesn't want to do, you should be okay. Of course that makes each person responsible for his own actions and for letting his partner know what he considers acceptable, but I believe that's the way it should be."

How then are we to let partners know what we consider acceptable? "Fortunately, I am a physically large person," said Jimmy, 47, a psychology doctoral student from Kentucky. "Ain't nobody doing nuthin' I don't want them to do," he added. We should all be so lucky. Most of the men I interviewed used a combination of nonverbal and verbal communication to convey their safer-sex guidelines. Saying only that you practice "safer sex" and leaving it at that doesn't mean very much unless you suggest what you will and won't do in bed—or wherever you have sex.

Some of the men I spoke with had found ways of communicating their standards without killing the spirit of sex: "I have two rules that I usually point out to my partners," said Harold. "First, anal sex means using a condom. Second, if we start doing something that I am not familiar with or feel uncertain about, they must stop if I tell them to. I like trying something new, but want to keep it within my safe-sex limits." Dudley, 42, who in chapter 13 discussed his relationship with an HIV-positive partner, Michael, said that when he has sex with other men, he is usually a "top man" but sometimes a "bottom":

A few weeks ago I was in San Francisco. I wasn't with Michael; I was traveling with some friends. I picked up a guy. I knew from the moment I picked him up that he really wanted me to be the top, so I was always in charge. Once we got back to the hotel, I basically said, "There are a few rules we're going to play with tonight." That's part of the S/M thing: "These are the rules." The first thing was that I had a glove. The second was that we'd wear condoms. He just said, "Yes, sir. Yes, sir."

I've never been with a top who I hadn't talked to ahead of time. Sometimes I think tops can get out of hand. But I'm a very pushy bottom. In that situation I would say, "Hey. Wait a minute here." I've never gotten into a situation where I wasn't able to get out or felt it wasn't right.

Austin is direct with partners who suggest things he is unwilling to do: "I just say, 'For me, this is the bottom line. This is where I feel comfortable. If you don't feel comfortable with that, this is not going to work for us. I have the rest of my life to think about, and this is just my decision.'"

BALANCING RISK AND PLEASURE

The challenge facing gay men in the age of AIDS is to find guidelines that balance risk and pleasure. Gay men are sometimes willing to discount desire and pleasure entirely in their search to avoid risk. Alan, 31, who in chapter 13 discussed safer sex with a positive partner, said that gay men should not dismiss pleasure from the equation: "One thing that irks me about safer-sex education is desire and pleasure's absence from the checklist of things to consider," said Alan. "If we ignore that, are we discrediting ourselves? The desire for pleasure is a big variable: How much are you salivating for that cock? How much is your asshole itching for that cock? Those are key elements in any decision-making process and can't be discounted. I'm not saying I'm not careful. I'm saying a key part of my decision is how badly do I want the sex. A lot of times that means doing it safely instead of not doing it at all."

Drew, a 30-year-old customer service representative from Pawtucket, Rhode Island, finds that acknowledging his sexual appetite is useful. He suggested that abstinence for long periods of time may be dangerous for him:

> If I haven't had sexual release for six months, I'm much more vulnerable than I am if I haven't had it for three. That's why I try to have sex more frequently, so I don't go, "Oh. It's a dick. I can finally suck it." If I have sex every two months, it's like, "Oh, it's just another dick. No big deal." I consider abstinence just like dieting. They say that people's weight fluctuates because people go on extreme diets. It's the same thing: people are starving themselves from sex. When they have it, they're going to binge. So you can imagine in a binge phase they may think, "Fuck the condoms."

Drew believes he actually reduces his risk by allowing himself some pleasure regularly.

Richard, 31, who in the beginning of this chapter mentioned using two condoms for sex, hopes that gay men who have been abstinent for a long time out of fear can find a way to have sex and still address their concerns for safety. "One of my wishes is that people establish guidelines they can live with that maximize both pleasure and peace of mind," he said. "Particularly peace of mind, because that is the piece that people find hardest to achieve. Pleasure is a little easier. Isn't there a way to find a place—a spot on the continuum—that you can live with?" Richard offered his own example: "I have sex with lots of people lots of times—with people who are positive, negative, and of unknown status. I'm an example that this can happen and there are others."

Austin seemed to me to have found a good balance between the desire to achieve pleasure but to avoid risk. For him, being sexually cautious was not something he felt resentment about. "I

don't have any resentments about having to practice safer sex,"
he said, "because I'm imposing my own rules. Nobody is telling
me to do this. I'm not mandated to do this. I'm making a choice.
Nobody's taking anything away from me. I'm giving myself my
life by making the decision to have safe sex, so I don't feel con-
strained." Austin did not particularly mourn the fact that some
forms of sexual intimacy were not available to him:

> It's very hot and erotic to be with a naked man. You
> don't have to be having anal sex or oral sex. To be with a
> naked man is a very hot thing. It's very nice to be close to
> somebody. I don't have to be focused on those things that
> I've chosen not to do.

Tucker, 31, who in chapter 15 compared protected sex in negative-negative couples to a war effort on the home front, was like
Austin in his confidence that safer forms of sexual interaction can
be satisfying. He went on to suggest that gay men may even have
an advantage over others in their capacity to enjoy safer sex:

> There are ways to get off without being unsafe, and I'm
> willing to do that. Even just jacking off with someone can be
> really hot and a lot of fun.
>
> Do you like Shakespeare? Do you know *Henry V*? At the
> end of the play, King Henry is going to marry Katharine,
> the daughter of the king and queen of France. He wants to
> kiss her but she says no, it is not the fashion for maids in
> France to kiss before they are married. Henry says, "We are
> the makers of manners, Kate."[2]
>
> Gay men redefine sex. How we fuck, straight people
> consider second best anyway. Anything to us can be sex
> because we don't have the same rules. We are not limited to
> putting Tab A in Slot B.

Tucker suggested that gay men—by virtue of their position in
our culture—have always taken the opportunity to express intimacy in new and striking ways. Our experience growing up as

sexual outcasts has equipped us well for the challenge of balancing risk and pleasure. "We've broken every rule that was made for us when we were in the closet in high school anyway. That's why we were so stigmatized," said Tucker. "We were thrown apart from the tribe from the beginning, so we can invent everything over for ourselves."

18

My Seed Is in You

Frank Ruggero

THERE WAS A TIME when I secretly wished to be HIV-positive. I sensed within the community a caring I hadn't seen before. It took the form of the AIDS Action Committee in Boston. I started as a volunteer there in 1983 or 1984. I witnessed so much loving and caring between caregivers and people who were infected that I was envious. I've always been looking for a community that is nurturing, caring, and inclusive. But I wasn't infected. I didn't think I was. I didn't know.

I used to think I needed to get love and affection by being sick. I don't believe that anymore. I've come to realize that a lot of the people I thought were giving love to the infected early on were in many ways fulfilling their own needs rather than taking care of others. It was creepy in a way. There was a time when my relationship with people who were ill was creepy too. I really wanted to save them.

When I think back to two men that had AIDS very early on, I remember being at one person's bedside at the hospital, to give him foot massages, clear his throat, and so forth. He wasn't a close friend; I was helping him because his family more-or-less orphaned him. Early on, I wanted to be what I thought others were to people who are sick. There were models I wanted to emulate.

The other person I was involved with was in the later stages of his illness. He and I slept together. We didn't have genital sex, but we kissed. I remember I stuck my tongue in his mouth. I wasn't thinking I might give him anything. I just wanted to probe, to kiss deeply. He said to me, "No. It's both for my good and your good." I wanted to care for him in a special way. But my caregiving was patterned on the caregiving I was most familiar with from my own family, which was not caregiving in the best sense. It was conditional and self-serving.

That's changed a whole lot. I am trying to figure out what the true way is for me to be caring. I have a friend now in the later stages of AIDS. He has had everything: pneumocystis pneumonia, cytomegalovirus, Kaposi's sarcoma. My relationship with him has been very different. I think the work I've done for myself to get at the core of my issues has helped me. I haven't been a doormat. I have had boundaries. The kind of caring I have for him is not so much to take care of him as to be there for him.

The only way I can be there for him is by being wholly with myself. That's a challenge in itself, to be present with myself and my emotions, whatever they are, whether anger, confusion, jealousy, rage, or sadness. In the past I have been reactive to my feelings. I've judged myself on the basis of what I'm feeling: "It's not right for me to be angry." I'm owning my feelings as best I can, and it feels good. I'm learning, little by little, how to take care of myself.

∂

It's been a process for me to come out fully as a gay man who is free to do what he wants, free from the shame and guilt associated with gay sexuality by culture or religion. I had a lot of shame—deep, deep shame—around wanting to give blow jobs, swallow semen, or get fucked.

Before AIDS, I would sometimes have a dry period for a long time, and then I would have anonymous sex with multiple partners in the course of a week. Invariably after those experiences, I would develop symptoms, and I would go for a test for sexually transmitted disease. The cultures and blood tests were always negative. That happened repeatedly for many, many years. My fear of sexually transmitted diseases is something it may take a lifetime to get rid of.

Part of me felt it was wonderful to have sex with as many men as possible, to pleasure other men and have my needs taken care of as well. A lot of the settings for anonymous sex were outdoors. Part of me felt, "It's beautiful, it's dark, the moon is out. There's a lovely breeze. There's an energy." Then on the other hand, "There are rats around here. Why do we have to do this in the dark? Why can't we be 'out'?" That conflict really points to our culture: we are not free to be who we are, so we need to hide.

Another part of me felt I was looking for a deeper connection, and it never happened with anonymous sex. I imagined that in a monogamous relationship my needs would be fulfilled. I'd be more involved with the person on an emotional level, and he'd be more involved with me. In a monogamous relationship, there is an opportunity to create a comfort level between two people: I can comfort him and he can comfort me. I value that. It didn't seem as though I was able to feel that kind of comfort in an anonymous setting. In my mind, there was little value in anonymous encounters.

So anonymous sex was a failure for me. It was a way for me to perpetuate the idea that I was a failure. I think it had a lot to do with my poor self-image. I felt defective anyway. This was a way to keep it going. I feel differently about that now. I don't hold the same value judgment against anonymous sex as I did before. It's probably a combination of material I've read and people I've met whom I respect and admire. And also just trusting myself.

It's not smooth sailing, by any means. I have times when the old stuff comes back. I may have an encounter and develop symptoms the next day—a sore throat, say—go to the doctor again, have a culture done, and it's negative. But there have been other times when I've had anonymous sex and felt it was just fine. It's a process.

When the AIDS epidemic started, I was petrified. I wanted to continue to be sexually active, but it was a confusing time, full of fear. Falling into the pattern of my fear of sexually transmitted diseases, I would get tested for HIV after an anonymous sexual encounter with exchange of body fluid. I've been tested four times.

I remember feeling quite horribly about not knowing whether somebody was positive or negative. You had to assume people were positive. Trust has always been a big issue for me: trusting myself or trusting others. What happened was it stirred up in me a lot of feelings about mistrust. Sex became more clandestine. If it was already repressed and we had to go to dark corners to have sex, it was getting even worse.

For a long time I assumed I was negative, that AIDS could not happen to me. I didn't feel I was part of the mainstream. I wasn't doing drugs and didn't think I was having as much sex as other people were. There was an underlying belief that I was negative and that I wouldn't contract it.

In a strange way it didn't matter whether I became infected or not. What mattered was if I infected somebody else. I was always afraid somebody else would become infected. If a person wanted to have anal sex and I was the top, I would insist on putting on a rubber. If there was no negotiation and the person just wanted to fuck me without a condom, I'd let him. If I wanted to suck a man off, I would, because I enjoy it so much, and it wouldn't matter to me that I would swallow the cum. It just wouldn't matter. But I feared that if I was infected and somebody blew me and swallowed, he might get infected. I would feel bad when that happened.

For the most part I was a bottom. A lot of the anonymous sex took the form of my servicing others, who would then walk away. Because of the form a lot of my sexual activity took—being receptive, passive, the bottom—I felt I could be at risk.

&

I struggle with low self-esteem and a tremendous amount of self-hatred. I have been very drawn to people who look rough, like horny heterosexual construction workers or homophobic athletes who want a blow job. There's a thrill in that. I think it's about abuse, about being bonded to one's abuser. In a strange way, I feel a person finds me attractive if he abuses me.

In my family, there was always a need for me to please others, because if I didn't, I would get punished. I got punished anyway, but I thought I needed to please. Because my parents' marriage was arranged, and because of conflicts between my mother and father, and because I was the only male child, I was placed in the position of surrogate husband to my mother. My part as a child who wanted to please was to be her caretaker from a very young age. There was what I consider sexual abuse: I remember sleeping with my mother, us being naked, and there being genital contact.

The shame I have today that I'm still working through is that I don't know whether I wanted it, whether I wanted to go back into the womb. But I have the feeling that I was being manipulated, that I was being used to take care of my mother in some way. I was estranged from my father and heard terrible things about him when I was young. I believed them, because very often he was drunk. He had alcohol for breakfast, lunch, and dinner. All I remember is his anger. And being a little fairy, and hearing him express that.

As a little boy, my sisters used to play with me like a little toy. They would paint my fingernails and put me in their hoop skirts. I loved the petticoats. I got off on it. It was okay for them to dress me up and paint my fingernails, but when it became clear I was getting into it, then I was called a fairy.

The other form of abuse that took place was with a sister who seemed to hate me from a very early age. There is a photograph of my family when I was two years old, and in it this sister is gripping my hand. I have a grimace on my face. I remember being physically abused by her, being beaten. She had one wonderful tactic: to stick her fingernails into my wrist until it started to bleed. The brunt of the abuse I experienced took the form of verbal abuse and criticism. I could not disagree with her. No one, in fact, could disagree with her. It was quite remarkable. I was literally her slave for years. I had to do everything she asked. There were no boundaries. She wanted to physically dominate me and keep me pinned down. She is a controlling person to this day.

Does this influence the way I express my sexuality? It must. I don't know whether I am in control by being passive, or if the other person is in control. I really don't know. That is a difficult question for me to answer.

§·

There was a time in 1984 and 1985 when I was abstinent, for a while anyway. The form my sex took was in fantasy. I remember telling other people to use condoms. I was invited to a red and black Valentine's Day ball and I wore a tuxedo with a red tie and carried a chocolate box. When I revealed its contents, it had condoms instead of chocolates. That was in 1984, and I felt hip.

I remember visiting a friend in New York City. I had an idea we might have sex. I told him I wouldn't swallow and I wouldn't take it up the ass without a condom. I did both of those things with him within an hour: I did swallow, and he did fuck me without a condom. It just happened. I felt some guilt and shame around that, because I was a mouthpiece saying, "Safe sex is important," and not doing it myself. For the most part I wasn't getting fucked at all. It was oral sex most of the time.

Along with talking a good talk, I did bring condoms with me. I wouldn't always use them, but I would bring them with me. If I was going to suck somebody off, I would say to myself, "You have a condom in your pocket," but I would never use it. I don't know if I have a strong connection between cause and effect, between my thinking and my actions. It seems as though there's a missing link. I don't always behave the way I think I ought to.

§·

Part of my nature is to not trust myself, to defer decisions to others. The people who were the most outspoken about not being tested were people I admired and respected, people at the forefront of the AIDS Action Committee, for example. They were strongly opposed to it. So for a while I was saying, "They must be right."

There were political implications: I didn't like the lack of confidentiality, and the idea of a government agency having a list of people's names. Most of the opinions strongly in favor of taking the test seemed to be coming from reactionary people, conservatives. There was talk about quarantine, isolating gay men and keeping them on an island somewhere. Putting a tattoo on your wrist, like in Nazi times. I remember agreeing it was not in my best interest to be tested.

Then I remember that opinion changing. Attitudes changed. People were saying it was better to know your status as early as possible, because either your sexual behavior would change or you would be able to have treatment early. I've forgotten which came first. It was important to know your status, or to know the status of another person, so you wouldn't infect another person or become infected. That was the value of testing at first. But I think soon after that they were offering AZT or pentamidine.

I don't know if I was really persuaded, but I took the test upon the suggestions of people I trusted. Many friends I had had sex with were dying: over 15 people I've had sex with are dead. I guess I wanted to see whether I was among the dying or among the living.

The first time I got a negative test result I was in disbelief. And also regret: I still wanted to be positive. I wanted to die more than I wanted to live. I am aware of my self-destructive tendencies. To be very honest, I have felt my life is such a mess that it would be better if I were dead than alive, because of the struggle. I've experienced a lot of despair in my life and a lot of hopelessness. Being HIV-negative means to me that I'm going to be alive for a while, especially if I have safer sex.

One part of my love of sex is swallowing cum. I feel as though the person—their seed—is inside of me, even though I'm not going to have a baby. It's valuable. I don't know if it's tribal, ancient, or what, but I think it's important to be able to drink another man and have him drink you. My very first lover fucked me, and as he was coming, he said, "My seed is in you for eternity." I felt a warmth of love when he said that, and when I fucked him, I said the same thing.

There are times when I want cum so badly that I fantasize going to a straight man who is uninfected or a gay man who is uninfected and asking him for his cum. Like going to a sperm bank and asking, "Can I borrow some?" I have fantasies about getting cum from a 16-year-old kid who has never had sex. I hate to make it sound like I'm addicted to a substance.

I know there are plenty of guys who don't like it. I had an experience with two men in an anonymous setting. We had been talking. We had established a kind of rapport. I wanted to blow both of these guys. One guy was an old pro. The other guy was new to the scene. He had voiced his concern about safe sex, and all he wanted to do was jerk off. When I introduced the idea of giving him a blow job, he seemed receptive to it. But it didn't happen. He said, "To tell you the truth, I really don't like oral sex." You know, I just don't believe that. Granted, I didn't know him well. I hadn't known him for a long time, but part of me intuits that he was trying to say, "No, I don't want it," and the best way he could do it was by saying, "I don't like oral sex." I know of very few men that don't like to get blown. I wonder if that's what our community is doing to itself.

A lot of my personal struggle has been learning to perceive myself as an empowered person with options and choices. When I was a kid, all I heard was, "You have no choice in anything."

I believe that having unprotected oral sex and swallowing cum is something I want, and I'm willing to take the risk. I've fucked somebody without a condom who was HIV-positive. I know they say that getting fucked without a condom is definitely the riskiest behavior. I don't think I would get fucked without a condom. I don't want to become infected. Fucking someone who is positive is less risky in my mind. I have taken that risk. There are times when I think I'm making a mistake. It's still unsettled. Being able to make choices has been a struggle for me all my life. I have believed that I cannot make choices. So this is a big coup for me, a real victory. I'm taking a stand, definitely. And in a strange way I think I'm dealing more realistically with my own mortality. I'm not inviting death. But I'm saying, "It might happen." I may choose not to be fucked without a condom, but I may continue to have oral sex and swallow semen and run the risk of having exposure.

On a metaphysical level, it doesn't matter whether I'm positive or negative, because I'm going to die some day. And that's not being fatalistic. I don't think so. It really is a matter of deep strength or faith or courage or something like that.

A lot of people—whether they are gay or straight—have a fear of being infected. People are afraid of death. There are people who are negative who stay away from people who are positive because they don't want to catch it. They don't want to be safe for the first six months of an ongoing relationship and then slowly slip and do things that are less safe.

As recently as January, I was involved with somebody who was positive. This guy was very handsome. I was very attracted to him physically and emotionally. I met him at a New Year's Eve party. He and I had a wonderful interaction; we were very present with one another. We sought one another out throughout the evening. He was drawn to me and I was drawn to him. Then we talked on the phone.

As I got to know him, I really wanted to suck his dick without a condom, and I did it. At that point, it *did* matter to me whether I got infected, but I still wanted to do it. We deep-throated like crazy. There was precum, but he wouldn't come in my mouth. That was his boundary. He was concerned that he was going to infect me. Part of me feels bummed out because of my inability to follow through. And I had unprotected anal sex with him. I was

213

the top. I just really wanted to fuck him without a condom. I was having trouble keeping myself hard with a condom. Put a condom on me and I get soft.

Other dynamics caused us to drift apart. What happened is something that happens to me often. I do work on myself emotionally through therapy, and I get in shape physically through exercise. I feel attractive enough to give it a try, but low self-esteem undermines that confidence. That little bit of confidence is like a bud. Before it can flower, I nip it. I start believing I'm not good enough, or the other person doesn't really like me. I start doing things to sabotage the relationship. I overeat. I stop doing exercises. If the person doesn't like smoking, I've picked up smoking. It's one of the deeply rooted core patterns I have.

There was also a lot of fear on my part of becoming positive if I became *willful*—let me use that word—and decided I wanted to. Let me put it this way: A lot of the sex we had involved tying him up. If he's tied up, I can do whatever I want. I can blow him and have him come in my mouth even if he doesn't want to. Even if his boundary is clear, and he doesn't want to exchange body fluids, and he wants me to wear a condom while I'm fucking him. If that's what I want, to be in control and be willful, then there's a chance. If we're in a relationship, I think there's always going to be a chance.

I've heard people whose opinions are very judgmental. There are gay men who condemn others: "He fucked around. That's why he got AIDS. He liked to get fucked every day. Look what happened to him." I've heard that a lot.

One of my sisters wrote me a letter and the tone was condescending: "AIDS is what happens to people who are not innocent. By the sheer fact that they are doing what they want to do, they are guilty. They are not innocent, and that's why they have AIDS. If you get AIDS now, it's your fault. You made a mistake. You should know better."

She doesn't know who I am. I tried to tell her by telling her I was gay, by coming out to her. In her mind, perhaps, a lot of what being gay is about is sex, so that's why the focus of the letter was about that. I think she probably would blame me if I became infected. I think she would be as caring as she could be, and sad to see me go, but I think on some level she would feel I did it to myself.

My mother is 80 years old. She certainly loves me, and knows I'm gay, but has a very hard time with it. She is deeply distressed. She doesn't understand my sexuality. She thinks a man and a woman are supposed to be attracted to one another in order to be human. There's a dick and there's a cunt, and one fits in the other. It doesn't work any other way. She's not a source of support. She's a source of anxiety.

I have told people that I've fucked somebody positive without a condom, and I've gotten reactions of horror, disbelief, and anger toward me. I believe their fear for themselves is behind that. A lesbian friend of mine, on the other hand, has compassionately voiced concern. I don't read it as disapproval. I read it as her saying, "Take precautions as much as you can."

Twelve-step work has been crucial to my process. The 12-step work includes Survivors of Incest Anonymous, Adult Children of Alcoholics, Sex and Love Addicts Anonymous, Overeaters Anonymous, and once in a while, Co-Dependents Anonymous. I probably am an alcoholic, but I don't go to Alcoholics Anonymous. Alcohol is not my substance of choice, but if there was a bottle of wine here, I'd probably finish it off. If there was a birthday cake, I'd eat the whole thing. I could abuse almost anything.

The issue is not the cake. It's not the wine. The issue is self-hatred. If I can soften my judgment of myself, then I'm better off. I've had a bottle of wine at dinner with a friend and had a rich encounter and didn't feel it was not sober. I've had food I'm not supposed to eat and it felt okay. I've had anonymous sex with people and felt okay about it. A dignity of self that I never had before is being restored to me. I can have my cake and eat it too.

The 12-step work allows me to see that I can manage my life if I do certain things. My goal is to be in conscious contact with a higher power, even though that higher power may be inside me. It's almost as if in my head there's one identity and self-image, and in my heart there's a different one. When there is more of a balance of heart and mind, that's the truer me.

The HIV-Negative Support Group that meets once a month in Boston has been remarkable. It's like I'm ripe: it's time for me to start talking about things that really matter to me, and that's where I talk. I don't always feel I'm understood. People sometimes try to give advice when it's not asked for. There's "cross talk," as we say in 12-step programs.

I learned a lot from the 12-step stuff about giving and receiving. There's a trust that develops in a group of people who come consistently. They begin to see that they can rely on the other people there. The people I rely on are the people who show up regularly. That's a form of service. Not only am I giving, but I am also receiving.

If I seroconverted, would that mean I couldn't come back to the HIV-Negative Support Group? That has been a real fear of mine, because I haven't been tested since my risky activity in January and February. If I were positive, I would have to be identified with a different group. There are support groups for positive people, but I would miss the people in our group.

೩

I don't know what it means to be a survivor. It's a mystery to me why I'm still here. I don't know what the hell this is all about, to begin with. I want to learn more about the spiritual transformation or awareness that has been a part of the AIDS epidemic.

A lot of times in the gay community there is a cult of beauty and youth that looks only at the outside. That's okay for some people, and it's okay for me sometimes. I don't deny that I am attracted to young men with great bodies—or older men with great bodies, even. But I'm also seeing other things. That inside stuff is what I feel is a lot more valuable. I place a value on it.

I have a friend who has AIDS right now and his body is covered with giant Kaposi's sarcoma lesions. He's had chemotherapy treatments and is very thin right now. If he said, "Let's make love. I want to be held. I want to be caressed," and he told me what he wanted and what he didn't want, I would definitely do it. It's not because he has great bulging muscles. It's because of who he is. The epidemic has changed that for me.

19

Retesting and Seroconversion

A CAT WITH NINE LIVES

"I see a lot of gay men who are just stuck, stuck, stuck on a testing treadmill," said Vernon, a 45-year-old HIV-test counselor who works in an urban health center. "It's like becoming a cat with nine lives: these guys come in thinking they only have so many negative tests in them, and one day they'll just use them all up."

With these metaphors, Vernon captures several important aspects of what being HIV-negative is like for many gay men. The "testing treadmill" attracts men who doubt the validity of their test results as well as those who are not sure about the risks they are taking in their sexual lives. Beyond this, Vernon suggests, some gay men reveal through repeated testing their conviction that becoming infected is inevitable, that it is only a matter of time before they seroconvert.[1]

Retesting and seroconversion are issues of concern primarily to those who test HIV-negative. Of course, many HIV-positive men are concerned that HIV-negative men not become infected. But testing HIV-positive eliminates the need to test repeatedly or worry about seroconverting. Testing HIV-negative, on the other hand, does not eliminate these concerns; it fuels them.

Testing negative sets men up for the possibility that they might test positive *after having tested negative,* an event with different psychological and social meaning than testing positive on a first test. Testing negative sets men up to view their HIV status as something they have a responsibility to protect. Thus, seroconversion may be interpreted as a failure of responsibility. Indeed, HIV-negative gay men sometimes see seroconversion as a betrayal not only of their own lives but of the gay community as a social entity. It is no wonder, then, that thoughts of retesting and seroconversion occupy HIV-negative gay men.

SITUATIONAL TESTING

Most of the men I interviewed were not on the "testing treadmill" that Vernon described. Nonetheless, many of them had retested at least once, usually because of concerns about the validity of their first test or about risks they had taken after it.

Ross, 37, who in chapter 11 explained his reactions to learning that his partner, John, was HIV-positive, got tested a second time because his first test had been done too soon to rule out HIV infection. "The second time was more stressful than the first," Ross told me. "The first test was done in reaction to the crisis of John testing positive. When I took the second test, I thought to myself, 'Shit, what if in the time period that wasn't covered by the first test I converted?'"

Ross said he would have been angry if he had "made it through ten years" of the epidemic only to seroconvert in the eleventh. "It's like when I was driving down to New Jersey this weekend: I was speeding all the way down, and about a quarter mile from the exit I nearly got pulled over by the cops." The stress of the second testing experience was so great for Ross that he never went back for the results. It was only through a later test that he was able to confirm he was HIV-negative.

Other men told me they had retested because of specific sexual situations they felt might have jeopardized their HIV-negative status. Robert, 40, whose narrative appears in chapter 4, tested after masturbating with an HIV-positive friend in Provincetown. Frank, 40, whose narrative appears in chapter 18, was considering getting tested after having sex with an HIV-positive partner without a condom. For these men, getting retested was not part of a regular pattern, but a response to incidents they deemed risky.

Other men told me they retested from time to time just to reassure themselves, even when they had taken no great risks since their last negative test. "I always practice safe sex," said Harold, 28, "but once in a while I like to be told that I am okay."

REGULAR TESTING

The need to be told that they are "okay" prompts some men to get tested on a regular basis, every six months or every year. Because there are steps to take to protect your health if you learn you are HIV-positive, some men choose regular testing as part of their routine health care. "There's no excuse for a person to not go at least once a year," said Drew, a 30-year-old customer service representative from Pawtucket, Rhode Island. "It's important to know, to catch it early. People who don't know their status are just not committed to their own health. That's what it comes down to for me anyway. I consider it just like going to the doctor once a year for a checkup: HIV testing is part of my regular routine."

When I asked men who tested every six months what was magical about that figure, some told me that it was related to the "window period," the time it generally takes HIV antibodies to show up after infection. It doesn't make sense to me that regular testing should be associated with the window period. If the purpose of regular testing is to identify HIV infection as soon as possible, then why not test every day? Perhaps the six-month figure is chosen because it is practical. Derek, 25, told me that testing twice a year was convenient: "My boyfriend and I got tested on our first anniversary. After that, since our birthdays are six months apart, we get tested on our birthdays—twice a year. Not because I don't trust my boyfriend, but because I don't trust the tests. It is reassuring to get a twice-a-year report card."

Gloria, 55, an HIV-test counselor, told me that many gay men test regularly because their sexual behavior leaves them feeling vulnerable. Like needle users in recovery who are surrounded by a culture where HIV is present, Gloria said, HIV-negative gay men experience HIV as an everyday presence in their lives. "If you believe that oral sex is a risk," she offered as an example, "then probably every man who has sex with men is in a window period when he gets tested. Some people are going to be in that window period for their whole sexual lives." It may be this feeling of continual vulnerability that leads some men to get tested regularly.

Gloria told me that HIV-negative gay men with HIV-positive partners are also among those who test regularly. Some couples use a significant anniversary date to do this testing every year. Gloria believes such testing often reveals in HIV-negative partners an emotional need to be attended to, rather than anxiety about HIV infection. "Their emotional risk is far higher than their physical risk," she said. "I encourage people whose partners are HIV-positive to come back if they need to. They have found a place where someone pays attention to them and talks about their needs. I think it's a real service. Some have asked, 'Do you think I'm abusing the system?' I don't think so."

CHRONIC TESTING

"I never feel completely clean," said Blake, 33. "I worry that I am a false negative. I have had six tests so far, and each time I have told myself that this one will probably be the positive one even though I have a real benign sex life." All the HIV-test counselors I spoke with had men like Blake among their clients, "chronic testers" who test repeatedly even when there is apparently little reason to do so. Such chronic testing, they told me, often has little to do with HIV.

Vernon told me that many men who repeatedly seek HIV testing are really dealing with "coming-out" issues that have remained unresolved. "I hear gay men say they're thinking about getting married to cure themselves, or they're totally closeted at work and are afraid to tell their families," Vernon said. "It's not about HIV testing. They're dealing with coming-out issues. If they're feeling bad just about being gay, they're likely to have higher levels of anxiety about HIV transmission, even in the absence of risk. It all flip-flops, one thing on top of another, like pancakes building up." Vernon sees his job as trying to unstack a few of those pancakes.

"AIDS and HIV have become the perfect net for displaced sexual anxiety," Vernon said. "Sex was always anxiety-provoking, frightening, mysterious, and confusing, even before HIV. People are not always able to separate their sexual anxiety from their HIV anxiety. They jumble it all together. I try to separate those things out."

Gloria is aware that some chronic testers use HIV testing as a way of seeking "permission" to continue risky behaviors, instead of changing them to reduce their risk for HIV. "Testers invite us into a sort of collusion," she said. "They think, 'You gave me a negative result and that means I'm okay.' What happens is they abdicate their responsibility." Gloria is careful in her counseling to address this permission seeking, making it clear to her clients that testing negative after risky behavior is not a rational basis for making decisions about future risk taking.

Alice, 40, an HIV-test counselor for the Red Cross, was even more outspoken about people not changing their behavior: "People who are being unsafe and after the fact coming in for testing—those are interesting individuals to talk to. All they are doing is asking, 'Am I infected yet? Am I infected yet?' In the meantime they are not doing anything to make sure that they aren't infected." Chronic testers sometimes even try to disguise the number of times they have tested, Alice told me. "They do all sorts of things," she added, "like sneaking to a different test site, thinking they're not going to see the same counselor. But since we go from site to site, they are often foiled."

Out of frustration, Alice has asked a couple of clients who test chronically if they want to be infected:

> With one particular person I said, "Do you want a positive test result? Is that what you want?" He said no, but I don't think he believed it when he said it. One individual actually said, "Yeah, it would be easier if I were infected." Because everyone else was. He wasn't actively trying to get

infected—it wasn't a death wish—but he just could not deal with getting a negative result. It was really very, very sad.

Alice suggested that anxiety about HIV sometimes masks other issues, such as guilt over sexual infidelity. "By putting everything on HIV," she said, "people don't have to deal with that guilt. They're afraid to test negative, because if they find out they're negative, then they're going to have to deal with their guilt, and they don't want to do that." Perhaps, then, chronic testing—in search of a positive result—is a way some people express a desire to be punished for their sexual behavior.

HELPING CHRONIC TESTERS

Gloria tries to refer chronic testers to other mental health resources available in the agency where she works. "I do it rather gently," she said. "I suggest there is much more going on for them than can be resolved by an HIV-antibody test. I don't close the door on HIV testing, but I always encourage them to rethink."

Gloria told me that some men who get HIV testing are struggling with substance abuse. The counseling session is a place to begin addressing this issue. She gave an example of her approach:

> Suppose somebody comes in who has been tested before. I say, "Why are you being tested again? What's going on for you?" And he says, "I was bad." I say, "Does that mean you've had risky sex?" And he says, "Yes. I was really stupid."
>
> That's my clue. I say, "Were you drinking or using drugs when this happened?" And he says, "Yes." That gives me an opening to say, "If you're getting drunk or using drugs and having unprotected intercourse, let's start with the alcohol or drugs, because that could happen again tomorrow or the next day for you." Sometimes they hear it.

Alice admitted that chronic testers are draining. "Individuals who are obsessed with HIV and refuse to get any sort of outside counseling are time consuming, frustrating for my staff, and difficult to draw the line with," she said. "I don't say, 'Don't call us anymore.' But in a way I want to say, 'We're done. We can't help you anymore. You really need to get some other kind of help.'" Alice believes individual counseling may be most appropriate for these testers. She recalled an abortive attempt to form a support group for chronic testers:

> Someone I know started a group in Boston for repeat testers who were consumed with the belief that they were infected. The group didn't work, because they all wanted individual attention. They didn't want to be in a group. They didn't want their story to compete with anybody else's, because their story was the most important. The leader told me he had to disband it. Everyone just vied for his attention. They all broke down and said, "I want a private counselor." So he just gave up on it. HIV really wasn't the issue.

When counseling gay men who exhibit great anxiety and yet modest risk for HIV, Vernon tries to get them to look at the many ways they have reduced their risk, rather than focusing on their anxieties. "Men beat themselves over the head because they once didn't use a condom," Vernon said. "I say, 'Hey, give yourself more credit. You've been safe 98 percent of the time.' He's not focusing on that. What does that say about his self-esteem?" Vernon believes that feelings of guilt about not always being "perfectly safe" arise from antigay sentiments in our culture, which have been incorporated into AIDS education:

> I think what is going on in the heads of some men I talk to is internalized homophobia. I have it too. How could I not? I was raised being made to feel afraid, ashamed, embarrassed, and guilty about the feelings I had for other men. AIDS education for gay men often makes us feel afraid, ashamed, embarrassed, and guilty if we have unsafe sex. It's reinforcing something that does not need reinforcement.

I don't want anybody to get this disease, I really don't. What bothers me is when I see people doing all the right things and still torturing themselves. It tells me what's been done to us gay men from the time we were boys. Internalized homophobia hasn't resolved itself in adulthood, and AIDS has made it worse. Working against that is a monumental task.

The desire to be 100 percent safe is often expressed by chronic testers, yet Vernon must point out to some men that their behavior contradicts this. "If a man is terrified he has HIV infection from having precum in his mouth," said Vernon, "but not terrified enough to use a condom for oral sex, I point out that inconsistency." Vernon encourages men to either change their behavior or recognize that some level of risk is acceptable:

I say, "You can't have it both ways. You can't keep testing, afraid that you've gotten infected through precum in your mouth, but not afraid enough to use a condom for oral sex. Either try to make the change or live with this as your own acceptable risk." People want certainty, but there is none. If you want to be 100 percent safe, be celibate. But you can minimize your risks, and you can minimize them dramatically.

Vernon hopes that men who are not engaging in high-risk behaviors will be able to trust their test results and trust what they are doing to maintain their HIV status. "Sometimes it actually happens," he told me. "Last week, a guy said, 'I'm not going to do this. I've done this seven times.' Another guy who had tested repeatedly said, without my prompting him, 'I thought I was coping with the epidemic by doing all this testing. Now I realize I was hiding behind the testing.'"

THE DESIRE TO SEROCONVERT

Although I suspect that most HIV-negative gay men hope to stay uninfected, there are many forces that work against that hope, and some men actually express the desire to seroconvert. I spoke with Wolf, a 46-year-old writer and AIDS activist, about the many reasons supporting the desire to seroconvert.

"I'm here watching friends around me being carted away, being chosen to get on the cattle cars and be shipped away," said Wolf. He had watched the film *Schindler's List* the day before I interviewed him. "I was named after my great-grandfather, who was killed by the Nazis when they invaded Poland. I relate what's happening within the gay community right now to what happened with my ancestors in Poland. I feel a strong connection." Wolf suggested that gay men sometimes feel fatalistic in the face of senseless mass destruction, and this fatalism can lead men to want to seroconvert:

> Some HIV-negative partners of HIV-infected men have told me, "I want to experience what my lover is experiencing." Or, if their lover has died, "I want to join my lover. It's lonely here without him. I'm going to get infected." I've heard that. Another thing is being fatalistic about survival: "I'm going to get it anyway. I might as well enjoy sex. I'm going to live my life as if HIV didn't influence me."

Wolf believes that repeated loss has taken its toll on gay men, especially AIDS activists. "People are becoming numb to the losses, to the deaths, to the sickness," he said. "A lot of us are walking zombies, dealing with this for so long, not seeing an end. The hope we had in the late eighties is dashed right now, and we don't see the light at the end of the tunnel." The immensity of these losses leaves some activists unable to grieve, damaging both their activism and their health. "Some people need to be in therapy to deal with underlying grief issues or they can't be effective activists," Wolf said. "Instead, they use activism as a way of not dealing with grief. And if you don't grieve, you don't grow. If you don't grieve, then feelings of fatalism, loss, and depression are going to be with you, putting you at greater risk—consciously or unconsciously—for infection."

For younger gay men, a different kind of despair may lead to seroconversion, a despair born from growing up in a society that devalues gay youth. "I hear in AIDS prevention circles the term 'passive suicide,'" said Wolf. "It refers to young people growing up in a homophobic, hateful society—especially young people living at home who have no support in their high schools and colleges—putting themselves at risk for AIDS as a way to passively kill themselves. They don't want to stick a gun in their mouth and pull the trigger. But because they grew up in a society which taught them to hide and to hate themselves, they are needlessly putting themselves at risk."

Another reason gay men may desire to seroconvert is that being HIV-positive appears fundamentally linked to gay identity. "Some people feel they are not 'gay enough' unless they are infected," said Wolf. "They feel that they are not heard or acknowledged if they're HIV-negative, that they are taken more seriously if they are infected—especially if they are involved in AIDS activism or the AIDS service industry." Wolf wondered whether some seroconversions could be the result of HIV-negative men seeking the attention they think HIV-positive men get. He offered an analogy from his past work:

> I taught disabled children for seven years. I saw parents who gave all their attention to their disabled child at the expense of their children who didn't have disabilities. The children without disabilities resented it. A lot of them acted out for attention. Some ran away as a plea for attention. One child feigned a limp in order to get attention from her mother. Maybe people are putting themselves at risk as a call for help, a call for attention, a call for acknowledgment.

That some gay men might take risks, or even seroconvert, as a call for attention reflects poorly on the gay community's ability to support all its members. We will suffer more losses if we cannot find ways to attend to the HIV-negative as well as the HIV-positive. We must find ways to assert that staying uninfected is valuable and to help HIV-negative gay men envision a future worth staying uninfected for.

THE RESPONSIBILITY TO STAY UNINFECTED

"It's the duty and responsibility of every uninfected gay man not to get AIDS," said Damien, 38. "If gay men keep going on, it shows people that we aren't doomed to die of AIDS, and that is very important." When I asked HIV-negative men what they imagined they would feel if they seroconverted, some told me they would feel they had betrayed themselves. Many more told me they would feel they had betrayed the gay community. They viewed staying uninfected not only as a personal responsibility but as a communal one.

I found this idea explicitly voiced in a 1989 AIDS brochure, which used the language of gay liberation to imply that the choice between sexual safety and danger is also a choice between community survival and suicide:

> The modern gay movement has certainly not fought for sexual liberty in the past two decades in order that gays might use that liberty to commit a collective suicide. . . . Choosing safer sex is thus not only a question of individual survival, but for gay men also a question of the collective survival of the gay community and its accomplishments. . . .
>
> In the era of the menace of AIDS, to "play riskily"—to refuse to take care of oneself and others—is a new form of gay *self-oppression.* Its destructive character includes the unexpressed message that gay men don't deserve a future, and that the struggles of the forces of gay liberation in the past two decades aren't worth preserving, defending, and enjoying.[2]

More recently, psychotherapist Thomas Moon developed this theme in several *San Francisco Sentinel* articles about gay men's psychology and health. "Clearly," Moon wrote in 1991, "the continued survival of the gay male community depends, in part, on as many of us as possible achieving an unambivalent commitment to survival." He added:

> HIV-negative men face many challenges—the challenge of avoiding unsafe sex, of enduring multiple loss, of supporting friends in their struggle against the disease, of struggling to keep the community alive, and of somehow living a quality life in the midst of a disaster. The challenges are daunting. They can be met successfully only by men who are unshakably clear about their commitment to survival.[3]

This theme was again expressed in a 1995 *Out* magazine article in which Michelangelo Signorile considered the responsibilities he would face upon getting retested after a risky sexual episode. "If I find I am negative," Signorile wrote, "I have a responsibility to keep myself that way, to beat back urges—no matter what fuels them and no matter how difficult they may be to fight off—to act in ways that put me at risk."[4]

I support gay men in using whatever motivations they need to remain uninfected, and feelings of social responsibility may serve this purpose for some men. But an emphasis on social responsibility may have drawbacks. Are we implying that if gay men are not sufficiently concerned about their own health then they should at least be concerned about the survival of the gay community? Is this message likely to encourage men to take care of themselves? Or does it merely make men feel ashamed when they have unsafe sex? Norms that support safer sex as a social responsibility may make it easier to practice safer sex, but do they also make it more difficult for gay men to discuss the unsafe sex they are having? Feelings of social responsibility that support rather than undermine gay men's mental and physical health need to be developed.

NIE WIEDER PLAGUE

Feeling continually responsible not only for oneself but also for a community in crisis can be exhausting. Wolf told me he felt he always has to be available to his HIV-positive friends when they need him. He described his commitment and fatigue this way:

I hate coming back to *Schindler's List*, but I just saw it last night. Schindler had to hold it together until after the war, because if he fell apart all the Jews would die. When the war was declared over, he broke down. At the end, you see him huddled in the snow in a mess. The Jews are coming to comfort him, after he saved them. I think in some ways, some HIV-negative people—including myself—feel they have to keep it all together too.

Perhaps HIV-negative gay men—whose immune systems offer resistance to opportunistic infections—believe they have no choice but to form a kind of Resistance against AIDS, struggling to ensure that the epidemic not get worse. "Nie wieder Krieg," say Germans who survived World War II, reminding us that wartime atrocities must happen "never again." Likewise, gay men who are uninfected sometimes feel a responsibility to act in ways that say, "Nie wieder plague."

THE LIKELIHOOD OF STAYING UNINFECTED

A 1991 report—based on Multicenter AIDS Cohort Study data from Baltimore, Chicago, Pittsburgh, and Los Angeles—estimated rates of seroconversion among gay men and suggested that there is a 30 percent chance that a 20-year-old HIV-negative gay man will seroconvert before age 30, and a 50 percent chance that he will seroconvert before age 55.[5] I am appalled and dismayed by these statistics.

Much as I dislike eliciting feelings of guilt in gay men about seroconverting, I believe it is important to discuss the seroconversion rates that gay men will need to achieve to keep a majority of gay men uninfected.

In my professional life, I edit high-school mathematics textbooks. Calculating the probability of remaining uninfected over time is not difficult if seroconversion rates are known. If the annual rate of seroconversion is r, for example, then the probability of remaining uninfected after one year is $(1 - r)$, and the probability of remaining uninfected after x years is $(1 - r)^x$. Unfortunately, the compounding effects of exponential functions work against us in this case. Even if the rate of seroconversion is only 2 percent annually, less than half of a group of uninfected 20-year-old gay men will remain uninfected by age 55, because $(1 - 0.02)^{35}$ is about 0.493.

Suppose seroconversion rates are constant across age groups.[6] The following table shows the age by which half of a group of uninfected 20-year-old gay men will be infected, based on various seroconversion rates.

Seroconversion rate (%)	Age when half will be infected
4.0	37
3.5	40
3.0	43
2.5	48
2.0	55
1.5	66
1.0	89

In order for half of a group of uninfected 20-year-old gay men to remain uninfected up to age 73—the life expectancy of an average 20-year-old man in the United States—we will need an overall annual seroconversion rate of less than 1.3 percent. If we are immodest enough to want more than two thirds of uninfected gay men to stay uninfected up to age 73, then we will need seroconversion rates under 0.76 percent.

How close are we to these rates? It is difficult to know, since a random sample of gay men is hard to establish. But recent studies do not offer an optimistic picture. Preliminary results of studies of men who have anal sex with other men, gathered in 1993 and 1994 for a vaccine-trial feasibility study, indicate annual seroconversion rates of 3.1 percent in San Francisco, and 2.6 percent in Denver and Chicago.[7]

Seroconversion is not inevitable for gay men. But for this to be the case, we need to keep rates of seroconversion extremely low.

Otherwise, it will be impossible to keep a majority of gay men uninfected. What rates of seroconversion should we aim for? What rates can we hope to achieve? What rates can we live with? These are questions gay men will have to acknowledge and discuss publicly.

LIVING WITH UNCERTAINTY

Testing HIV-negative leaves gay men with an uncertainty they must find a way to live with: an uncertainty about whether they will become infected. Some men try to handle this uncertainty with repeated HIV testing, even though HIV testing cannot predict the future. Others remove this uncertainty by becoming infected. But seroconversion is certainly not the healthiest way of handling uncertainty about HIV status.

I made a list one day of all the things I would do if I learned that I had seroconverted. Among the items were these: I would exercise more. I would eat better. I would play my violin again. I would finish reading Shakespeare. I would spend more time in Venice.

Looking over the things I had listed, I realized I didn't have to be HIV-positive to do most of them. The last item on my list was this: If I seroconverted I would invite my friends over for a party to celebrate the end of worrying about seroconverting.

Perhaps I can find a better reason to invite my friends over. Maybe we can find other things to celebrate.

20

Yeah, Ma, I'm Okay

Nathaniel McNaughton

PEOPLE WANT DESPERATELY to be a part of the gay community, and the gay community is so intertwined with HIV infection that they want to either be HIV-positive or believe themselves to be at risk for it. It's hard to say, "I am uninfected and I'm going live my life." You can't possibly do that, because HIV is so overwhelmingly a part of our culture. How many people do we know who walk around with a sense of pride that they're HIV-negative? That's very rare. Nobody wants to be seen that way. That has a swaggering quality that's anathema to many gay men.

Look at all the people who feel, even today, that they should have been positive because they saw their friends and lovers get sick and die. I think it's difficult to be apart from a culture, apart in many cases from a longtime lover. It's hard to grasp that a lover is now able to sit in community with friends at a coffee klatch and talk about who's on AZT and DDI, and who has a lesion and who doesn't. The HIV-negative man is totally beyond the pale of this discussion. Because he's HIV-negative, he's out of the loop. There is no Boston Living Center for HIV-negative men.

I do HIV-test counseling as part of my work. Last night I gave a young man his HIV-test results. He was negative, and he suddenly felt labeled. He felt there was a neon sign hanging in front of him flashing, "HIV-negative. HIV-negative." And he didn't like it. I didn't want to just let him out the door with an HIV-negative result, pat him on the back, and say, "Go have an ice cream cone, pal." I said, "What is this all about? What is behind this for you? You're 19 years old. You feel like you're wearing a scarlet letter that says HIV-negative." And he said, "It's so weird. I've always felt I was going to get this. I've always felt I was going to be HIV-positive, just by virtue of who I was. Now that I have this label, I don't know if I want to tell anybody."

There's an etiquette to not talking about HIV status, because then you're all on the same level. Even if you know you're negative, you might not want to come out and say you're negative because then you can no longer say, "We're all equally at risk. We're all equally infectious. And let's all play safe." That's a great strategy for safer sex, but the downside for the man who knows he's HIV-negative is that he cannot grasp and deeply incorporate that identity and move on.

There are HIV-negative men who believe themselves to be negative in their deepest gut but put out a public persona that implies, "I might be positive, or I'm at risk for being positive." That's not necessarily so, but they want to believe they are at risk because that puts them in brotherhood with other people. They don't want to be seen as not vulnerable because that would put them above it all, and they don't want to do that. They don't want to be distanced from their gay male friends.

In most discordant couples, the negative one wants to stay negative and the positive one wants the negative one to stay negative. They don't express any deep-seated need for the negative one to become like the positive one. Where I've experienced that in my counseling work, there are other unhealthy things going on.

For example, there was a couple I saw in which one person was negative, the other one positive. Their entire relationship was based on incredibly unsafe sex. The negative one was always getting fucked by the positive one. No condoms. Always with ejaculation. Sometimes even with rectal bleeding. The negative one had alcohol abuse issues going on and did not want to change his behavior. I would say, "You need to look at this. You need to deal with this, and you need to be in communication with each other about this." But they would come back and report continued unsafe sex, time after time. Eventually, in this particular scenario, the negative man did become positive.

The man had a beatific glow on his face when he found out he was positive. He had been expecting this for so long, and finally the desired outcome was achieved. What was going on for him was that he desperately wanted to keep this relationship alive, and the positive one wanted to dump him. The negative one desperately wanted to keep it alive, so he desperately wanted to continue the sexual behaviors. I think he wanted to show the positive one the extent to which he was willing to go to prove his love.

That glow on his face was something I will never forget. He really felt triumphant that he had become HIV-positive. It's frightening to sit with people who are that clear about it. It's like sitting with someone who wants to commit suicide, in many ways.

No sooner had he seroconverted than the couple continued their sexual behavior, but they continued it with condoms. They instituted condom use immediately following the seroconversion. I don't know what that means. All I can tell you is that's what happened.

ﻌ

There are people who think it's important to keep sex alive in the way that we knew it. It's a cultural phenomenon: the way we have sex has cultural meaning to us, and people want to keep that alive. I have known people who wanted to continue unsafe sex, not so much because they wanted to become infected, but because it was imperative to them as standard-bearers of gay culture to continue to do things they felt were integrally a part of gay culture.

One recent example comes to mind. This man went to a bathhouse, lay down on a cot with some lube, spread his legs, and four people came in and fucked him. He didn't know them, he didn't know their antibody status, and he was clear as a bell about the fact that he wasn't drinking, he wasn't on drugs. What he wanted was the experience—the gay cultural experience—of being in that setting and doing those things. He deeply missed that, not as somebody who had previously experienced it, but as somebody coming into a culture which that had once been a part of. He wanted not to *reexperience* it, but to experience it for the first time. The man was 23. He was born in 1970.

And what happened to this young man? He became HIV-infected. When he came in for HIV testing, he made an appointment to get his results with his lover, who was HIV-positive. They had a monogamous relationship which was very safe. They were set up for their appointment on a Tuesday. He called on Monday and said, "Can I come in today and get my results and then come back tomorrow and pretend I'm getting them for the first time?" I didn't have any reason to refuse him, so I said yes. He came in and found out he was positive and then had to figure out how he was going to tell his lover. Because of the safe structure of their relationship, his lover knew that he was not the one who had infected him. An incredibly complex scenario.

More often than not, people I know who have seroconverted were having unprotected receptive anal sex. Alcohol or recreational drug use was often, but not always, a part of it. It really stemmed from other things going on in their lives: being tired of safer sex, being nostalgic for unsafe sex, being angry and depressed, feeling overwhelmed by the epidemic and engaging in unsafe sex as a stress reliever. There's an irony there.

One man who I counseled had been in a relationship with a known HIV-positive partner for a long time and they had very safe sex. The negative one was younger, kind of footloose-and-fancy-free. The negative one really liked to get fucked. But the positive one was 40, established, determined to protect his lover, determined to always use condoms. And so they always did. The younger one, when he was removed from this structured relationship, fell into—tumbled into—unsafe sex with multiple partners. This is a man who would drink 20 cocktails in an evening. He was fucked in a nine-month period by dozens of different men. He decided to get tested, and when I gave him his results, they were positive. He sat down and said to me, "I knew it. I knew it. I knew I was going to be positive."

Another man was in a similar scenario: a structured relationship with a known HIV-positive partner. That wasn't the unsafe thing. There wasn't anything unsafe about that. Safe sex was the norm for that couple. When that relationship broke up, the negative one was a free bird, able to have sex again in the way he may have desired and long wished for and hoped to do again. He went out and did it with people of unknown status and became positive. Can you imagine? Staying safe and being committed to safe sex with an HIV-positive man for so many years, and then being removed from that situation and being at risk.

Gay men are growing older, just like everybody else, and some gay men are going to die of things like heart attacks, liver cancer, and automobile accidents. The surviving partner is at risk in the same ways, I believe, as these other men.

I personally know of one couple, for example, both of whom were in their fifties and HIV-negative. They were going to go off to California and have a wonderful retirement together when— boom—one of them died of a heart attack. It was a total surprise, like a doorknob coming off in your hand. The next time I saw the survivor, he crumbled in my arms, sobbing. The feelings he expressed of loss, rage, and grief were very similar to the feelings that I've heard from those who have lost partners to AIDS.

I think this man is at extraordinary risk for HIV acquisition, but I have no idea where he is right now. His phone number is disconnected. I can't find him through the mail. This is a man who had been committed to safer sex, who had seen tons of his friends and lovers die of HIV infection, and who was planning to be in this negative-negative relationship for the rest of his life. This man is out there alone in the world and I believe at very great risk. He may be dead now. I have no idea.

A young man I know whose substantially older lover died of liver cancer is adrift in a fog. It was a deeply profound father-son relationship for the two of them, and he is continuing to seek that out. He has multiple sex partners now, looking for the daddy that he lost. And he is continuing to seek that out with older men, who are probably more likely to be HIV-infected. They are not necessarily going to infect him on purpose. How do they know if they are HIV-infected? There are still people who don't get tested. They might infect him because they want to believe they are not HIV-positive.

I've seen sadness and depression and anger and frustration, coupled with nostalgia and an overwhelming sense of "I'm so exhausted by the HIV epidemic, my God, I think I'll just have unsafe sex." And that's what happens.

የ

In 1987, somebody who I had counseled several times showed up for his HIV-test results four months late, and he had seroconverted. Every time since then when somebody is late, it's a red flag to me that they might have done something they are afraid to come in and find out about—for two reasons, at the very least: because *they* don't want to find out they are positive, and because they don't want *me* to know. A rapport develops between me and the clients I see over time so that the way I feel about them—the way they *perceive* that I feel about them—is important to them. It makes them feel that they have let me down, that they have betrayed our work together, if they seroconvert.

One such client was a man whose very reasonable safety net was that when he went out, he went out with his friends, his cousins, and his brother. It was a gay network of friends that supported each other in not drinking too much, not going out with somebody who looked like a suspicious, shady character, however they construed that.

Well, one time he went out and he didn't have those people with him. I can't tell you how much not being with that peer group was his risk factor, more than anything else. I don't know that to be true, but when he inserted that into his tale, it rang for me as being his risk factor.

He drank a lot, probably about ten beers. It was close to Christmas, it was snowy, it was romantic. He was lonely, he met a guy, they went home. The way he tells it, the guy apparently was hung like a horse. The condom didn't fit. The condom busted. They said, "Well, let's do it without it." He had rectal bleeding. The guy came inside him and was gone the next morning. He never saw him again.

This man didn't tell me this story until 18 months after it happened. I saw him in December. He was sick not long after that, what I now believe was acute HIV infection. In April he seroconverted. He told me it must have been oral sex. He stuck to that story for more than a year. Then this story I've just told you started to spill out. Not as a new story. He just sort of *reviewed* it, as though he had told me many times and was just telling the tale again. I was hearing it all for the very first time.

This is a man who was deeply, deeply invested in staying HIV-negative, for his own sake, and for the sake of his mother, because his mother had already lost children to HIV infection. She knew he was HIV-negative. She supported his continued HIV negativity. They never talked about it, but she always knew when he was going for an HIV test. And when he came home after getting his results, she always asked him if he was okay. That was her code word for "Are you still HIV-negative?" And he would always say, "Yeah, Ma. Yeah, Ma, I'm okay." After he seroconverted, he went home that day, and his mother said, "Are you okay?" And he said, "Yeah, Ma, I am." And he has continued to say that to this day because he cannot bring himself to tell her.

❦

These people are not crazy, not in the least. We are talking about nurses and priests and AIDS educators and respectable college librarians: people who have their feet on the ground and know a lot about HIV. These people are a microscopic reflection of the gay community at large. These kinds of things must be happening out there in the world to people who are not seeking HIV testing or counseling.

We have patted ourselves on the back for the incredibly decreased rates of unprotected receptive anal sex. Look at how gonorrhea has gone way down. And yet, to be completely frank with you, the pats on the back are a little too premature, when people seroconvert at their fifteenth HIV test, after not only being educated 14 times, but getting HIV-negative test results 14 times. There aren't too many people walking around with 14 HIV-negative tests under their belt. To be positive on the fifteenth means that information doesn't do enough.

I have tried to embrace people in exactly the same way in their new HIV-positive identity as I had always done in their HIV-negative identity. I have to respect people and not treat them any differently. To support them taking care of themselves and doing what they need to do to be as healthy as possible, and to not contribute to any bad feelings they have about what happened.

A recent seroconverter has pretty much come to terms with it. This is somebody who had been determined to stay HIV-negative for the rest of his life. Who knew that this man, of all the men I've worked with, would become HIV-positive? But he did. He has imbued our conversations with the same passion about life as he always did. He used to say he was always going to be HIV-negative; now he says he's going to be the longest-living HIV-positive person ever. I'm delighted that his character is unchanged.

But he does admit that down the road he might need medical care. If somebody—a doctor, a nurse, a counselor—asks him, "Do you know when you became HIV-infected?" and he says, "Well, I know it was in the summer of 1991," he is petrified that the response is going to be, "Well, you should have known better, pal." He is petrified that he is not going to get the same supportive, loving care that people have gotten who went before him, because they "didn't know any better." This epidemic came out of nowhere, and there were all of these "innocent victims."

I have never said to anybody, "You should have known better." I don't believe I even think that in my private moments. I hear from people the incredible weight they're carrying around, whether it's seronegative guilt, exhaustion with the epidemic, or wanting to align themselves with their seropositive friends and people who have died. I know they are carrying that weight around and possibly don't have places to go with it. This is very heavy.

៛

When people seroconvert, I feel, "That could have happened to anybody. That could have happened to me." I could have a fight with my lover and go out and have unsafe sex with somebody else, I suppose, if I had a couple of cocktails. I don't think I would do that, but I don't see myself being so far beyond that. For these guys who seroconverted, things were going on in their lives that just melded together to make it possible for this to happen—even the guy who lay down on the cot in the bathhouse. I can't point a finger at this person, even in my own private moments, and say, "You shouldn't have done what you did." I may express sorrow, but not condemnation.

I think my parents view me as somebody who will not get AIDS. I think they believe that because I do AIDS-related work, I won't get it, unless I stick myself with a needle, or something like that. They think that by being a health-care worker and a counselor, I effectively separate myself from the great wide world of people at risk for HIV infection.

My worry is this: For what portion of my work have I done that myself? Did I effectively remove myself from the world because the world was a dangerous place? By being on the front lines and witness to so much cumulative tragedy, was I in fact separating myself from it? Was I so separate from it that I believed it would not personally affect the integrity of my body?

If I felt that way on some level about myself and my own work, it was clearly knocked to bits by the fact that some of the recent seroconverters have been AIDS workers, people who ministered around AIDS issues as educators or priests or nurses. Those people, perhaps even more than all of the other people, were "just like me." If I were to become seropositive now, not only would it be a blow to me, my family, and my friends, but—right or wrong—it would be a big let-down for all of the people I have counseled over the years. I don't think this is right, but people hold me in a certain kind of esteem. People put me on a pedestal. People think, "This is somebody who is going to be the standard-bearer."

I want to stay negative anyway. I have absolutely no interest in becoming HIV-positive. I have a lover who is HIV-negative. We had a commitment ceremony in June of 1991. We have always viewed our relationship as a committed relationship that is exclusive of sex outside the relationship. If either of us ever wanted to have sex outside, it would be something we would need to talk with one another about beforehand. It's never come up. I'm not saying it won't, but it hasn't. He says he hasn't had sex with anybody outside of our relationship, and I believe him. I haven't had sex with anybody outside of our relationship, and he believes me. Is it always going to be this way? I don't know.

I have faith in the monogamy of gay men. Not of every gay man, but of some gay men in couples. I have seen that happen. The HIV-negative man, even one in a couple with another HIV-negative man, is not permitted to rise above the much-fabled promiscuity of gay male culture. That much-fabled promiscuity is culturally valuable: a lot of people still talk about it, a lot of people miss it, a lot of people hold nostalgia for it. What we're doing is stereotyping. We're saying that gay men are promiscuous. A gay man in a couple will *of course* be promiscuous or his lover will *of course* be promiscuous. Somebody will step out on the relationship, and because of that you must always use latex when you are having sex with each other.

I think it's homophobic to presume that gay men are going to step out of their relationships. That is unfair to gay men. To assume that a heterosexual married couple—where both people test negative—should not have to use condoms if the woman has some other sort of birth control, and not assume that two gay men could do the exact same thing, is homophobic. There are no other ways to put it. The assumption is that heterosexuals are going to be more monogamous than we are.

Two HIV-negative gay men who continue to use condoms for anal sex or oral sex are continuing to align themselves with a beleaguered community: "If the gay community has to do this, then I have to do this too." That may have merit in certain ways. People who have gone beyond that have a type of private strength to rise up and say, "I see what's necessary in other people's situations. But it's not necessary in mine." It may sound like denial, but it's completely different. That private strength only wells up when somebody has looked very carefully at his situation and said, "You. Me. This is what we're going to do. This is the commitment that we make." It comes from communication with one another, and it's based on trust.

When two people are negative and they ask whether they should continue to use condoms, all I can do is tell them that you can never know for sure if somebody is going to have sex outside the relationship: "That's where communication is a lot more important than latex. You need to decide for yourselves." Privately I want to say, "Go for it." I can't do that in my position at the agency I work for, and I don't. I've tried to insert this topic into the agenda when the agency talks about safer sex. I've tried to ask, "What if two people are negative?" There's always somebody who will say, "Yeah, well, you can never tell." My coworkers rise up against me and say, "We're not going to discuss that." People don't want to defy the standard line.

I want to see the agency, and safe sex education in general, grow to a point where we can accept that there are HIV-negative men in our midst who are not at risk for HIV infection. That's just the way it is.

※

I think we are all survivors. We're survivors of friends and lovers. We're survivors of what might have been. We're survivors of a kind of holocaust, although I don't really want to use that word because I respect the Holocaust as an incredibly violent and horrifying span of events.

Working as an HIV counselor, I have been privy to the deaths of nearly a hundred people. Every one of those people was special in his own way. Every one of them was delightful, even the pistols. I'm fortunate to have been witness to their stories. They have brought profound things to the table, and I consider myself lucky to have witnessed that. I remember all of those people, and I don't want to forget them.

Do we have a responsibility to tell the story? Do we have a responsibility to keep in our hearts the stories of people who have died? Do we have a responsibility to teach the world what we've witnessed? I don't know if we have a responsibility. That's what I'm going to do, for the rest of my life. I want to be a historian of, a documentor of, a tale-teller of this whole process. To continue to put in people's consciousness that this is something that happened. I want them to know what this was like. Because a whole helluva lot of people who I think were pretty damn eloquent about the experience of this epidemic are dead now. And if they can't talk about it anymore, and if they can't teach, then I want to. I want to keep their hard work and goodwill alive to the extent that I am able. I don't think it's the responsibility of every HIV-negative gay man.

I think there may be an unfortunate assumption that the gay male HIV-negative survivor is shut up in a cell somewhere, wrapped in Saran Wrap, friendless and alone, or covered with warts like a toad and nobody wanted to date him anyway. There's not a lot of sexy glamour to being HIV-negative. I think the world looks at us as "you little librarians, under mushrooms there." I want gay life to be more than that.

I want people to stay safe so they can be alive and healthy, and so they can further the very special contributions of gay men on the planet, particularly since we've lost so much. I hope that a lot of HIV-negative gay men will want to, so gay male culture will be more than just cumulative tragedy, so we will be able to thrive in ways that teach the world that we are made up of more stuff than just surviving HIV.

It hasn't just been ordinary gay men who have died, although it *has* been ordinary gay men. It has been many extraordinary gay men who have died as well. We have lost a great deal: a lot of momentum, a lot of art, and music, and brilliant thought, and wittiness. And those of us who remember what has faded, those of us who remember that brilliance—oh, I *will* say it: We *do* have a responsibility to keep it alive. I hope a lot of other people feel that way.

21

HIV-Negative Identity

One day in 1994, as I walked to the Boston Public Library in Copley Square, I saw a teenager with a small white button pinned to his chest. In bold black letters the button proclaimed, "HIV–." I had never seen such a thing and was immediately overcome by curiosity and revulsion. I wanted to ask the youth where he had gotten the button, and at the same time I wanted to shake him by the shoulders and berate him for flaunting his HIV-negative status. "How dare you wear that button!" I wanted to exclaim. "Don't you realize how offensive it is to HIV-positive people?"

Instead of confronting the youth, I walked on, puzzled at my emotional reaction. Why was I so disturbed by his button? After all, I had spent the past few years facilitating a support group for HIV-negative gay men. I was beginning to think that adopting an "HIV-negative identity" might help men remain uninfected. Couldn't wearing an "HIV–" button be an aspect of HIV-negative identity? And yet I bristled at it.

What I was forced to confront when I saw the youth wearing an "HIV–" button was my own ambivalence about my HIV-negative status and the propriety of disclosing it publicly as an aspect of my identity. To wear an "HIV–" button seemed like an affront to the HIV-positive. It struck me as boasting, rubbing one's own good fortune in the face of those less fortunate. My reaction may have been a form of survivor guilt: I was reluctant to publicize my HIV-negative status out of deference to the HIV-positive.

Born in 1963, I grew up on the cusp of the AIDS epidemic, influenced by sexual mores both before and after the epidemic began. I share with gay men older than myself the idea that one should not boast about being HIV-negative because that status is not something one has earned. Like Simon Watney, quoted in chapter 9, I sometimes think that my being uninfected is largely a matter of the whim of fate, and that I have an obligation to recognize an essential solidarity with infected gay men. And yet I share with the button-wearing youth—and others who have become sexually active in the era of AIDS—the idea that being HIV-negative is a kind of achievement, something to be celebrated, encouraged, and prized. So I at once want to proclaim my HIV-negative status and yet be mute about it. Can I adopt an attitude that embraces survival if I am ashamed to proclaim being a survivor?

TWO T-SHIRT DESIGNS

Paul, 35, whose narrative appears in chapter 6, told me that when he designed a T-shirt for a gay pride parade, a friend who saw his preliminary design suggested that he make two versions. Paul was repulsed by the idea:

> He suggested that I have two sets of T-shirts made up—one that had a negative symbol in the pink triangle and one that had a positive symbol—so that people would be able to recognize immediately whether the person was positive or negative. I just had this visceral reaction: "You can't do that."

The friend who suggested two designs had recently learned he was HIV-negative after fearing for many years that he was HIV-positive. "He was kind of grandiose about it," Paul said, "and it bugged me." Paul did not think uninfected gay men should go around wearing their HIV negativity on their sleeves, so to speak. "A pink triangle is a symbol of community," he said. "If you start differentiating a positive sign and a negative sign within it, it's a community divided, don't you think?"

When I pressed Paul about this, asking how he felt about HIV-positive gay men who wore buttons or T-shirts advertising their HIV-positive status, he said this seemed different: "To hear about somebody doing that when they're positive seems okay. Somehow, if people do that when they're negative, it doesn't seem right. Isn't that interesting: it's like a double standard. Flaunting your negative status seems arrogant."

Paul agreed with me when I suggested that perhaps the reason for this double standard is that being HIV-positive is a stigmatized position, an "outgroup" identity. To claim that being HIV-negative is an "outgroup" identity that deserves to be acknowledged may seem as bizarre as a "heterosexual pride" parade or a "white power" rally. There is no weight to the "stigma" of being HIV-negative.

What Paul pointed out is that expressing an HIV-positive identity is acceptable in gay culture—perhaps even viewed as courageous—but that expressing an HIV-negative identity is unacceptable—perhaps even viewed as insensitive and divisive. Alan, 31, elaborated on this idea when he told me that the Boston HIV-Negative Support Group was a good idea, but that HIV-negative identity was not:

> The issue isn't that we're HIV-negative. The issue is that we're HIV-negative *in the context of this crisis.* The crisis is the problem. What do you do when you're not sick, you haven't tested positive, but your community is in crisis? The support group is a great idea, because that's what they deal with.
>
> But HIV negativity is not the issue, and building an identity around it outside the context of the support group I see as being very damaging and not useful. Because outside that context it is about alienation, and it is about division, and it is about superiority.

The challenge that HIV-negative gay men face is this: How do we go about valuing our HIV-negative identity without alienating or devaluing HIV-positive men?

THE DEVELOPMENT OF HIV-POSITIVE IDENTITY

Gay men have a history of taking symbols of oppression and turning them into icons of identity. The pink triangle used by the Nazis to mark homosexuals in concentration camps has been adopted as a symbol of gay identity. More recently, the epithets "faggot" and "queer" have been reclaimed by some gay activists as terms of empowerment. It did not surprise me, then, that when HIV-positive gay men found themselves a stigmatized minority within a minority, they reacted by claiming "HIV-positive" as an identity rather than a label.

At a gay and lesbian health conference in Houston in 1993, I saw oversized T-shirts with the slogan "HIV+" emblazoned across the front in pink letters almost a foot high. For an HIV-positive person to wear such a T-shirt is to display his HIV status to the world without shame and to force passersby to confront their feelings about people with HIV. Wearing such a T-shirt—like wearing a pink triangle—is a way of making visible something invisible, of making public something private, of turning a stigma into a symbol of identity.

Even more controversial than T-shirts proclaiming one's HIV-positive status is the practice of tattooing "HIV+" on one's body. When a conservative commentator suggested that HIV-positive drug users be tattooed on the arm and HIV-positive gay men be tattooed on the buttocks, his idea was dismissed as reactionary, recalling as it did the identification of concentration camp prisoners by Nazis. That gay men might *tattoo themselves* is an act with a very different—and potent—political meaning. Such tattooing—which has been reported in the Pacific Northwest—is a deliberate establishment of identity that marks one's difference from others in a visible way. It reveals the stigmatization that HIV-positive status bears in our culture, and expresses—in the tattoo's permanence—the ineradicability of HIV within the body.

In contrast to the permanence of HIV positivity is the impermanence of HIV negativity. This impermanence may be the chief reason that it is difficult to establish an HIV-negative identity. To put it bluntly, no one would tattoo "HIV–" on his body, because being HIV-negative is not a fixed characteristic.[1]

THE FRAGILITY OF HIV-NEGATIVE IDENTITY

"I'm bugged by this HIV-negative identity stuff," said Alan. "I think it's a fucked-up thing to build an identity around, because it's variable. It's not something that you can say at any given moment is the truth." HIV-positive identity, on the other hand, is much clearer. If you are infected with HIV, your HIV status is not "variable." The difficulty of establishing HIV-negative identity is thus partially related to a dissymmetry inherent in HIV testing: HIV-positive test results are considered reliable indicators of HIV status, but HIV-negative test results are not.

I have mentioned in earlier chapters that many gay men do not believe their negative test results. This disbelief sometimes indicates that they feel they do not deserve to be uninfected or that they believe that becoming infected is inevitable. Even when men do believe their test results, being HIV-negative sometimes seems like a provisional status, something precarious that could be lost at any moment. It is difficult to build an HIV-negative identity if men are reluctant to claim it as something they deserve or something they expect will continue.

The fragility of HIV-negative identity became especially clear to me at a 1994 HIV-prevention summit I attended in Dallas. During the conference, a group of HIV-positive and HIV-negative gay men gathered to discuss whether AIDS education should address men of different HIV statuses differently. When these men introduced themselves and announced their HIV status, the HIV-positive men invariably said that they were HIV-positive. Sometimes they mentioned the date when they were diagnosed with AIDS. The HIV-negative men, on the other hand, did not say that they were HIV-negative. Instead, they said things like, "I tested negative in September of 1989" and "I was negative the last time I was tested," as if they could never be sure of their HIV-negative status. I'll bet that if someone marketed buttons or T-shirts with the slogan "HIV-Negative (So Far)" they would have sold well at that conference.

THE ABSENCE OF A CONDITION

Another reason that HIV-negative status seems an improbable thing to organize an identity around is that it is defined by the absence of a medical condition rather than the presence of one. Dudley, 42, who in chapter 13 discussed being in a positive-negative couple with Michael, put it this way:

> I can't imagine somebody going around saying, "I *don't* have breast cancer, isn't that fabulous?" But I do know people who go around saying, "I had breast cancer and I *survived* it." I look at survivors as people who have had something and survived. But what would be the point of going around saying, "I'm *not* living with AIDS"? It doesn't make a lot of sense.
>
> I don't identify with the concept of HIV-negative identity. I'm just a healthy gay person, and part of my being healthy is that I happen to be HIV-negative and intend to stay that way.

Dudley suggests that an HIV-negative identity is equivalent to saying that one is "not living with AIDS." But as the men I interviewed have made clear throughout this book, being HIV-negative *is* a form of "living with AIDS." That HIV-negative status is defined by the absence of a medical condition does not mean that HIV-negative gay men do not have a unique position and an identity associated with it. Nor should it dissuade us from developing an HIV-negative identity and supporting others with that identity. Precedents for this kind of support already exist: there are support groups for spouses of terminally ill patients, for children of alcoholics, and for siblings of schizophrenics, to cite just a few examples.

The very precariousness of HIV-negative status should inspire us to develop HIV-negative identity in order to maintain it, just as recovering alcoholics develop a "sober" identity even though that sobriety may be difficult to maintain. Self-help groups that encourage gay men to stay sober offer a model to consider when looking for ways to encourage gay men to stay uninfected. Like sobriety, HIV negativity is a state of being that can be lost by doing something pleasurable. The difference is that when an alcoholic in recovery falls off the wagon, he can get back on. When an HIV-negative gay man falls off the HIV negativity wagon, he cannot.

I don't want to suggest that the sexual behavior that threatens HIV negativity is comparable to addiction, but I do believe that the principle of mutual support that underlies 12-step groups may be useful for HIV-negative gay men. Information about forming HIV-negative support groups appears in the appendixes. We need to support such groups and find other ways to "sponsor" HIV-negative identity.

HIV-NEGATIVE PRIDE

At a January 1995 steering committee meeting for the Boston HIV-Negative Support Group, one man suggested that the group march with a banner in the next gay pride parade. The suggestion raised in me the same discomfort that the HIV-negative button on the teenager's chest did.

Much as I support the idea of HIV-negative identity, the concept of "HIV-negative pride" struck me as bizarre. The word "pride" sometimes connotes "feeling superior," and that troubled me. But "gay pride" is really just a synonym for "gay self-esteem." There's nothing wrong with that, so what could be wrong with the concept of "HIV-negative pride"? The self-esteem of uninfected gay men is important, and celebrating it might even help uninfected men stay uninfected.

If my own conflicting feelings about marching in a gay pride parade as an HIV-negative gay man are any indication, though, it is unlikely that this will happen soon in Boston. There are too many forces militating against it: shame about being HIV-negative, reluctance to identify oneself as a "survivor" in an ongoing epidemic, uncertainty about HIV-negative status, and the simple desire to be quiet. All these forces conspire to make it difficult to develop, support, or advertise HIV-negative identity. As a result, I believe few HIV-negative gay men will want to make their presence visible in gay pride parades.

To measure just how far we are from that point, I invite readers to examine how they feel carrying this book around. Do they experience discomfort? Are they afraid of what people will think of them? How many readers, I wonder, will hide the cover or spine of this book from view so that others won't see what they're reading?

22

We Want Kansas City Trucking

James Douglas

ONE THING THAT TROUBLES ME is that I tend to use pornography for behavior control. I know this really sounds awful, but sex for me is something to be managed and controlled, and it's associated with need and disease. It's really hard to deal with. If I can manage my sexuality by watching a video, reading *BEAR* magazine, or whatever turns me on, I manage it. Phone sex has been like that for me. I used to have really unsafe, bizarre fantasies on the phone. That seemed relatively healthy, as long as it wasn't ever acted upon. I don't do it any more because of the cost.

But what really turns me on is unsafe sex, and the videos I really like are the old ones, where everything goes. It's all this wonderful sex, no holds barred, and at the same time I don't know if I'm being responsible. It's like somehow allowing unsafe sex to happen. It bothers me that that's what I watch.

I've talked to friends and they are struggling with some of the same things. We want *Kansas City Trucking*. We want the unsafe tapes, so we can live out those fantasies. The problem for me is I think there is a direct relationship between my seeing unsafe pornography and acting unsafely. That's not the only thing that influences my behavior, but there's a direct relationship between what I watch and what I want to do. In some way I'm allowing those images to model my behavior. And that's very disturbing. It does not feel okay.

I don't think it's about being sex-negative. I think it's about not having the appropriate safer-sex-positive images there, so that those can be substituted in some way that feels satisfying. Is there just simply no erotic safer pornography that we can watch? Do I not know about it? Am I aiding and abetting somehow by doing this? Every time I watch, at least once during the session, I have this thought: "I wonder if that's when HIV infection happened?" I know some of the stars are dead now.

It feels at times like a betrayal of the work I do as an HIV educator. I can share it with my closest friends, but it would be hard for me to admit in a work situation that this is true for me.

For me, visual pornography is very powerful. I know I have acted unsafely after looking at pornography. The unsafe behavior I might do is mostly oral sex: letting someone come in my mouth. The funny thing is that I don't even like it. It's very erotically charged for me, but the actual act I find pretty distasteful. It's not logical. Because the risk associated with oral sex isn't so clear, that's the boundary I play with. I haven't had unprotected anal sex in a long time; I think the last time was a few years ago.

In 1986 I took a part-time job in a sexually transmitted disease clinic in New Hampshire that was based in a feminist health center and had a clientele of gay men. Ostensibly I was hired to do STD counseling, but I got trained in HIV counseling and that's all I ever did there.

I didn't feel ready to get tested myself for a few years. The first time I got tested was in 1990. What I said to myself was what I told clients: I had a choice about whether to get tested, and I would make my decision based on my behavior and what I knew about HIV. I had had limited risk behavior at that point.

I don't know if not having been tested made me more neutral as a counselor. Maybe it did. I was not invested in having a client test unless the client wanted to. I was invested in the process for the client—education, learning, and making a decision—not so much the end result of the test. I felt that if I had the choice not to test, then so did everybody else.

I did disclose to some clients that I had not had the test. Some would challenge me. They would get angry: "How can you do this if you haven't had the test?" I sometimes disclosed why: "I have a lot of information, so I can make that decision based on my risk. So far I have not felt the need to test."

I would handle that differently now as a counselor. I wouldn't necessarily disclose information about myself, because I'm not sure the client needs to know whether I've tested to make the decision for himself. I would say, "The counseling session is about your decision to test, not about mine. Whether I've tested or not doesn't help you make your decision." I think the focus needs to be on the client's decision.

I had had a relationship of about three months with a man named Rusty who lived in Boston. When the relationship ended, we didn't see each other for a year and a half. I saw him at the beginning of the From All Walks of Life fund-raiser, and he had lost 40 pounds. It was clear that he was sick.

He told me he had AIDS. He had been diagnosed with pneumocystis pneumonia four months after we had broken up. I was very concerned about him. He was a person I loved very much. I had known the relationship couldn't work, but I always had a fondness for him, a special feeling. I also realized that I had put myself at risk with him. It wasn't substantial, but we had had anal sex with each other. I had penetrated him, he had penetrated me, without condoms. Neither of us had come inside each other, but some of the intercourse had been pretty rough, and I remembered him precumming a lot. Given what I know about HIV, he probably had virus in all his body fluids when we had sex. So I realized I was at risk to some degree.

Finding out that Rusty had AIDS was a difficult thing for me. I was not in great shape at work and actually asked to be excused from seeing clients for about two months. Because I was one of the only counselors who knew how to draw blood, I became a phlebotomist for a few months. I had a clinical supervisor, a nurse-psychologist, and was able to talk with her about the issues in my life in relation to the work I was doing. That was helpful. One of the things my clinical supervisor said to me was, "You're really at risk for being unsafe, because you are strongly identified with this fellow. One of the easiest ways for you to be like him is to be infected. I just want you to know that." She was very on-the-ball about that.

Like clockwork, I went out and started having unsafe sex. In July, I had anonymous sex with a man and let him fuck me without a condom. After he pulled out, I realized he had a lesion on his penis. I flipped out. I didn't know what the lesion was. I went to the doctor, got tested for syphilis and everything else. I didn't feel he had come inside me but didn't really know. It was scary. I realized afterwards, "My clinical supervisor was right." I was caught up in my emotions about the loss or potential loss of Rusty. My identification with Rusty was strong, and it was even worse because we couldn't be lovers. I was just sick about him being HIV-positive and having AIDS. I hated it, and all the pathology came down. It wasn't conscious at all. It felt beyond my control.

I got tested in August because it was so in-my-face. I felt, "This is a reason, I guess, to finally do this." I went to a counselor I knew and respected a lot. He had trained me. I knew he was HIV-positive and that he knew Rusty. I went to him because of the familiarity. I tested negative. It wasn't inclusive of the unsafe episode in July, but it answered the questions about Rusty.

When I got a negative result back, I didn't tell anybody for a while. It wasn't like, "Oh boy, I'm negative!" It was more like, "This is an awful process." I wasn't necessarily happy, because I was aware that other people went through the process and got other news. I felt it was a grave process. It's grave whatever your result is. Part of the gravity for me was understanding that I could have heard something different. It gave me more compassion for all of us, whatever the results of our tests. That is part of the responsibility of being negative: to not think of yourself as Other, to see the commonalities along the way. The process of being at risk, and finding out about that, is a brotherhood in itself, regardless of your antibody status. Recognizing that gravity lessened the apartheid between HIV-positive and HIV-negative people for me. I don't feel so separate from HIV-positive men.

Giving someone a positive result years ago, I spent a long time with the client in a posttest counseling session, sometimes with the client's partner present, and tried to help them manage what was happening. There wasn't a lot we could do for people in 1986 and 1987 in terms of treatment, so a lot of it was psychosocial support. People who were testing positive—mostly gay men—felt very alone. This was in New Hampshire. It took us about a year to develop a support group for people who were positive.

I'm working now in Boston, where there are a lot more people testing positive. When we see gay men testing positive now, sometimes there's no reaction emotionally at all. It seems they've expected it. They know a lot of people who are positive. They feel there is something they can do, and they want to start right away. On the surface, it seems like less of a crisis. They might cry at home, they might grieve by themselves, but there is a matter-of-factness about it that is shocking. I never thought I'd see this, but counselors now report almost-routine positives.

We used to see negative results as routine. We used to treat them so. They were usually pretty quick; we felt we didn't have to spend much time. My philosophy about that has changed over the past couple of years, partly through the HIV-Negative Support Group, and partly from the literature being published around these issues. Now when I train people, I tell them that a negative result is never routine. I have a protocol for giving clients a negative test result.

First of all, we normalize the clients' reactions about the result, whatever they are. We don't assume clients are going to be overjoyed. If their partner is positive, if their best friend just died, if they lost a lover a year ago, we're not going to assume they are going to be happy about this.

It's important to check out whether clients believe the results. I think we sometimes assume that because the results are negative, and because that's "good news," clients will believe the test was right. So we check that out with them.

We discuss the result within the context of their lives. If something significant has happened in relation to HIV infection in a client's life, the test result is going to be seen in that context. I remember one man who tested because his brother was diagnosed with AIDS. He didn't know what to do about it. He knew he wasn't at risk. He needed somebody to talk to about that event in his life. He got some risk-reduction information along the way, but his need was to sort out—with somebody he could trust—what to do. That was the context of the HIV test for him.

When I teach people about counseling and testing, we brainstorm a list of 20 or 30 reasons why people test, and most of them are pretty good. They are all reasons that people really bring in: from domestic violence to a new relationship. The list can be pretty long.

I see gay and bisexual men testing to get support around being safe. They often see it as a time when they can check in with somebody about behaviors and ask one more time about what they're worried about. The test may not be the most important piece. Having someone to talk to is. If somebody is reaching out for help, and the test isn't exactly the focus, that's not a problem for me. For the Centers for Disease Control, in terms of funding, that's a problem. But for me as a counselor and supervisor, it's not a problem.

૬

What we try to provide at the hospital HIV-test site I manage is a place where people are not going to be judged about their behaviors. We try to not slap people on the hands and not make them feel bad about themselves. We try to find out what successes they're having and build on that.

I was sitting with a client yesterday. He referred to himself a couple of times as "stupid" because he hadn't been practicing safer sex. Every time he said it, I stopped him and said, "Don't beat yourself up. You're not being stupid. Education doesn't equal behavior change." He needed to hear that many times. He feels he's "too stupid" to practice safer sex, he's "too stupid" to use a condom. Part of the intervention was to get him to see that it was not about being stupid or smart; it was about learning some facts about condoms, understanding that it was a process, and building on the successes he had.

I think it's the same as using fear to scare adolescents about AIDS: fear and shame only raise anxiety, lower self-esteem, and lead to acting out. If people don't feel good about themselves and are shamed by somebody in the community and feel even lousier, what happens is they act out unsafely. You usually do things that make you feel worse. That worries me. I don't think fear and shame work. They've never worked for me. The reality is that the times when I am able to make better decisions come from *not* feeling punished.

We say to clients that if they take semen into any part of their body, either the mouth, vagina, or rectum, they are at risk for infection. But they are the people who decide what their line is. We can't be the safe-sex police. We can't make people do anything differently by wanting them to. The only thing that is really unacceptable for me is if the behavior isn't consensual.

Sometimes clients will say, "My partner wanted me to be unsafe," or, "My partner asked me not to use a condom and I couldn't say no." Often it's with the steady partner where there is a breakdown. The same man might have anonymous sex with many different partners and be safe every time with those men, but with the steady partner can't say no, can't negotiate that.

There are all kinds of norms. Some people believe it's not safe to have somebody penetrate you wearing a condom and come while they are inside you: you always withdraw, even with a condom. That isn't the norm for other people. I would want to hear what the client felt was safe. I would want the client to tell me what was important to him about the kind of sex he was having.

I don't think you can talk about safer sex without finding the meaning of sex for somebody. If the client says, "I'm not going to use a condom for anal sex, even though I know my partner is positive, and I'm still worried about being infected," the person knows what could happen. The only thing to do is to find out why that person is doing that. What does it mean to that person?

This happens a lot with mixed-status couples: they have intermittent unsafe sex. One thing a counselor can do is to ask, "What's going on when you're unsafe? What are the conditions? What are the feelings? Is it after an argument? What does it have to do with the availability of things to use?"

Unsafe sex might be the only way a person knows how to tell his partner that he loves him: it's an expression of love. For lack of being able to verbalize feelings, people act unsafely, because that seems to be a more profound verbalization. Sometimes people need help figuring out how to say what they want, how to say what they need, and to understand that they don't have to be unsafe. That's longer-term work than just HIV counseling can do, but the HIV counselor can certainly be the person who illuminates that issue for the client. It might be the first time the client hears it spoken about like that. You might be able to get that person to work with a therapist to learn how to express love in ways that are less unsafe.

§.

Sometimes I feel the struggle is how to be a sexual gay man. It's that basic. And if you've tested HIV-negative, it seems more loaded to me: there's more to lose. It's hard for me to know what to do because I don't have a regular partner. What do I do with my sexuality? What do I do with my need to be close to people? Does being gay mean that we have a different kind of sexuality, a different kind of focus on relationships than straight people? I don't know the answer to that. It's compounded by HIV. HIV is just one more thing to worry about.

My professional self is pretty secure, but my gay male identity is not as secure, is subject to everything every other gay man is subject to. The combination feels interesting. I struggle with my own repression around sex. I am not always positive about being sexual. Even though people assume I'm pretty liberal, pretty free, and pretty comfortable—because I can talk about sex in a very positive, nonjudgmental way—I'm not comfortable about sex.

Why I like hearing Eric Rofes speak is that he seems to be comfortable with his sexuality. He talks about it in relation to his struggles. It's very easy to see him as a sexual man. It's right up there on stage when I hear him talk. I respect that. I would feel good working with clients if people had a clear view of me as a sexual person, in an appropriate way. A counselor's sexuality should not be part of the session, but if you're comfortable with yourself, it comes through. At times I am comfortable with myself and it probably does come through. At other times I might be separated from it.

I sometimes go to rest areas or other places to cruise, and I run into HIV-test clients there. I handle it by acting matter-of-fact: "Hi. How are you doing? It's okay that we've met here. It's not a problem for me." I'm not sure that it isn't a problem for me in some ways. I think, "What am I going to do? Do I have a right to a sexual identity? Do I have a right to cruise—to have anonymous sex—being a health-care worker?" I would probably go to some lengths to avoid that situation, not wanting clients to see me at a place where risks are taken. Certainly it's possible to have safer sex at those places, but I think some risk is inherent in having anonymous sex there. I've watched people having unsafe sex. I wonder, "What's my responsibility here? Should I be handing out condoms? Should I stop people?"

In the absence of a partner, I've really been looking for some way to be sexual that feels safe and connected to people. But it's been hard for me to make room for that. I did a Body Electric weekend last April and I'm going to do another one in October. It involves erotic massage. You're essentially taught how to have a full-body orgasm without ejaculation. You're in contact with many different men. It's very heart-centered and very orgasmic. In a way, it feels like the antidote to some of the struggles I've had.

⁊●

I don't think the answers are easy. I worry about people continuing to operate with the belief that if you have information about HIV prevention, you're all set, when there's absolutely no evidence that that's true and a lot of evidence to the contrary. It's always hard to work with people long term around changing behavior.

The lie is that everybody is practicing safer sex. That's the lie we have lived with in the gay community. It's simply not true, and the thing that worries me is that people don't know where to go to get help. I don't like community norms that feed into people feeling bad about themselves, not being able to talk about what is really bothering them.

There isn't enough sensitivity in the gay community to people's struggle with being safe. There aren't many places where a person can be honest and not be judged. Often people feel judged by their peers, and then they close up and are not likely to open up again. I don't know how to build maintenance and support for longer-term behavior change into a community.

Just about every gay male friend has told me that they have had at least one episode of unsafe oral sex within the last year. These are guys that know a lot about HIV. If that's so, then in any group of gay men, a lot have been unsafe within the last year, but very few are willing to talk.

There needs to be a different format for AIDS education. It should not be huge halls filled with gay men. In a large group, it's hard for people to feel safe. I don't think it feels safe for people to share something that they feel would be judged, or forbidden, or taboo. I'm hoping that in smaller groups, people will feel safer. Even the HIV-Negative Support Group is too big at times for people to feel they can really share some of the things that are going on for them. There needs to be a sense of confidentiality so people can disclose difficult stuff.

§a

One of the myths about HIV is that people who do this work always practice safer sex, always do everything right, and don't struggle with these issues as much as anybody else. I've had to allow myself to be human and not beat myself up about my own struggles. I hope I don't talk to clients or teach people in such a way that I convey having it all together. When I say to somebody, "Behavior change is a struggle and it takes time," I'm really cutting myself slack. That doesn't invalidate my work.

That whole thing of "practicing what you preach" is probably the rawest form of conflict. I worry that if others knew I was not always practicing safer sex, it would invalidate my work or invalidate me.

A couple of times, a gay colleague has admitted that he and his partner have unprotected sex. They've been together for years. The only contact my colleague has had outside the relationship has been absolutely safe. It was an admission: he was sort of confessing to me that they weren't having safer sex. I found myself thinking, "It's such a novel idea. I wonder what that's like. To do that and not worry. To do that and have it be an expression of the relationship." It's been so long since I've been in a relationship of duration, I haven't experienced that myself: having a partner and being able to make that decision about unprotected sex.

Gay couples are under a microscope in terms of what they do and what they don't do. It's almost like the only way to be good and gay now is to practice safer sex. If we're practicing safer sex, that somehow redeems our sexuality. Somehow we're supposed to do this without questioning it.

§a

A psychologist said something to me once about the belief that if you do this work, you'll be spared. I think many people, including me, still operate from that principle: because I am essential to the fight—which is bullshit—somehow I will be spared. I know it's not true logically, but I operate from such principles. It's like insurance against becoming infected myself.

I still find myself assuming that people who do AIDS work are HIV-negative, that somehow they—if anybody—should know how to protect themselves. I should know better. Seroconversion could happen to me. It's very clear to me that it could happen.

I've thought about what it would feel like to seroconvert, in relation to my work. I think it would be very difficult for me to worry about judgment: it's the supreme failure as a health educator, in some ways. It's also at the same time a real admission of how hard the struggle is.

When I'm teaching providers HIV counseling, I have an HIV-positive speaker come in to talk. I don't want people to leave the course without some sense of what it feels like or means to test positive for HIV. I thought about what it would mean to teach my course knowing I was HIV-positive. One of the questions I asked myself was, "Would that give me more validity? Would I have more credibility?" I don't know the answer. I don't want to become positive to prove the point.

It's been a while since I've tested. I've had risky sex since then, so I don't know what my status is. But I often think of myself as negative. My last antibody test is a part of my identity. I think my work is tied to that identity. I don't think it's dependent on it, but I think it's tied to it.

I think it's important to talk about an HIV-negative identity, as long as it's not at the expense of the connections we have with HIV-positive people. Whether I'm HIV-positive or HIV-negative as I continue to do this work, I'm still *me* doing this work, with my sensibilities and my values. That's what's really important, not what my antibody status is.

Maybe there are parallel conditions for people who are infected or not infected that we are not seeing. Some agencies offer services to everyone affected by HIV. They don't separate people into groups by HIV status during their workshops. It's hard to pay attention to common needs if there are polarized needs. HIV-negative people have some needs that are different from HIV-positive people's, but maybe they're not as divergent as we think.

I struggle with staying HIV-negative. That's part of the mission of the HIV-Negative Support Group, and that's partly what we do in posttest counseling sessions with clients who test negative.

Where does wanting to stay negative come from? Does it come from loving yourself? Or does it come from being afraid of HIV? Maybe that is the issue for me personally: it's about fear and my conflicts about sex, not about loving myself and saying, "I deserve to be happy sexually and to be free of infections."

What are you willing to do to stay negative? For some people, that can involve being absolutely crazy, to the point where you're obsessing about it night and day, as some people in the HIV-Negative Support Group seem to do. The way they operate is to not get infected at any cost. I have to fight against wanting to judge men who are paranoid about getting infected and who will do anything to avoid it.

A person getting infected is not the ultimate tragedy. There are many things that are more grievous losses than your antibody status. There are bigger things in life to lose than your HIV negativity: your integrity, your sense of compassion. Part of the trick here is to keep HIV in perspective.

What I'm imagining is this Faustian bargain, where you bargain that you'll never get HIV, but you lose your soul in the process. That's the struggle, to not let that happen. One of the questions you asked is what this book could do: it's somehow to prevent people from becoming zombies.

The gay male community is being ravaged by the epidemic, and there are plenty of people who would like to see us all dead. One way to respond is this: "Love your community enough to feel good about yourselves." In a sense, the survival is in that. If we can't get in touch with the goodness in ourselves, what we end up doing is effecting our own Final Solution. That's real. I don't think that's abstract.

HIV-negative people need to talk about and deal with this, because they are dealing with something they could lose at any moment. Each time you have sex, you are dealing again with the possibility, so there's incredible stress in terms of living with that potential loss. That's not recognized. We focus on the completed loss, not the potential loss. The completed loss of HIV-negative status clearly has terrible stressors involved. But the potential loss does too.

Men are afraid to talk about their HIV-negative status. We've had a lot of descriptions about the lives of people who are positive. I think there is a responsibility for HIV-negative men to talk about the complexity of what it feels like to be HIV-negative, and to articulate it. That's why I'm grateful for the HIV-Negative Support Group, and this book, and the work that Eric Rofes and Walt Odets are doing. We're starting to describe it. It needs to be described. It takes a kind of courage, because people may not want to hear it.

છે.

We have a mistaken notion that survivors are not traumatized. We know that's not true. We know that people need to be taken care of if they've been traumatized. If you admit that survivors are traumatized by the experience of survival, they need care. Survivors of concentration camps were scarred in some very profound ways. You couldn't turn back the clock.

We don't often connect survival with transformation. We connect it with escaping from things. We escape the infection. We escape the concentration camp. But it *is* about transformation. When I train HIV-test counselors, I talk about the psychological aspects of testing positive, what that means in terms of identity change. Transformation probably happens as much for people who are negative. I don't think we talk enough about the subtle identity changes that people who are negative go through.

I hope my definition of survival gets more complex, because oftentimes I do it a disservice. Often when we think of the word "survivor," we think of it as being "successful," or we think of it as meaning "unscathed." That's unrealistic. I can't identify with it when I think about it that way. I *can* identify with surviving with marks, surviving as a changed person because of the experience.

23

"Fog," "Faith," and "Atlantis"

Mark Doty

FOG

The crested iris by the front gate waves
its blue flags three days, exactly,

then they vanish. The peony buds'
tight wrappings are edged crimson;

when they open, a little blood-color
will ruffle at the heart of the flounced,

unbelievable white. Three weeks after the test,
the vial filled from the crook

of my elbow, I'm seeing blood everywhere:
a casual nick from the garden shears,

a shaving cut and I feel the physical rush
of the welling up, the wine-fountain

dark as Siberian iris. The thin green porcelain
teacup, our homemade Ouija's planchette,

rocks and wobbles every night, spins
and spells. It seems a cloud of spirits

numerous as lilac panicles vie for occupancy—
children grabbing for the telephone,

happy to talk to someone who isn't dead yet?
Everyone wants to speak at once, or at least

these random words appear, incongruous
and exactly spelled: *energy, immunity, kiss.*

Then: *M. has immunity. W. has.*
And that was all. One character, Frank,

distinguishes himself: a boy who lived
in our house in the thirties, loved dogs

and gangster movies, longs for a body,
says he can watch us through the television,

asks us to stand before the screen
and kiss. *God in garden,* he says.

Sitting out on the back porch at twilight,
I'm almost convinced. In this geometry

of paths and raised beds, the green shadows
of delphinium, there's an unseen rustling:

some secret amplitude
seems to open in this orderly space.

Maybe because it contains so much dying,
all these tulip petals thinning

at the base until any wind takes them.
I doubt anyone else would see that, looking in,

and then I realize my garden has no outside, only *is*
subjectively. As blood is utterly without

an outside, can't be seen except out of context,
the wrong color in alien air, no longer itself.

Though it submits to test, two,
to be exact, each done three times,

though not for me, since at their first entry
into my disembodied blood

there was nothing at home there.
For you they entered the blood garden over

and over, like knocking at a door
because you know someone's home. Three times

the Elisa Test, three the Western Blot,
and then the incoherent message. We're

the public health care worker's
nine o'clock appointment,

she is a phantom hand who forms
the letters of your name, and the word

that begins with *P.* I'd lie out
and wait for the god if it weren't

so cold, the blue moon huge
and disruptive above the flowering crab's

foaming collapse. The spirits say *Fog*
when they can't speak clearly

and the letters collide; sometimes
for them there's nothing outside the mist

of their dying. Planchette,
peony, I would think of anything

not to say the word. Maybe the blood
in the flower is a god's. Kiss me,

in front of the screen, please,
the dead are watching.

They haven't had enough yet.
Every new bloom is falling apart.

I would say anything else
in the world, any other word.

FAITH

  "I've been having these
awful dreams, each a little different,
though the core's the same—

we're walking in a field,
Wally and Arden and I, a stretch of grass
with a highway running beside it,

or a path in the woods that opens
onto a road. Everything's fine,
then the dog sprints ahead of us,

excited; we're calling but
he's racing down a scent and doesn't hear us,
and that's when he goes

onto the highway. I don't want to describe it.
Sometimes it's brutal and over,
and others he's struck and takes off

so we don't know where he is
or how bad. This wakes me
every night now, and I stay awake;

I'm afraid if I sleep I'll go back
into the dream. It's been six months,
almost exactly, since the doctor wrote

not even a real word
but an acronym, a vacant
four-letter cipher

that draws meanings into itself,
reconstitutes the world.
We tried to say it was just

a word; we tried to admit
it had power and thus to nullify it
by means of our acknowledgement.

Oh I know the current wisdom:
bright hope, the power of wishing you're well.
He's just so tired, though nothing

shows in any tests, Nothing,
the doctor says, detectable;
the doctor doesn't hear what I do,

that trickling, steadily rising nothing
that makes him sleep all day,
vanish into fever's tranced afternoons,

and I swear sometimes
when I put my head to his chest
I can hear the virus humming

like a refrigerator.
Which is what makes me think
you can take your positive attitude

and go straight to hell.
We don't have a future,
we have a dog.
                    Who is he?

Soul without speech,
sheer, tireless faith,
he is that-which-goes-forward,

black muzzle, black paws
scouting what's ahead;
he is where we'll be hit first,

he's the part of us
that's going to get it.
I'm hardly awake on our morning walk

—always just me and Arden now—
and sometimes I am still
in the thrall of the dream,

which is why, when he took a step onto Commercial
before I'd looked both ways,
I screamed his name and grabbed his collar.

And there I was on my knees,
both arms around his neck
and nothing coming,

and when I looked into that bewildered face
I realized I didn't know what it was
I was shouting at,

I didn't know who I was trying to protect."

ATLANTIS

I thought your illness a kind of solvent
dissolving the future a little at a time;

I didn't understand what's to come
was always just a glimmer

up ahead, veiled like the marsh
gone under its tidal sheet

of mildly rippling aluminum.
What these salt distances were

is also where they're going:
from blankly silvered span

toward specificity: the curve
of certain brave islands of grass,

temporary shoulder-wide rivers
where herons ply their twin trades

of study and desire. I've seen
two white emissaries rise

and unfold like heaven's linen, untouched,
enormous, a fluid exhalation. Early spring,

too cold yet for green, too early
for the tumble and wrack of last season

to be anything but promise,
but there in the air was white tulip,

marvel, triumph of all flowering, the soul
lifted up, if we could still believe

in the soul, after so much diminishment . . .
Breath, from the unpromising waters,

up, across the pond and the two lane highway,
pure purpose, over the dune,

gone. Tomorrow's unreadable
as this shining acreage;

the future's nothing
but this moment's gleaming rim.

Now the tide's begun
its clockwork turn, pouring,

in the day's hourglass,
toward the other side of the world,

and our dependable marsh reappears
—emptied of that starched and angular grace

that spirited the ether, lessened,
but here. And our ongoingness,

what there'll be of us? Look,
love, the lost world

rising from the waters again:
our continent, where it always was,

emerging from the half-light,
unforgettable, drenched, unchanged.

CONCLUSION

Looking to the Future

I was 23 years old when I told my father I might not live another five years. We were seated in armchairs 15 feet apart in my parents' formal living room. I had just returned from a year traveling in Europe after graduating from college in 1985. My Grand Tour was supposed to have opened my eyes to the limitless horizons of a young man fresh out of college. Instead, as I discussed career plans with my father, I spoke of the difficulty of planning a future when the presence of AIDS left me uncertain how long I might live. I had not yet taken an HIV test.

Across the room my father sat baffled and fearful. Why was I afraid I wouldn't live another five years? Had I done something unsafe? Was I infected with the AIDS virus? I told him that I had little reason to think I was infected, but that since I did not know, I had to assume I might be. One consequence of this assumption was an inability to plan for the future. Years of pretending or assuming I might be infected had taken their toll. It became clear to us both at that moment how profoundly AIDS had affected me. A son in his early twenties was speaking like a man in his eighties.

Before HIV testing existed, the fear of already being infected kept many gay men like me occupied with the present rather than the future. Now that HIV testing exists, the HIV-negative are offered some solace in learning that they are uninfected, but the possibility of becoming infected in the future looms large and sometimes seems inevitable. Envisioning the future is something that should occupy HIV-negative men but often does not.

CONTEMPLATING FEWTOPIA

Contemplating a future in which many of our friends and lovers will be gone—a "fewtopia"—is a bleak prospect. David, 35, who in chapter 9 compared being HIV-negative to being in a spinning aircraft, used another image to express his despair when thinking about the future:

> I want to use the analogy of being in the eye of a hurricane, walking towards it. I can see the violence of the storm, still increasing, and wonder what will be left of the fields out there, of the towns, of the friends. Will the hurricane leave any seeds in the fields after it tears out the plants? Will it leave pieces of wood that we can rebuild with? Will it leave any friends, or will even the places they are buried be hidden?
>
> I cannot answer what being gay in those future times will be like, but I can answer what it is like to be gay today: it is to see the shadows of death color everything one loves, to take a last loving glance at the bars and the streets every time one is there, and toast to the friends and the neighborhoods, before the storm descends in earnest.

This kind of grim thinking is sometimes shared by the HIV-positive, who in perverse moments voice thanks that they will probably not live to see such a diminished future. In an essay about the psychological toll of AIDS on uninfected gay and bisexual men, Walt Odets quotes a 23-year-old HIV-positive gay man: "I'm sometimes glad to think that in ten years I'll be dead. By then the only gay people left will be those whose lives were ruined by watching the rest of us die."[1]

Feeling that life is not worth living and that there is no future worth looking forward to is natural when one has been widowed. Such feelings pass with time, when mourning has done its work. What HIV-negative gay men face now, however, is a kind of continuous and unremitting grief. Not content with one sweep through us—causing one great round of loss—HIV seems intent on plaguing us without end, and its cussedness in foiling our attempts to fight it is daunting. We see people dying now and more people becoming infected. We call it the "second wave" or "third wave" of infection, but in the end all it points to is more loss and more grief.

I am not surprised that some men question whether remaining uninfected is important. Having lost much and facing future losses, who is to be so presumptuous as to say that "life is really worth living after all"? Indeed, there is something about the consistency of life in a plague that makes a future that is livable and desirable seem distant indeed.

LIVING IN THE PRESENT

Envisioning a future is particularly difficult for people living with partners who are HIV-infected. Cathy, 27, a social-work graduate student whose partner Louie has AIDS, told me that she focuses on living in the present:

> Louie's in A.A., so he's got a mindset of "one day at a time," which I have found very difficult to adjust to. He used to ride a motorcycle across country saying, "We'll stop where we stop." He was always like that. In his mind there's a way to think about the future without planning. I'm learning a little. I still don't quite get it.
>
> Louie will say things like, "I'm going to be there to see you graduate," which is at least three years away. I don't even think about my graduation. It's too far. I don't keep the appointment book that I used to. It's more important for me to stay home and watch TV with Louie at night than to go to a lecture on HIV vaccines, which a year ago I would have gone to. My priorities are different. I try not to plan things too far in advance.

Cathy thinks in terms of the rest of Louie's life as opposed to the rest of her life. "What am I going to do for the rest of my life?"

she mused. "I have no concept. What am I going to do for the rest of his life? That's easier. I know what I'm going to do. I want to be with him."

NOT WANTING TO CELEBRATE

Some men told me their difficulty in looking toward the future came from not wanting to celebrate life, as if doing so would somehow dishonor those who have died or offend the HIV-positive who are faced with life-threatening illness.

Randy, a 31-year-old social worker, talked with me about his decision to become a parent, something that had been a lifelong goal of his. After months of discussion with his partner and a woman interested in coparenting, Randy decided to become a father. He was expecting a child when I interviewed him:

> I think the most interesting thing to say about parenting in the age of AIDS is that it's something I've wanted to be really quiet about. I feel social awkwardness about it, especially around HIV-positive people for whom becoming a biological parent is not an option.
>
> It came up last night after I went to the movies. On the way out, I fell in stride with two people I know who are HIV-infected. Then behind us came a friend whose lover is positive. It was beginning to be overwhelming for me, at the end of a long day when I wanted a night away.
>
> When we got to the end of the sidewalk where we were going to part, one of the three men said, "Oh, so congratulations on your baby!" One of the other two knew, but I had told him not to tell people. He said, "Oh, well, I guess the secret's out." I said, "Yeah." The third guy, who was pretty sick, had a real strong reaction to it. His explicit reaction was not about AIDS at all, but the tone was bitter: "Well, I hope you know the people really well." Would the reaction have been so strong were he not facing the end of his life right now?
>
> If I were a straight man, I think his reaction might have

been, "Big fucking deal. You're having a baby. That's so unconnected to my life." I've found talking about becoming a father much more difficult as a gay man, partly because it's predicated on "negative" sperm.

I feel also that it's about wanting to have a private celebration rather than a public one. I don't want to celebrate during the age of AIDS. That's what it's really about. That is the profound thing here. It's really a hard time to do that, for me.

One of the greatest challenges facing HIV-negative gay men these days is to find a way to celebrate their futures and build lives worth living, without feeling that by doing so they are abandoning the HIV-positive. To embrace life is not to dishonor those who have died or give affront to those who are ill.

ENVISIONING THE FUTURE

A negative HIV test can be an opportunity to reframe one's attitudes toward the future. Edward, 39, described how his reluctance to plan for the future changed when he tested negative:

It took a fair amount of time for me to figure out that I had not been planning ahead, that I had taken my sights of the future and brought them close in, to within two or three years, and was not thinking about anything further than that.

All of a sudden the realization came down on me that I had a life to live. It was like a fog lifted: "You have to start thinking about getting old. That could possibly happen." Retirement issues used to be something that would just go right over my head, because who was thinking about retirement? I wasn't able to plan until I realized that there was this enormous possibility opening up.

Austin, 36, told me that he had gotten tested partly to learn whether he should go ahead with some of his lifelong plans. "If the test was negative," he said, "I was going to proceed with the things I had been dreaming of for a long time, liking buying some land. If I was positive, I wouldn't go through with that. I wouldn't be around long enough to get through all the hassles." When he tested negative, he found that he could fulfill some of his dreams, but at a cost to a friendship:

> I experienced a transition in my relationship with a friend who was diagnosed with AIDS. The transition came when I realized that my life was going to go on and he was going to die. I was in the process of buying some land, and I brought it up in a conversation with him and his parents. We were talking in a restaurant about what I was going to do with this land in Maine, how I was going to build a cabin and all this stuff.
>
> After that, when we were alone, I said to him, "I just need to know how you feel about that." He was very sick. He said, "I really can't talk about it." And I realized that there were some things that I couldn't talk about with him, because I was planning for a future and he was planning for how long he was going to live, and it wasn't going to be much longer.

Although Austin was sad that he could not share some of his dreams about the future with his friend, he has not abandoned dreaming. "I am still able to have my goals and my dreams, and talk about them with different people," he said. "Some people can talk about it and some people can't. It depends on their perspective. I have a friend who is very sick right now but is interested in what I'm doing with my house and wants to come visit."

ACCOMMODATING THE VIRUS

Looking at the narrative chapters in this book, one reader responded by asking me, "Am I supposed to be proud of these people because they can talk about their problems?" He implied that many of them had not been very successful in resolving their anxieties and issues about being HIV-negative.

When I hear people call for "resolution" of difficult issues, I remember what I have learned by reading about trauma and chronic illness, and I switch the conversation to how people can "accommodate" their anxieties. Accommodation, not resolution, seems to me a more fruitful avenue. I don't expect anything more than that.

What does it mean to accommodate HIV? For me, accommodating the virus means accepting the epidemic as a lifelong event in my life. Accommodating the virus means not nurturing unrealistic hopes of medical advances. Accommodating the virus means acknowledging that seroconversion among gay men will continue and is a possibility in my own life. Accommodating the virus means recasting my concept of life expectancy, perhaps even redefining—I am 32 now—what it means to be "middle-aged."

When I think about the future of gay men, I am optimistic about our ability to face the challenge that AIDS poses. We can find ways to accommodate the virus without actually harboring it in our own bodies. We can find ways to incorporate our losses without letting them destroy us. We can allow ourselves to experience the despair that AIDS engenders in us without letting that despair rule us. And perhaps we can even take our uncertainty about the future and turn it to our advantage.

THE WAY WE LIVE NOW

In 1986 Susan Sontag published a story in the *New Yorker* called "The Way We Live Now."[2] In this fictional account, Sontag presents a near-complete alphabet of friends and lovers—from Aileen to Zack—who recount the ways in which they have been profoundly changed by the unnamed life-threatening illness of an unnamed central character. When I read the story, I imagined the emphasis in the title resting on the penultimate word—"The Way We *Live* Now"—because the story speaks to me about how our lives have been affected by AIDS, even when we are not ourselves infected with HIV.

Meditating on the uncertainty of the future has made me wonder if another reading of Sontag's title is possible, one which puts the emphasis on the last word: "The Way We Live *Now*." AIDS forces us to confront our mortality, to recognize the uncertainty of the future, and to live in the present. AIDS has changed the way we live the now.

"AIDS has challenged me to look at things I was taking for granted," said Todd, a 26-year-old pianist. "It has made me realize I'm not immortal. I may not have the rest of my life to accomplish the things I've set out to do. Indeed, what does 'the rest of my life' mean? AIDS has made me focus on the fact that all we really have is right now." This understanding has fueled Todd's creative output as a composer. "I used to be one of those people who said, 'When I learn enough counterpoint, I'll write an orchestral piece,'" he told me. "That's bullshit. I'm writing an orchestral piece now."

Starting an HIV-Negative Support Group

THIS MATERIAL PROVIDES an overview of how a peer-led support group was formed for HIV-negative gay and bisexual men in Boston in 1991. I hope you can use our group as a model for creating a support group in your own community.

ORIGINS

The Boston HIV-Negative Support Group was founded in March 1991 by Jim Brinning, Gay Male Health Educator at the AIDS Action Committee of Massachusetts, with the assistance of Robb Johnson, Coordinator of the Living Well Series at the Fenway Community Health Center of Boston.

Brinning was alarmed to find that men who had once tested HIV-negative were subsequently testing HIV-positive. Johnson recognized that providing workshops and support for the infected did not address the whole epidemic. Together they felt it was important to target educational efforts specifically toward HIV-negative gay and bisexual men, to offer them support in adopting and maintaining behaviors that help them stay HIV-negative.

MISSION

After a few successful meetings had taken place, those who were interested in formalizing the support group gathered to hammer out a mission statement that reflects the purpose of the group:

The Boston HIV-Negative Support Group provides a forum in our community in crisis for HIV-negative gay and bisexual men to receive educational and social support. Educational support to encourage informed decision-making will include discussions about HIV transmission, safer sex, and testing. Social support will include peer-led explorations of the social and emotional issues that arise from knowing one's HIV-negative status.

Our mission statement mentions both educational and social support because we feel each component is insufficient alone. Social support without education does not allow us to make informed choices about safer behavior. Education without social support can likewise fail, offering us information but no opportunity to discuss how to implement it in our lives.

PARTICIPANTS

People participate in the support group for a variety of reasons. Some have just been tested and are curious to hear about others' experiences. Others are considering retesting. Some are single and wondering how to date or have sex as HIV-negative men. Others are in relationships, sometimes with HIV-positive partners. Some are grieving the loss of friends and lovers to AIDS. Most participants are from Boston, but some come from suburbs, and others come from as far away as Cape Cod, New Hampshire, and Rhode Island.

Here is what some participants said about why they participate:

I find in some mixed groups, as soon as HIV-positive men find out you are HIV-negative a wall goes up; they back off, stop talking. I guess there is a feeling that the safety of the situation goes away. You find that a difference of serostatus does make a difference.

When I am in groups that include HIV-positive men, I sometimes feel I have to withhold comments or questions that might be offensive to people with HIV.

The level of urgency, emotional intensity in groups with HIV-positive men can sometimes be overshadowing. Any issues that HIV-negative men have take a back seat, are not as significant.

I like the feeling that I am not isolated. I sometimes feel like everyone in the gay community is infected or dying, and I need to know that others like me are learning to survive.

I want to hear about safer sex from other HIV-negative men, because they are in the same position as I am. To hear about safer sex from an HIV-positive man, while welcome, may not seem applicable to me. I understand the motivation of an HIV-positive man to help me avoid becoming HIV-positive, but I still prefer to speak with others who are negative and struggling with my issues.

Seroconversion is a major concern of mine. I find the support group helpful as a point of identification and support.

FORMAT

The free drop-in group meets from 7 to 9 P.M. on the third Thursday of every month. Attendance has fluctuated between 20 and 40. New participants are always welcome, and there is no fee.

During 1991 our meetings took place at a church in Copley Square, Boston. The AIDS Action Committee made donations to the church for the use of the space. Since 1992 the meetings have been held at the new facilities of the Fenway Community Health Center.

There are two kinds of meetings. The first is a general discussion. The group divides into smaller groups for informal discussions led by volunteer facilitators. Groups of six to eight seem to work best. After about an hour and three quarters, these small groups reconvene to spend 15 minutes summarizing the issues that were raised. Frequently this leads to further discussion.

The other kind of meeting begins with an opening presentation by a speaker or panel on a specific topic. These presentations are usually brief, lasting between 20 and 40 minutes. The rest of the meeting is spent in small discussion groups, which may begin by responding to the presentation topic if they wish.

These two meeting structures reflect the two-fold approach implicit in our mission statement. The general discussions embody social support, and the presentations embody educational support. In practice, there is often little distinction between what is "social support" and what is "educational support." In the past we strictly alternated the two kinds of meetings. Recently we have planned more discussion topics, and we hope to keep them limited to the first half hour, to allow ample time for small-group discussion.

ORGANIZATION

A steering committee of half a dozen volunteers organizes the meetings. The steering committee meets every few months, usually for an hour before a monthly meeting. The steering committee reviews the evaluations that have been handed in by participants and discusses suggestions for future meeting topics. When planning future meetings, the steering committee members assign one person to coordinate each meeting. Coordinators are responsible for obtaining speakers if a discussion topic requires it. They also make sure there are enough small-group facilitators available and help run the meeting.

Steering committee members often volunteer to facilitate the small-group discussions. One responsibility of the facilitator of small groups is to ensure that basic ground rules are followed.

GROUND RULES

In order to help the meetings run smoothly, we have implemented a few ground rules that we state at the outset of each meeting. These ground rules will be familiar to anyone who has worked in group settings, such as encounter groups, therapy groups, or recovery groups.

First, what is discussed at the meetings is confidential. We encourage people to share what they have learned with others, but to do so in a way that doesn't identify any participant without his consent. Often people give first names only. This ground rule is intended to preserve people's privacy and to encourage them to be frank in discussions.

Second, we ask people to speak from their own experience and refrain from attacking others. The discussions often raise controversial issues. This ground rule encourages openness in sharing views and discourages people from harming each other. It is the responsibility of the small-group facilitator to see that no participant dominates the discussion or uses the forum as an opportunity to attack others.

DISCUSSION TOPICS

Meetings have included presentations and discussions on a range of topics. Appendix B contains open-ended discussion questions that we have used to encourage conversation in some of these areas:

- Grief and loss
- Dating in the 1990s
- How to use condoms
- Intimacy with and without sex
- Disclosing one's HIV status
- Relationships with HIV-positive men
- Dealing with diverse definitions of safer sex
- Developing relationships between men
- Can unprotected sex ever be safe?
- Self-esteem, substance use, and sex
- Repeated HIV-antibody testing

OBSTACLES

When the HIV-Negative Support Group was formed, we feared there would be some opposition from HIV-positive gay men. We feared they might ask, "Why would there be such a group? What could you possibly talk about?" How could we presume to have legitimate needs?

Here is how some participants addressed this concern:

> Some HIV-positive men see a group that is restricted to HIV-negative men as separatist, divisive, or elitist. I see it as a way for us to address our own issues, so that we are better able to be more inclusive. I feel stronger and better able to respond to my HIV-positive friends after I have been offered an opportunity to vent some emotions and feelings among HIV-negative men.

> I resent the fact that support groups for HIV-positive gay men are seen as natural and healthy, whereas support groups for HIV-negative gay men are seen as offensive, self-absorbed, or counterproductive.

> By having a place where I can exorcise some issues, I am more prepared to deal with my HIV-positive friends from a calm, interested perspective. I am less likely to worry about "bringing up" inappropriate issues with my HIV-positive friends, because some of these issues I can deal with in a different location.

> I think that HIV-negative men first have to identify their own issues before they can productively address them with their HIV-positive friends. We should recognize our anger, resentment, and despair so that we can move beyond it.

The group is meant to meet the needs of the HIV-negative so that we can be a part of our community, not set ourselves apart from it. We anticipated backlash from HIV-positive men, but such backlash has been reported only anecdotally.

One way that we have attempted to involve HIV-positive men is to invite them to participate in at least one meeting each year. For example, one meeting involved three positive-negative couples discussing their relationships. Another meeting presented a panel of speakers who had seroconverted.

Another obstacle we faced is that the drop-in nature of the group causes the discussions to lack continuity. Newcomers often have to unburden themselves of pressing issues that have already been handled by others who have been attending meetings regularly. Ongoing participants dislike having to explain their positions over and over. We are beginning to address this obstacle by dividing into small groups that accommodate those who are committed to attending regularly and those who are just "testing the waters." We call one the "ongoing" group and the other the "newcomers" group.

Recently, an additional response to the lack of continuity inherent in our drop-in group has been devised. A closed, time-limited group run by two professional HIV-test counselors is offered on a monthly basis at the Fenway Community Health Center. It consists of three two-hour sessions spread over three weeks. Based in structure on similar groups already in place for people who have found out they are HIV-positive, this new group is more directed and less freewheeling than the ongoing monthly support group.

Another obstacle we are just beginning to face is the complexity of the role of group facilitator. In the time-limited group, the facilitators are professionals, and their approach is more psychologically informed. In the monthly peer-led group, the facilitators are volunteers, often with little training, and sometimes preoccupied by their own needs for support. How much should they disclose about their own lives? Should they participate as equal members or take a more neutral role as conversational mediators? We are currently developing a training program for facilitators and exploring ways that volunteer facilitators can rotate out of that role to become participants on a regular basis. How this will influence later facilitation remains to be seen.

OUTREACH

The meetings are advertised in the local gay newspaper, as well as in the newsletters and telephone information of both sponsoring organizations: the AIDS Action Committee and the Fenway

Community Health Center. Fliers that list topics for the upcoming six meetings are posted and handed out to participants. Word-of-mouth advertising has brought many new participants.

Annual letters describing the mission of the group are sent to the HIV-test cites administered by the Department of Public Health in Massachusetts. Fliers to photocopy are included in these mailings.

We have also created a brochure that discusses issues that face people receiving an HIV-negative test. The brochure lists the discussion group as a resource and offers quotations from participants on a range of topics that confront HIV-negative gay and bisexual men. This brochure is available at HIV-test sites.

Having fliers and brochures available when people receive negative test results is useful for HIV-test counselors, especially when they see repeat testers who might benefit from more ongoing support than a posttest counseling session allows. Some of our recent participants have been referred from HIV-test sites in this way.

IMPACT

Here are some comments from participants about the usefulness of the group:

> A support group for HIV-negative men helps us realize that it's not inevitable to get HIV. It's not a train that's going to catch up to us and run us over.

> I find that participating in the support group has made it easier to reenter sexual relationships, to communicate more effectively about safer sex. After hearing the struggles and successes of other men, I am more prepared to negotiate safer sex.

> By speaking with other HIV-negative men and HIV-positive men who formerly tested negative, we learn to see what forces impel us to engage in unsafe behavior, and what obstacles block us from behaving in safer ways.

I find that participating in the support group has made it easier for me to get retested. I feel that I have a support system.

I appreciate the support I get from others in helping me stay HIV-negative. I like knowing that others support me in my decision to be healthy, and that I can learn from them. It is important for us to voice our decisions to stay uninfected. That is an important first step in safer behaviors.

Discussion Questions

FACILITATORS of the Boston HIV-Negative Support Group have used some of these open-ended questions to begin conversations.

DEALING WITH GRIEF AND LOSS

- What losses due to AIDS have you experienced, on a personal or community level?
- How is the way you feel about yourself affected after a significant part of your life is gone?
- What are some of the ways you've expressed grief?
- What might be signs of unresolved grief?
- Some grief counselors talk about a "grief cycle" and about how long it should take to process a loss. Do these grief theories apply when someone suffers repeated losses?

TESTING ISSUES

- How does the uncertainty of the HIV test affect your feelings about yourself and others?
- How do you deal with fear or anxiety that the HIV test might not be accurate?
- What are some of the good things you get from being tested?
- What issues remain unresolved after the testing process?

ATTITUDES TOWARD RETESTING

- What feelings have you experienced after getting tested?
- How do those feelings change with time, and when do your feelings lead you to consider another HIV test?
- Are there unique issues that arise during retesting that you did not experience during your first HIV test?
- How is the quality of your life affected by retesting?

HIV AND DISCLOSURE

- Who have you told about your HIV-negative status?
- What advantages or disadvantages are there to disclosing your HIV-negative status?
- Should HIV-positive men disclose their status to sexual partners? Should HIV-negative men?
- How do you bring up the subject of your status with others, positive or negative?
- How is your sexual behavior influenced by knowing the HIV status of your partner?

BEING WITH HIV-POSITIVE FRIENDS AND LOVERS

- What feelings do you have about HIV-positive lovers?
- What questions would you *not* pose to people who are positive?
- In what ways do you feel you can be intimate with someone who is HIV-positive?
- What feelings do you have when with your HIV-positive friends?
- How do you feel when your lover or friends begin to talk about being HIV-positive? When they're sick?
- In what way does knowledge of HIV status affect your choice of friendships?

IS IT EVER SAFE TO HAVE UNPROTECTED SEX?

- Is sex without condoms always unsafe?
- Is it difficult for us to discuss the unprotected sex we have?
- Is it ever important to have unprotected sex?

- Does "unsafe" mean different things for HIV-negative and HIV-positive people?

SELF-ESTEEM, SUBSTANCE USE, AND SEX

- How do you know a person has high or low self-esteem?
- What do drugs and alcohol do for self-esteem?
- Does it seem as if gay men around you drink and drug more or less than before AIDS?
- What do drugs and alcohol do for sex?
- What are some "pick-me-ups" that work to help you feel better about yourself when you're feeling down?

TIMES I'VE HAD UNSAFE SEX — OR WANTED TO

- What circumstances cause you to want unsafe sex?
- When have you actually engaged in unsafe sex?
- What feels different about wearing a condom? Why would not wearing a condom feel different?
- When you have wanted to have unsafe sex and didn't, what stopped you?
- Is it ever unsafe to negotiate safer sex?

SEX TALK: LEARNING TO SAY HOW AND WHEN

- What are some of your success stories regarding good communication with sexual partners?
- How do sexual roles (top/bottom, daddy/son, master/slave) affect your ability to talk about sex with your partner?
- What are your fears about discussing sex with your partner?
- How does the kind of relationship you have with your partner (fuck buddy, friend, lover, trick) affect the way you talk about sex?
- Describe an erotic experience that challenged your rules about sexual safety. How would talking with your partner have made the sex safer?
- How can you practice talking about sex?

THE ROLE OF OUR SEXUAL FANTASIES

- How have your fantasies changed since AIDS appeared?
- How does concern about HIV influence your use of pornography?
- To what extent do your fantasies involve safer sex?
- How do your fantasies influence your practices?
- What emotions does fantasizing about unsafe sex bring about?
- How do your fantasies compare to what you do in reality?

SEROCONVERTING

- What is your life like being HIV-negative?
- How do you feel your life would be different if you seroconverted?
- What pressures, if any, do you feel to become infected? How do you handle those pressures?
- How would you react to seroconverting? To whom would you reveal this? How might they respond?
- What changes would you make in your life if you were HIV-positive?
- How would you feel about a friend who seroconverted?

WHAT'S IN OUR FUTURE?

- How often and how clearly do you think about your future?
- How far into the future do your dreams and fantasies go?
- How easy is it to talk about your future with friends? Does it differ depending on their HIV status?
- What are some of the things you're looking forward to in your life?
- Do you have concerns or worries about the future?
- What are your thoughts on growing older as a gay or bisexual man?
- Do you think of yourself as a survivor of the AIDS epidemic? What does that mean to you?

APPENDIX C

Resources

To find a toll-free telephone number in your area for information about HIV and AIDS, call the National AIDS Hot Line in the United States at 1-800-342-AIDS.

HIV-NEGATIVE SUPPORT SERVICES

To be listed in a nationwide directory of support services for HIV-negative gay and bisexual men, to find out whether such services exist in your area, or to learn how to establish them if they do not, write to this address:

HIV-Negative Support Network
P.O. Box 126
Boston, MA 02117-0126

Include a self-addressed stamped envelope, and indicate whether you wish your name and contact information to be listed in the directory.

NEWSPAPER ARTICLES

Frutchey, Chuck. "Negatives Being Negative." *San Francisco Sentinel*, 12 October 1994: 22.

Gagnon, John. "Losing Ground against AIDS." *New York Times*, 6 January 1994: A21.

Goleman, Daniel. "Holocaust Survivors Had Skills to Prosper." *New York Times,* 6 October 1992: C1+.

Graham, Renee. "The Negative Experience." *Boston Globe,* 21 January 1992: 51+.

Gross, Jane. "Second Wave of AIDS Feared by Officials in San Francisco." *New York Times,* 11 December 1993: 1+.

Hurst, Lynda. "Survivors Deal with Constant Guilt." *Toronto Star,* 7 February 1993: A10.

Kaiser, Charles. "Overcoming a Death Wish." *New York Times,* 30 November 1992: A15.

Moon, Thomas. "Survivor Guilt in HIV-Negative Gay Men." *San Francisco Sentinel,* 14 November 1991.

———. "The Problem with Prevention." *San Francisco Sentinel,* 20 July 1994: 26.

———. "Prevention Taboo." *San Francisco Sentinel,* 17 August 1994: 22–23.

———. "A Failure of Nerve." *San Francisco Sentinel,* 26 October 1994: 26.

Natale, Richard. "Walking Wounded." *Los Angeles Times,* 1 July 1993: E1+.

Navarro, Mireya. "Left Behind by AIDS." *New York Times,* 6 May 1992: B1+.

———. "Healthy, Gay, Guilt-Stricken: AIDS' Toll on the Virus-Free." *New York Times,* 11 January 1993: A1+.

Pelfini, Andrew. "To Be or Not to Be HIV Negative." *San Francisco Sentinel,* 29 August 1991: 42.

Schoofs, Mark. "Can You Trust Your Lover? Gay Couples Weigh the Risk of Unprotected Sex." *Village Voice,* 31 January 1995: 37–39.

Tommasini, Anthony. "This 'Test' Is Both Positive and Negative." *Boston Globe,* 3 December 1993: 54.

Tuller, David. "Uninfected Gays Suffering, Too." *San Francisco Chronicle,* 19 March 1993: A1+.

Van Gorder, Dana. "Staying Negative." Three-part series. *San Francisco Sentinel,* 28 December 1994: 18+; 4 January 1995: 18+; 11 January 1995: 20+.

Warner, Michael. "Unsafe: Why Gay Men Are Having Risky Sex." *Village Voice,* 31 January 1995: 32–36.

JOURNAL AND MAGAZINE ARTICLES

Barber, Charles. "AIDS Apartheid." *NYQ,* 3 November 1991: 42+.

Caldarola, Tom, and Michael Helquist. "Counseling Mixed Antibody Status Couples." *Focus: A Guide to AIDS Research and Counseling* 4.9 (1989): 1–2.

Clendinen, Dudley. "When Negative Meets Positive." *GQ,* October 1994: 237+.

Dilley, James, and Thomas Moon. "Supporting Uninfected Gay and Bisexual Men." *Focus: A Guide to AIDS Research and Counseling* 8.6 (1994): 1–4.

Evans, Frederic. "Dating and Disclosure in the Gay Nineties." *Wellspring,* May/June 1993: 16–17.

Gochros, Harvey L. "The Sexuality of Gay Men with HIV Infection." *Social Work* 37.2 (1992): 105–109.

Grothe, Tom, and Leon McKusick. "Coping with Multiple Loss." *Focus: A Guide to AIDS Research and Counseling* 7.7 (1992): 5–6.

Gupta, Sunetra, and Roy Anderson. "Sex, AIDS and Mathematics." *New Scientist,* 12 September 1992: 34–38.

Holleran, Andrew. "Notes on Celibacy." *Christopher Street* 110: 8–10.

Huggins, James, et al. "Affective and Behavioral Responses of Gay and Bisexual Men to HIV Antibody Testing." *Social Work* 36.1 (1991): 61–66.

Kaal, Herman. "Grief Counseling for Gay Men." *Focus: A Guide to AIDS Research and Counseling* 7.7 (1992): 1–4.

Kaiser, Charles. "Tempting the Virus." *QW*, 1 November 1992: 23–26.

Kippax, Susan, et al. "Sustaining Safe Sex: A Longitudinal Study of a Sample of Homosexual Men." *AIDS* 7.2 (1993): 257–263.

Odets, Walt. "The Homosexualization of AIDS." *Focus: A Guide to AIDS Research and Counseling* 5.11 (1990): 1–2.

———. "The Secret Epidemic." *OUT/LOOK*, Fall 1991: 45–49.

———. "AIDS Education and Harm Reduction for Gay Men: Psychological Approaches for the 21st Century." *AIDS & Public Policy Journal* 9.1 (1994): 1–18.

———. "Why We Stopped Doing Primary Prevention for Gay Men in 1985." *AIDS & Public Policy Journal* 10.1 (1995): 1–31.

Rogers, Patrick. "Surviving the Second Wave." *Newsweek*, 19 September 1994: 50–51.

Schochet, Rachel. "Psychosocial Issues for Seronegative Gay Men in San Francisco." *Focus: A Guide to AIDS Research and Counseling* 4.9 (1989): 3.

Signorile, Michelangelo. "Unsafe Like Me." *Out*, October 1994: 22+.

———. "Negative Pride." *Out*, March 1995: 22+.

Silvestre, Anthony, J., et al. "Factors Related to Seroconversion among Homo- and Bisexual Men after Attending a Risk-Reduction Educational Session." *AIDS* 3.10 (1989): 647–650.

Sontag, Susan. "The Way We Live Now." *New Yorker,* 24 November 1986: 42–51.

Tighe, John Charles, ed. "Sexual Relapse." *HIV Counselor Perspectives* 1.1 (1991): 1–8.

Weisend, Tom. "Mixed Status Couples." *Wellspring,* March/April 1993: 12.

BOOKS

Aggleton, Peter, Graham Hart, and Peter Davies, eds. *AIDS: Social Representations, Social Practices.* Philadelphia: Falmer Press, 1989.

Bateson, Mary Catherine, and Richard Goldsby. *Thinking AIDS: The Social Response to the Biological Threat.* New York: Addison-Wesley, 1988.

Bettelheim, Bruno. *Surviving and Other Essays.* New York: Knopf, 1979.

Boccaccio, Giovanni. *The Decameron of Giovanni Boccaccio.* Trans. Frances Winwar. New York: Random House, 1955.

Cadwell, Steven A., Robert A. Burnham, Jr., and Marshall Forstein, eds. *Therapists on the Front Line: Psychotherapy with Gay Men in the Age of AIDS.* Washington, DC: American Psychiatric Press, 1994.

Crimp, Douglas, ed. *AIDS: Cultural Analysis, Cultural Activism.* Cambridge: MIT Press, 1988.

Dietrich, David R., and Peter C. Shabad, eds. *The Problem of Loss and Mourning: Psychoanalytic Perspectives.* Madison, CT: International Universities Press, 1989.

Dilley, James W., Cheri Pies, and Michael Helquist, eds. *Face to Face: A Guide to AIDS Counseling.* San Francisco: AIDS Health Project, 1989.

Epstein, Helen. *Children of the Holocaust: Conversations with Sons and Daughters of Survivors.* New York: Bantam, 1979.

Fee, Elizabeth, and Daniel M. Fox, eds. *AIDS: The Burdens of History.* Berkeley: University of California Press, 1988.

Flannery, Raymond B. *Post-Traumatic Stress Disorder: A Victim's Guide to Healing and Recovery.* New York: Crossroad, 1992.

Froman, Paul Kent. *After You Say Goodbye: When Someone You Love Dies of AIDS.* San Francisco: Chronicle Books, 1992.

Gill, Anton. *The Journey Back from Hell: Conversations with Concentration Camp Survivors.* New York: Avon, 1988.

Herman, Judith Lewis. *Trauma and Recovery.* New York: Basic Books, 1992.

Jäger, Hans, ed. *AIDS Phobia: Disease Pattern and Possibilities of Treatment.* Trans. Jacquie Welch. New York: Halsted, 1988.

Johnson, Julie Tallard. *Hidden Victims: An Eight-Stage Healing Process for Families and Friends of the Mentally Ill.* New York: Doubleday, 1988.

King, Edward. *Safety in Numbers: Safer Sex and Gay Men.* New York: Routledge, 1993.

Kleinman, Arthur. *The Illness Narratives: Suffering, Healing, and the Human Condition.* New York: Basic Books, 1988.

Mack, Arien, ed. *In Time of Plague: The History and Social Consequences of Lethal Epidemic Disease.* New York: New York University Press, 1991.

Matsakis, Aphrodite. *I Can't Get Over It: A Handbook for Trauma Survivors.* Oakland: New Harbinger, 1992.

Miller, James, ed. *Fluid Exchanges: Artists and Critics in the AIDS Crisis.* Toronto: University of Toronto Press, 1992.

Monette, Paul. *Borrowed Time: An AIDS Memoir.* San Diego: Harcourt Brace Jovanovich, 1988.

———. *Love Alone: 18 Elegies for Rog.* New York: St. Martin's Press, 1988.

Odets, Walt. *In the Shadow of the Epidemic: Being HIV-Negative in the Age of AIDS.* Durham, NC: Duke University Press, forthcoming.

O'Malley, Padraig, ed. *The AIDS Epidemic: Private Rights and the Public Interest.* Boston: Beacon Press, 1989.

Overall, Christine, and William P. Zion, eds. *Perspectives on AIDS: Ethical and Social Issues.* Toronto: Oxford University Press, 1991.

Patton, Cindy. *Inventing AIDS.* New York: Routledge, 1990.

Shelp, Earl E., Ronald H. Sunderland, and Peter W. A. Mansell. *AIDS: Personal Stories in Pastoral Perspective.* New York: Pilgrim Press, 1986.

Slaby, Andrew E. *Aftershock: Surviving the Delayed Effects of Trauma, Crisis and Loss.* New York: Villard Books, 1989.

Sontag, Susan. *Illness as Metaphor and AIDS and Its Metaphors.* New York: Doubleday, 1990.

Vargo, Marc. *The HIV Test: What You Need to Know to Make an Informed Decision.* New York: Pocket Books, 1992.

Watney, Simon. *Policing Desire: Pornography, AIDS and the Media.* Minneapolis: University of Minnesota Press, 1987.

Watstein, Sarah Barbara, and Robert Anthony Laurich. *AIDS and Women: A Sourcebook.* Phoenix: Oryx Press, 1991.

Notes

PROLOGUE: BOCCACCIO'S LESSON

1. Giovanni Boccaccio, *The Decameron of Giovanni Boccaccio,* trans. Frances Winwar (New York: The Modern Library, 1955), pp. xxiii–xxvii.

INTRODUCTION: CLIMBING TO ANGELS LANDING

1. Human immunodeficiency virus (HIV) is generally considered the cause of acquired immunodeficiency syndrome (AIDS). Some theorists dispute this, suggesting that HIV is unrelated to AIDS or is just one of several cofactors necessary for disease progression. I cannot say whether these theorists are correct. Nonetheless, my investigation of the ways in which HIV-negative gay men have been affected by the epidemic—and of the significance of HIV testing—does not depend on knowing the actual cause of AIDS. If we find out that something other than HIV causes AIDS, this does not change the historical fact that our fears, concerns, and anxieties about the epidemic were largely shaped by our belief that HIV causes AIDS.

2. I use the phrase "HIV testing" in this book because it is more commonly used by gay men and is shorter than "HIV-antibody testing." The latter phrase is more accurate, because the

ELISA and Western-Blot tests currently in use detect the presence of antibodies to HIV, rather than HIV itself.

CHAPTER 5: CONSIDERING TESTING

1. For example, a 1991 Michigan survey of 1,689 men who have sex with men found that 514 had not been tested. The most common reasons for not testing were "I'm not at risk" (43.4 percent), "I'm not sure I could handle a positive test result" (34.4 percent), and "I don't want to know the results" (26.1 percent). Less common reasons were "I was afraid that having the test might lead to discrimination against me" (22.6 percent), "I was worried that others would be told my test results" (14.6 percent), and "I don't think the test has much value" (7.4 percent). Multiple responses were allowed. See Bureau of Infectious Disease Control and Midwest AIDS Prevention Project, *HIV-Related Attitudes and Risk Behaviors among Men Who Have Sex with Men: Findings of the Fourth Michigan Survey* (Lansing: Michigan Department of Public Health, 1992), p. 5 and table 12.

   Similar results were found in 1990 surveys in Massachusetts and North Carolina. See AIDS Action Committee, Community Education Unit, *A Survey of AIDS-Related Knowledge, Attitudes and Behaviors Among Gay and Bisexual Men in Greater Boston, Massachusetts: A Report to Community Educators* (Boston: AIDS Action Committee, 1991), pp. 1, 27; and North Carolina Department of Environment, Health, and Natural Resources, Division of Epidemiology, *An HIV-Related Community Assessment Survey of Gay and Bisexual Men in North Carolina: A Report to Community Health Educators* (Raleigh, NC: Department of Environment, Health, and Natural Resources, 1993), pp. 11–12.

2. Discussions of the lack of positive correlation between HIV testing and risk reduction are found in the following essays, collected in *The AIDS Epidemic: Private Rights and the Public Interest*, ed. Padraig O'Malley (Boston: Beacon Press, 1989):

Marshall Forstein, "Understanding the Psychological Impact of AIDS: The Other Epidemic"; Michael Gross, "HIV Antibody Testing: Performance and Counseling Issues"; and Susanne B. Montgomery and Jill G. Joseph, "Behavioral Change in Homosexual Men at Risk for AIDS: Intervention and Policy Implications."

CHAPTER 9: REACTIONS TO TESTING NEGATIVE

1. Simon Watney, "The Possibilities of Permutation: Pleasure, Proliferation, and the Politics of Gay Identity in the Age of AIDS," in *Fluid Exchanges: Artists and Critics in the AIDS Crisis,* ed. James Miller (Toronto: University of Toronto Press, 1992), p. 347. Italics in the original.

2. Because it takes some time after infection with HIV for antibodies to develop, the tests currently in use—which detect antibodies rather than HIV itself—are not foolproof. Experts disagree about the time it takes for antibodies to be produced, but in general, most people infected with HIV develop antibodies within six months.

3. The chance of testing error is minuscule but not nonexistent. The preliminary test currently in use, the ELISA test, is designed to err in the direction of telling people who are uninfected that they are infected, rather than telling people who are infected that they are uninfected.

4. In San Francisco and a few other urban gay communities in the United States, the number of HIV-positive gay men is estimated to be equal to or slightly greater than the number of HIV-negative gay men. Because there is no easy way to establish how many gay men are in any base population, such estimates are hard to evaluate.

5. From a draft manuscript by Walt Odets. For more about the psychological issues facing HIV-negative gay men, see Walt Odets, *In the Shadow of the Epidemic: Being HIV-Negative in the*

Age of AIDS (Durham, NC: Duke University Press, forthcoming).

6. Marshall Forstein, "Suicidality and HIV in Gay Men," in *Therapists on the Front Line: Psychotherapy with Gay Men in the Age of AIDS*, ed. Steven A. Cadwell, Robert A. Burnham, and Marshall Forstein (Washington, DC: American Psychiatric Press, 1994), p. 121.

CHAPTER 11: DIVISION BY HIV STATUS

1. Charles Barber, "AIDS Apartheid," *NYQ*, 3 November 1991, p. 42.

2. Ibid., p. 45.

3. Ibid., p. 68.

4. Ibid., p. 44.

5. Dudley Clendinen, "When Negative Meets Positive," *GQ*, October 1994, pp. 238–239.

6. Ibid., p. 239.

7. Ibid.

8. For more on the analogy between the biological and social responses to HIV infection, see Mary Catherine Bateson and Richard Goldsby, *Thinking AIDS: The Social Response to the Biological Threat* (New York: Addison-Wesley, 1988).

CHAPTER 15: NEGATIVE-NEGATIVE COUPLES

1. Susan Kippax, June Crawford, Mark Davis, et al., "Sustaining Safe Sex: A Longitudinal Study of a Sample of Homosexual Men," *AIDS* 7.2 (1993), pp. 257–263.

2. The Kippax study notes that agreements about sex outside relationships are common. Among the 82 men who had regular partners (a sample that included HIV-positive, HIV-negative, and untested men), 74 percent had a clear agreement

on sexual practice outside their regular relationship. Among those men, 39 percent had agreed to no sex outside the relationship, 23 percent had agreed to "safe sex" outside the relationship but not in the relationship, and 36 percent had agreed to "safe sex" both outside the relationship and in the relationship. This last group contained those HIV-negative men who practice safer sex even with HIV-negative partners.

3. For example, see Gay Men's Health Centre, "Relationships: Your Choice" (South Yarra, Australia: Victorian AIDS Council, 1994), which presents a list of steps that gay men in negative-negative couples might take before deciding not to use condoms. Among the steps are these: "Discuss and promise each other that you will avoid anal sex outside the relationship, or that if you or your partner fuck with anyone else, condoms will be used. . . . Discuss and promise each other that if either of you slips-up or has an accident with unsafe sex outside the relationship, you will *tell the other* immediately and go back to safe sex until you've both been tested again. . . . Agree that either partner can *insist* on using condoms again . . . and that it won't mean the end of the relationship. *Don't punish* your partner for being honest."

See also AIDS Committee of Toronto, "Can You Relate? Safer Sex in Gay Relationships: Think about It, Talk about It" (Toronto, Canada: AIDS Committee of Toronto, 1994), which offers this: "Some gay men, when they get into a relationship, stop using condoms for anal sex (fucking) because they feel that caring for someone or being in love is all the protection they need. . . . If you are both *truly* HIV–, and you both *never* do anything to put yourselves at risk outside the relationship, you can stop using condoms. But it often isn't that simple. . . . Ultimately, the choice is up to you. But decisions about condom use need to be based on more than just caring for someone. If you don't think you, as a couple, are willing and able to deal with the many issues that are involved, then play it safe."

CHAPTER 17: DECIDING WHAT'S UNSAFE

1. Robyn M. Dawes, *Rational Choice in an Uncertain World* (San Diego: Harcourt Brace Jovanovich, 1988), p. 29.

2. The passage Tucker referred to is from Shakespeare's *Henry V*, act V, scene ii, where Henry first addresses an interpreter and then Katharine herself:

> *King Henry.* It is not a fashion for the maids in France to kiss before they are married, would she say? ... O Kate, nice customs curtsy to great kings. Dear Kate, you and I cannot be confined within the weak list of a country's fashion. We are the makers of manners, Kate, and the liberty that follows our places stops the mouth of all find-faults. ...

CHAPTER 19: RETESTING AND SEROCONVERSION

1. "Seroconversion" is sometimes used synonymously with "HIV infection," but it is helpful to make a distinction. Technically, "seroconversion" refers not to HIV infection but to a biological event made evident by two HIV tests: the movement from the absence to the presence of HIV antibodies in the bloodstream. In popular usage, "seroconversion" often refers to the psychological event of learning one is HIV-positive after learning one was HIV-negative.

2. Mattia Morretta, ed., *Dire, fare, baciare ... Il sesso al tempo dell'AIDS* (Milano: Associazione Solidarietà Aids, 1989), pp. 11–12. The translation is mine.

3. Thomas Moon, "Survivor Guilt in HIV-Negative Gay Men," *San Francisco Sentinel*, 14 November 1991.

4. Michelangelo Signorile, "Negative Pride," *Out*, March 1995, p. 24.

5. These statements are based on the report's estimates of rates of seroconversion for various age groups: 4.4 percent for men

ages 20–25, 2.5 percent for men ages 25–30, 1.5 percent for men ages 30–45, and 1.0 percent for men ages 45–55. See D. R. Hoover et al., "Estimating the 1978–1990 and Future Spread of Human Immunodeficiency Virus Type 1 in Subgroups of Homosexual Men," *American Journal of Epidemiology* 134.10 (1991), pp. 1190–1205.

6. In reality, younger gay men probably have higher seroconversion rates than older gay men. Mathematical models can take this into account by multiplying expressions of the form $(1 - r)^x$ using different rates for different ranges of years. The estimate in the Hoover study cited above, for example, that only half of a group of uninfected 20-year-olds is likely to remain uninfected by age 55, is supported in this way:

$$(1 - 0.044)^5(1 - 0.025)^5(1 - 0.015)^{15}(1 - 0.010)^{10} = 0.507$$

Realistic goals for seroconversion rates will have to acknowledge that rates are likely to be different for different age groups.

7. These results are preliminary findings of the Sexually Active Men (SAM) study funded by the federal Centers for Disease Control and Prevention and the National Institute for Allergies and Infectious Diseases. The study included 1,769 participants but excluded men who reported never having anal sex in the previous year. See David Olsen, "Study: Gay Men Seroconverting at High Rate," *Bay Windows*, 26 January 1995.

CHAPTER 21: HIV-NEGATIVE IDENTITY

1. The idea that someone might tattoo himself as "HIV–" seems preposterous. Interestingly, however, a "–" symbol can be changed into a "+" symbol by adding a vertical stroke. In perverse moments of fancy, I imagine that someone who has tattooed himself as "HIV–" could change it to "HIV+" if he seroconverts. In this way, the apparent permanence of an "HIV–" tattoo contains an implicit flexibility that reflects the

impermanence of HIV-negative status and the one-way nature of HIV infection.

The same tension between apparent permanence and implicit flexibility is found at the Vietnam Veterans Memorial in Washington, D.C. When prisoners of war and those listed as missing in action are found to have been killed in action, the cross symbols next to their names are changed to diamond shapes by carving away additional stone.

CONCLUSION: LOOKING TO THE FUTURE

1. Walt Odets, "The Secret Epidemic," *OUT/LOOK*, Fall 1991, p. 49.

2. Susan Sontag, *The Way We Live Now* (New York: Noonday Press, 1991). Originally published as a short story in the *New Yorker*, 24 November 1986, pp. 42–51.

Contributors

Names followed by an asterisk are pseudonyms.

৯়

ERIC ROFES, 40, is an author and community organizer living in San Francisco. He is a board member of the National Gay and Lesbian Task Force and has served as Executive Director of the Los Angeles Gay and Lesbian Community Services Center and San Francisco's Shanti Project.

GIOVANNI BOCCACCIO (1313–1375) was an Italian poet, story-teller, and friend of Petrarch. He wrote the *Decameron,* a collection of bawdy tales, after the Black Death raged through Florence in 1348.

ANTHONY TOMMASINI, 45, is a freelance writer and pianist. He has written for the *New York Times* and the *Boston Globe.* For more than five years he volunteered for the AIDS Action Committee hot line in Boston. He lives in New York City.

SANDRO COSTA*, 23, works in a newspaper distribution office. He studied aerospace engineering and English literature at the University of Southern California.

ROBERT NEWMAN*, 40, is a health-care administrator who lives in a Boston suburb. Living and coming out in San Francisco in the mid-seventies was his major formative experience as a gay man. Single, but looking, he enjoys hiking, classical music, and traveling.

PAUL FIELDING*, 35, is manager of the furniture department in a department store. He grew up in a lower-middle-class rural town in Connecticut. He enjoys interior decorating, buying and selling antiques, and hiking. Paul has lived alcohol- and drug-free for the two years since his interview and hopes to continue on a healthy path of recovery.

CLAUDE DUPONT*, 34, was raised in Haiti. He is the regional coordinator for an agency that does corporate training about disability issues in the workplace.

SAM PAPPADOPOULOS*, 30, has an A.S. degree in animal science, a B.S. in education, and hopes to pursue a master's in social work degree. He has volunteered for the Boston HIV-Negative Support Group, Boston Jacks, and community events that raise awareness of HIV in underserved communities.

MATTHEW LASALLE*, 31, is a meeting planner for an insurance company in Boston. He grew up in New Hampshire. Influenced by his relationship with an HIV-positive partner, he has become more active in AIDS volunteer work, most recently by organizing a corporate team for the Boston–New York AIDS fund-raising bicycle ride.

DON WILLET*, 33, works in the field of HIV prevention and education. He believes HIV-negative men need to envision a place for themselves in the future in order to remain uninfected. He and his partner of 12 years are new adoptive parents of a 10-year-old boy.

RYAN JOSEPH*, 52, manages a desktop publishing group at a university in Boston. He is active in the school's gay and lesbian caucus, participates in an HIV/AIDS support group there, and has produced brochures on resources available for people with AIDS and people who have tested HIV-negative.

FRANK RUGGERO*, 40, a first-generation Italian-American, is in recovery, working for spiritual, mental, and physical balance. He finds art and restoration projects nurturing. He volunteers at a gay health center and at a rehabilitation center. He has been a fan of Barbra Streisand all his life.

NATHANIEL MCNAUGHTON*, 34, is an HIV educator whose work includes HIV-test counseling. He grew up on a farm in the Midwest and rode a horse to his one-room schoolhouse. He enjoys reading Chinese poetry.

JAMES DOUGLAS*, 44, trains HIV-test counselors and coordinates HIV counseling, testing, and support services for a metropolitan public health department. He stopped working as a visual artist in 1987, partly in response to the AIDS epidemic. He is currently back in the studio exploring images related to eroticism, gender, survival, and loss. His Radical Faerie name is Cupcake.

MARK DOTY, 41, has published three books of poetry: *Turtle, Swan; Bethlehem in Broad Daylight;* and *My Alexandria,* which won the National Book Critic's Circle Award and the Los Angeles Times Book Award and was nominated for the National Book Award. His companion of 12 years, Wally Roberts, died of AIDS in January 1994. He lives in Provincetown, Massachusetts.

ABOUT THE AUTHOR

WILLIAM I. JOHNSTON, 32, grew up near Boston and graduated from Harvard College in 1985 with a degree in visual studies. From 1987 to 1993 he worked on the hot line of the AIDS Action Committee of Massachusetts. Since 1991 he has been a volunteer facilitator of the Boston HIV-Negative Support Group. He lives in Watertown, Massachusetts, and is a mathematics textbook editor for Houghton Mifflin Company. *HIV-Negative* is his first book and his first book design.

ACKNOWLEDGMENTS

The author thanks the following for their help: Robert Aron, Frank Berndt, Gail Beverley, Warren Blumenfeld, Arlen Brown, Steven Cadwell, Barry Callis, Audrey Carneski, David Casti, Woody Castrodale, Chwee Lye Chng, David Christina, Ken Cinelli, Carol Cosenza, Sean Crist, Prentice Crosier, Terry Dash, Inês Esteves, Elizabeth Evans, Richard Fleming, David Gray, Ralph Hakim, Ray Hardin, Paul Hastings, Doug Hein, Audrey Helou, Sue Herz, Michael Howe, Joe Huffman, David Johnson, Robb Johnson, Jeff Jones, Marvin Kabakoff, James Kaczman, Eric Kristensen, Walter Kulecz, Alon Lavie, Matthew Lena, Michael London, Andrea Lonon, Michael Malamut, David Martin, Malinda Matney, Richard Mattoli, Laurie McDonald, Cynthia McKeon, James McQueston, Brad Miyasato, Tom Moon, Ken Nimblett, Walt Odets, Steve Palmer, Maurice Plourde, Danielle Potvin, Daniel Reid, Eric Rofes, Mark Rosenstein, Helen Rubel, Jim Sacco, Rachel Schochet, Jim Sellers, Michael Shelton, David Sheppard, Charles Solomon, David Speakman, Jeffrey Stone, Henrik Storner, Larry Stratton, Kit Wessman, James Wood, and E. J. Zita.

❧

Index

Anal sex, 42, 192
  abstinence from, 22, 24, 26, 83, 108,
    171–172
  with condoms, 26, 28, 108, 111, 132,
    183, 191, 245
  without condoms, 17–18, 20–21,
    110, 131–132, 158–159, 173–174,
    197, 208, 210, 213–214, 236–238,
    260, 267
  with ejaculation, 110, 236–238, 260
  without ejaculation, 36, 259
  with HIV-negative partner, 21, 24,
    111, 159, 173–174, 245
  with HIV-positive partner, 20–21,
    28–29, 48, 108, 212–214
  with unknown-status partner,
    17–18, 46, 131–132, 208, 260
Angels Landing, 1–2, 9–10
Anthony [Tommasini] (age 45), 11–15,
    321
Antibody envy, *vi*
Anton (age 31), 195
Anxiety, *vii*, 83–87, 156–157, 169–170,
    288–289
Apartheid, based on HIV status, 63–64,
    125–128, 142, 261
Arthur (age 30), 104
Attribution theory, 197–198
Audrey (age 32), 77
Austin (age 36), 59, 105, 197, 200–202,
    287–288
Avoidance
  of the HIV-positive, 26, 117–119,
    122–123
  of plague carriers, *xi*
AZT (azidothymidine), 71, 76, 181, 235

Barber, Charles, 125–128, 146, 316
Bart (age 39), 196–197
BEAR magazine, 257
Bearing witness, *v, viii*, 13, 97, 246–247
Bingeing, after abstinence, 201
Blake (age 33), 41, 80, 196, 222
Blood
  attitudes toward tainted, 39–40
  donation restrictions, 39
  fear of infection through, 11

Boccaccio, Giovanni, *xi–xii*, 313, 321
Body Electric workshops, 265–266
Boston HIV-Negative Support Group,
    4, 6, 7, 28, 52, 87, 216, 251, 261,
    269, 291–299
Boston Living Center, 117, 235
Brendan (age 43), 196
Brent (age 36), 199
Brinning, Jim, 291
Buzz (age 37), 122, 196

Cal (age 42), 62, 168–169, 196
Catholicism, 31, 85
Cathy (age 27), 145–146, 148, 150–152,
    285–286
Celebration, muted, 286–287
Claude (age 34), 83–87, 95, 98, 169, 322
Clendinen, Dudley, 128–129, 316
Coming-out issues, in chronic testers,
    222
Condoms. *See* Anal sex; Oral sex; Sex
    with condoms
Cruising, 50–51, 207, 265
Cum. *See* Anal sex; Oral sex; Semen
Cytomegalovirus, 206

Damien (age 38), 97–98, 229
David (age 35), 34, 102–103, 284
Dawes, Robyn, 197–198, 318
Dehumanization, 119
Denial, *vi–vii*, 17–18
Depression, *vii*, 6, 20–21
Derek (age 25), 90–91, 170, 197, 221
Designing Women, 19
Disaster, reactions to, *v–viii*
Disclosure
  of HIV-negative status, 12, 25, 69,
    98–99, 109, 112, 123, 135, 198–199,
    249–250, 255–256
  of HIV-positive status, 124, 127–128,
    134, 162, 251–252
  questions about, 302
Discordant couples. *See* Positive-
    negative couples
Discrimination, based on HIV status,
    57–58, 73–74, 107–108, 113–114,
    122–129

Symptoms, searching for, 20, 33–36, 45,
55, 108, 131, 206–207

T-cells, 70, 72, 76, 134
Television programs, on AIDS, 19, 34
Testing. *See* HIV testing
Testing HIV-negative. *See* Reactions to
testing HIV-negative
Testing HIV-positive. *See* Reactions to
testing HIV-positive;
Seroconversion
Todd (age 26), 78–79, 91–92, 290
Tommasini, Anthony, 11–15, 321
Trauma, *vi–vii*, 270–271
Trust, in couples, 28, 159, 171–175,
184–185, 245
Tucker (age 31), 31, 178–179, 202–203
12-step groups, 215–216

Uncertainty, 154, 233, 289–290
Unprotected sex. *See* Sex without
condoms
Unsafe sex
after learning of partner's HIV-
positive status, 196–197, 260
in others, 195–196
invention of, before HIV testing,
41–42
persistence of early definitions
of, 42

Unsafe sex *(cont.)*
questions about, 303
reasons for, 17–18, 163, 185–186,
195–198, 263–264
as response to trauma, *vii*
in self, 196–197
subjective meanings of, 193–194
variety of definitions of, 191–193
videos showing, 257–258

Vernon (age 45), 219–220, 222–223,
225–226
Vietnam War, *vii*, 96–97
Virtual HIV, 168–169
Vulnerability, feelings of, after testing
HIV-negative, 119–121, 195

Watney, Simon, 93–94, 250, 315
Western-Blot test, 275, 314
Wojnarowicz, David, 127–128
Wolf (age 46), 227–228, 230–231
Women quoted. *See* Alice, Audrey,
Cathy, Gloria
Woody (age 52), 129–130

Youth, gay, 17, 228

Zion National Park, Utah, 1–2, 9–10
Zombies, *vi*, 269
Zwickler, Phil, 127–128